The Undercover Messiah and His Coming Kingdom

The Undercover Messiah and His Coming Kingdom

Messiah as Prophet, Priest, and King

JIM R. SIBLEY

Foreword by Mark M. Yarbrough

WIPF & STOCK · Eugene, Oregon

THE UNDERCOVER MESSIAH AND HIS COMING KINGDOM
Messiah as Prophet, Priest, and King

Copyright © 2025 Jim R. Sibley. All rights reserved. Except for brief quotations in critical publications or reviews, no part of this book may be reproduced in any manner without prior written permission from the publisher. Write: Permissions, Wipf and Stock Publishers, 199 W. 8th Ave., Suite 3, Eugene, OR 97401.

Wipf & Stock
An Imprint of Wipf and Stock Publishers
199 W. 8th Ave., Suite 3
Eugene, OR 97401

www.wipfandstock.com

PAPERBACK ISBN: 979-8-3852-2830-0
HARDCOVER ISBN: 979-8-3852-2831-7
EBOOK ISBN: 979-8-3852-2832-4

VERSION NUMBER 04/16/25

Scripture quotations taken from the (NASB®) New American Standard Bible®, Copyright © 1960, 1971, 1977, 1995, 2020 by The Lockman Foundation. Used by permission. All rights reserved.

Scripture quotations marked HCSB have been taken from the Holman Christian Standard Bible®, Copyright © 2017 by Holman Bible Publishers. Used by permission. Christian Standard Bible® and CSB® are federally registered trademarks of Holman Bible Publishers.

Scripture quotations marked KJV have been taken from the King James Version of the Bible.

Henry F. Lyte, "Abide with Me," in *The Lutheran Hymnal* (St. Louis, MO: Concordia Publishing House, 1941). Public domain.

Charles Wesley, "Come, Thou Long Expected Jesus," in *A Collection of Hymns for Social Worship, More Particularly Designed for the Use of the Tabernacle Congregation in London*, edited by George Whitefield, 7th ed. (London: William Strahan, 1754). Public domain.

Philip P. Bliss, "Hallelujah! What a Savior!" in *Gospel Hymns No. 2: As Used by Them in Gospel Meetings*, edited by P. P. Bliss and Ira D. Sankey (New York: John Church/Biglow & Main Co., 1876). Also as, "'Man of Sorrows,' What a Name," *Baptist Hymnal* (Nashville, TN: Convention Press, 1975). Public domain.

Johnson Oatman, "Holy Holy, Is What the Angels Sing," in *Seventh-day Adventist Hymnal* (Hagerstown, MD: Review and Herald Publishing Association, 1985). Public domain.

To Kathy,
The wife of my youth and
My best friend,
Who has shared
My highest hopes and
My greatest joys
From the ends of the earth and back again.
מצאתי אותה כפי נפשי חפצה:

Contents

List of Illustrations | ix
Foreword by Mark M. Yarbrough | xi
Preface: Our Destination | xiii
Acknowledgments | xv
Abbreviations | xvii
Introduction: The Undercover Messiah | 1

Part 1: The Messiah in the Pentateuch | 11
1   The Prophet Like Moses | 13
2   The Alternative Priesthood | 21
3   The Coming King | 30

Part 2: The Messiah in the Prophets and Writings | 39
4   Messiah as the Prophet Like Moses | 41
5   Messiah as the Priest Like Melchizedek | 56
6   Messiah as the King Like David | 69

Part 3: The Messiah in the New Testament | 77
7   Jesus as the Prophet in the New Testament | 79
8   The Arrival of Jesus, the Prophet Like Moses | 96
9   Jesus, the Prophet, in Samaria and in Galilee | 105
10 Jesus, the Prophet, in Jerusalem | 119
11 When Did Jesus Begin His Priestly Role? | 132
12 What Does His Priestly Order Tell Us About His Ministry? | 149
13 What Does He Do? He Saves Us! | 154
14 What Does He Do? He Transforms Us! | 162
15 Jesus as the King in the New Testament | 172

Part 4: The Messianic Kingdom | 195
16   The Messianic Kingdom in the Hebrew Scriptures | 197
17   The Messianic Kingdom in the New Testament Scriptures | 206

Epilogue: What Shall We Do? | 225
Appendix 1: The Three Offices of Messiah | 229
Appendix 2: The "Generation" of Matthew 24:34 | 236
Appendix 3: Views of the Kingdom | 242
Bibliography | 255
Scripture Index | 271

List of Illustrations

Figure One   The Alternative Priesthood | 28
Figure Two   The Pattern of the Pentateuch | 30
Figure Three   Sermon on the Mount | 109

Foreword

INTERESTINGLY, THERE HAS EMERGED a renewed curiosity and interest among people today in the person and history of Jesus. So much has been written on the topic from deep scholarly works to more popular treatises that present Jesus as a culturally relevant religious guru who promises to give you a good life.

Thankfully, the Bible makes plain from cover to cover that the second Person of the Trinity, Jesus Christ, God's Son, resembles nothing of the culture's imagery of him and is so much more—in fact, he's infinitely more.

In this great new book by Jim Sibley, *Undercover Messiah and His Coming Kingdom: Messiah as Prophet, Priest, and King*, you will come face to face with the Jesus of the Bible. And you will discover that he has been revealed to us and to the world in three very distinct aspects of his identity and ministry—*Prophet, Priest,* and *King*.

Jim Sibley, having lived in Israel for many years, and as a diligent researcher and careful theologian, has brought together these wonderfully related aspects of Messiah's ministry in one volume, that begins with a compelling look at the Old Testament descriptions of Messiah and closes with a thrilling look at Messiah's redemptive and victorious work as developed and revealed by the New Testament writers.

I invite you to come to this study with a fresh and open mind, and a willingness to think deeply and theologically about the subject of this book . . . Jesus Christ, the Messiah, our Prophet, Priest, and King.

Once you do, you will be equipped with a helpful and insightful set of hermeneutical categories to guide a lifetime of careful study, accurate interpretation, and practical communication of the Scriptures, all through the lens of the Person and wonder of Jesus Christ the Messiah.

I assure you this will be a journey you will be glad you undertook.

Preface
Our Destination

THIS STUDY BEGAN WITH a quest for answers about the Messianic Kingdom. Several things became apparent: (1) the Kingdom needed to be viewed in light of the kingship of Jesus, the Messiah, (2) his kingship needed to be explored in relationship to his other anointed offices of Prophet and Priest, and (3) this study needed to begin with the Old Testament.

A careful study of Old Testament prophecies concerning these offices of Messiah sheds light not only on the Kingdom, but also on the Messiah in the New Testament. By giving attention to these prophecies, it will be clear that although Jesus was born to be the King of the Jews, he first needed to serve as our Moses-like Deliverer and as our Melchizedek-like Priest.

Therefore, this book has a dual focus. The original questions about the Kingdom have been answered, but this original quest has almost been overtaken by a desire to give Christians a deeper understanding of Jesus himself. Recognizing Jesus as the Prophet like Moses in his earthly ministry opens the Gospels like nothing else. Seeing Jesus as our great High Priest illumines his current role and ministry to us. Embracing the reality of Jesus as our coming King infuses our lives with confidence, purpose, and hope. Jesus the Son of God and divine Messiah provides for our deepest need—forgiveness for sin and fellowship with the Father.

Acknowledgments

THE JOURNEY FROM A personal search for answers to the publication of this book was a lengthy one, and its completion has been dependent upon the Lord and a host of his people. Needless to say, my wife, Kathy, has not only been a prayer partner and encourager, but she has been a valued and excellent consultant I have relied upon throughout our married life. Our daughters, Betsy and Laura, their families, Ken and Ann Sibley, and other family members, as well, have been faithful in praying for this project for years.

I want to express my sincere gratitude for the support and encouragement I have received from Dr. Erez Soref and One For Israel. One of my great joys was the privilege of serving on the faculty of Israel College of the Bible. The daily interactions with valued colleagues were especially helpful and greatly valued.

Dr. Robert Jeffress, pastor of First Baptist Church Dallas, afforded me the opportunity to teach through the material in this book several times on Sunday evenings. To the staff and to the church members who came, listened, and questioned, I owe deepest gratitude, for "iron sharpens iron."

Indebtedness is especially due to the late John H. Sailhamer and to Walter C. Kaiser Jr. In particular, John Sailhamer's works have opened the Scriptures of the Old Testament as those of no other. Others whose works have been especially helpful and insightful are those of Craig Blaising, Seth Postell, Michael Rydelnik, and Mark Yarbrough. I am also honored that Mark Yarbrough has written the foreword, especially in the midst of his very busy schedule during the Centennial Year of Dallas Theological Seminary.

Expressions of deepest gratitude are due to Ana Bobo, a gifted editor, who juggled an already full schedule to help this book see the light of day. I can never repay my debt of gratitude to Diana Cooper, former student and administrative assistant, whose attention to detail and format have been essential for the book you hold in your hands. Help with graphic design by Jennifer Cheatham was exactly what was needed. Assistance from Frank Ball and the staff of Roaring Lambs has also been very helpful in navigating this new world of publishing.

Particular gratitude is due to David and Maxie Hecht, J. S. Gruner, Ron and Catherine Boney, and many others who have faithfully prayed for the preparation and publication of this book at every stage of its development. Your prayers have been answered, and I am grateful for your unwavering support and friendship. Olivier Melnick has offered helpful consultation and input. Nevertheless, in spite of this invaluable assistance, mistakes and errors are almost inevitable. For these, I take full responsibility.

Matthew Wimer, Managing Editor, and the staff at Wipf and Stock Publishers have guided me through the publication process with patience and competence. Thank you for your faith in the manuscript.

A definite set of convictions has guided this work: the authority and inerrancy of the Bible, a canonical or "close reading" method of interpretation, the direct fulfillment of prophecy, and the premillennial and pretribulation rapture of the church. It perhaps goes without saying that there are many godly authors and students of the Bible who do not share all the views presented here on the Kingdom or of the Messiah. This is true of some whose intellect and devotion are greatly appreciated and whose friendship is deeply cherished. My goal, and that of these authors, has been to rightly divide the Word of God to the best of our ability. May the Lord help us as we faithfully study and apply his Word. To God be the glory!

Abbreviations

b. Sota	Babylonian Talmud, Sota
b. Sukkah	Babylonian Talmud, Sukkah
BDAG	A Greek-English Lexicon of the New Testament and Other Early Christian Literature, 3rd ed.
BDB	Enhanced Brown-Driver-Briggs Hebrew and English Lexicon
Eccl. Rab.	Ecclesiastes Rabbah
HALOT	The Hebrew and Aramaic Lexicon of the Old Testament
HCSB	Holman Christian Standard Bible
HOL	A Concise Hebrew and Aramaic Lexicon of the Old Testament
KJV	King James Version
LXX	Septuagint
m. Sukkah	Mishna, Sukkah
m. Tamid	Mishna, Tamid
MT	Masoretic Text
NASB95	New American Standard Bible (1995)
NIV	New International Version
NJPS	Tanakh, a New Translation of the Holy Scriptures according to the Traditional Hebrew Text

Introduction
The Undercover Messiah

THE EMMY AWARD-WINNING TELEVISION show "Undercover Boss" originated in England in 2009 and has franchises in twenty countries. It's a reality show where high-level corporate executives anonymously take up jobs, often blue-collar jobs, at their own companies. They hope to discover how the rank-and-file employees view their positions and to identify those whose talents could be put to better use elsewhere. What makes the show work is that the employees don't realize their boss is among them at first. Instead, they get to know a "regular guy." By humbling himself, or herself, the executive gains more respect, not less.

The use of "undercover" may need a word of explanation when applied to the Messiah. An undercover policeman assumes an identity that is not his own—perhaps that of a gang member. An undercover agent may seem to be loyal to one country, but he or she may actually work for another country. These are assumed identities. When we speak of the undercover Messiah, though, it is not because his roles are fake or deceptive. It is because his roles as Prophet and Priest are largely unknown and unrecognized, even though they were prophesied centuries earlier in Israel's Scriptures. Most people then (as now) were seeking a political solution to life's problems rather than a spiritual one. They were only interested in Messiah as King.

But before we consider these specific roles, it is important to identify the two major characters in the Bible: Israel and the Messiah. Mark Yarbrough, the President of Dallas Theological Seminary says that as a literary "character," Israel gives cohesiveness to the tremendous diversity of the Bible. The Bible is composed of sixty-six books, written by prophets, fishermen, shepherds, farmers, soldiers, kings, and tax collectors. The books were written in three languages over a period of at least fifteen hundred years. The Bible consists of narratives, poems, prophecies, visions, letters, and genealogies. Israel is the glue that holds it all together and shows us how it all forms one continuous revelation.[1]

Yet Israel is not the main character of the story; instead, Israel is the guide. The Jewish people are presented as sinners, no better or worse than Gentiles, but God has chosen them for a purpose. If we are sensitive to what the Scriptures teach regarding Israel, God will use his people to guide us in our understanding of his Word. Israel is the key to the Bible!

If Israel is not the hero of the Bible, who is? The Messiah. The story of Israel points to him. Yarbrough says:

> The central character of the master narrative [i.e., of the Bible] is that of Israel, with Israel's Messiah as the hero of the grand story. To miss this perspective . . . is to avoid large portions of Old Testament scriptures and focus on personalized salvation in Christ. While the latter is true and essential, the total story is much more. God's redemptive process is one of total reclamation based on his promises. That is why we wait for his return, in this current mess and state of confusion, to bring a kingdom where Jesus, as the righteous King reigns.[2]

Before looking at Messiah's different functions, understand that he cannot be viewed entirely apart from the people of Israel. These two, the People of Israel and the Messiah, are linked together with the same vocabulary. For example, both are called the seed of Abraham,[3] God calls both "My servant,"[4] and both are given priestly functions.[5] No one can interpret Scripture correctly without a clear understanding of what it says about both.

Nevertheless, the goal is to gain a better understanding of Messiah, of Jesus. When we think of him, we need to understand that, as the focus and central character of the biblical story, he was to serve in several

---

1. Yarbrough, "Israel and the Story of the Bible," 53–56.
2. Yarbrough, "Israel and the Story of the Bible," 55–56.
3. Of Israel, see Ps 105:6, see also, Gen 22:17–18; of Messiah, see Gal 3:16: "Now the promises were spoken to Abraham and to his seed . . . that is, Messiah." For a discussion of the distinction between singular and plural uses of "seed," see Collins, "A Syntactical Note (Genesis 3:15)," 144.
4. Of Israel, see Isa 41:8–9; 44:1; of Messiah, see Isa 42:1; 49:3 (see also vv. 5, 6); 50:10; etc.
5. See Exod 19:6; Ps 110:4.

different ways. My desire is to highlight Scripture passages that reveal the development of these roles.

Understanding these personal offices not only helps us learn more about Jesus, but such an understanding also brings clarity regarding his Kingdom. For to have a kingdom at all, it is necessary to have a duly authorized king who is actually reigning. The study of all three messianic roles is crucial for correctly interpreting the biblical promise of the Messianic Kingdom. When we consider Jesus as ultimate Prophet, great High Priest, and true King, the New Testament suddenly makes much more sense.

To understand the offices of the Messiah, we must turn to the Old Testament. Even though the Old Testament comprises almost three-fourths of the Bible, many Christians are not so familiar with it. For the sake of time, we cannot deal with the material in the Old Testament as thoroughly as we might wish. Nevertheless, this Old Testament background is vitally important. For these reasons, I encourage you to read and study the passages we discuss here on your own.

Think of this book as a journey through the Scriptures to the Messianic Kingdom. As we begin our hike through the Hebrew Scriptures, this first stretch through the Old Testament might be more difficult and less familiar, and perhaps a bit steep in places. Then it levels out and gives a fantastic view. You can't really appreciate the view if you haven't climbed the trail. But seeing Jesus in and through the Old Testament makes it worth the effort, for this is how he was intended to be viewed.

On the road to Emmaus, when Jesus taught the confused and defeated disciples about himself, he did not review the events of his life—his teachings, miracles, or crucifixion. Instead, "beginning with Moses and with all the prophets, He explained to them the things concerning Himself in all the Scriptures" (Luke 24:27).[6] This has been called "the Emmaus Code,"[7] but it really isn't a code at all. Nevertheless, the fact remains, if we want to enrich our understanding of Jesus, we must begin "with Moses and with all the prophets."

We will begin by looking at the first five books of the Bible. These books are often referred to as the Pentateuch. They are also known as the Torah. The two words are virtually interchangeable. Although the Torah

---

6. Unless otherwise noted, the *New American Standard Bible* (1995) [NASB95] is used throughout. "Christ" has been changed to "Messiah." In the Appendices, the *Holman Christian Standard Bible* [HCSB] is used, unless otherwise noted.

7. Limbaugh, *The Emmaus Code*.

appears in our Bibles as five separate books, it is better to understand them as five parts of one book. In 2 Chronicles 25:4, it is referred to as "the book of Moses," and in Nehemiah 8:1 as "the book of the law [or *torah*] of Moses." Although *torah* is often translated "law," it also means "instruction."[8] Part 2 will continue with the remaining books of the Old Testament. Following that, we will see how this information affects our perception of Jesus. After all this, we can better understand what Scripture has to say about the Messianic Kingdom.

Earl Ellis, a highly respected theologian and New Testament scholar, after a lifetime of study, teaching, and writing, said, "I remain convinced that the use of the Old Testament by the New Testament writers is the primary key to their theology and, thus, to the message of God that they taught the early church and that they continue to teach the church of today."[9] Remember, when the New Testament church *was* the New Testament church, it did not possess the New Testament! This is important, for the messianic message is central in the Old Testament and vitally important for understanding the New Testament.

THE MESSIANIC MESSAGE OF THE OLD TESTAMENT

Kevin Chen writes, "Rightly appreciated [the Pentateuch's] dense, highly concentrated Messianic content shows where [its] center of gravity lies. Salvation will come through the seed of the woman, not through the Sinai/Deuteronomic law which will be given later."[10] The prophecy of Genesis 3:15 is the beginning of what has been termed "the offspring hope,"[11] and it is a major theme of Scripture. Because of the sin of man, all nature has been corrupted. Humanity has been seriously compromised. God will send a person born of a woman who will defeat Satan and restore creation to God's design. When will this Deliverer come? How will we know him? These are among the central questions the Bible was designed to answer.

Seth Postell points out that "a primary function of the book of Genesis in the Torah is to blaze a trail leading from the seed of the woman in

---

8. "Torah" is also used in secondary ways in Judaism. For example, it can refer to the entire Old Testament or to the literature of later rabbinic traditions (the so-called "oral torah").

9. Ellis, *The Old Testament in Early Christianity*, ix.

10. Chen, *The Messianic Vision of the Pentateuch*, 91, n. 50.

11. G. Ortlund, "Resurrected as Messiah," 756–59.

Gn 3:15 to the coming Messiah in Gn 49:8–12." If this is true of Genesis, what of the Gospels? Postell continues, "Matthew's purpose in beginning his Gospel with a genealogy is to trace the line of the promised seed to the person of Jesus."[12]

In his first epistle, the Apostle Peter indicates that when the prophets were given revelations about the coming Messiah, they were anxious to know more about the circumstances and timing of his arrival. Likewise, even the angels were simply beside themselves to know how God's plan would unfold. The mental picture I have is angels on tiptoe, looking over the banister of heaven, straining to see the story of Messiah play out following his birth in Bethlehem (1 Pet 1:10–12).

The truth is, the entire Old Testament is pregnant—it is expectant. It is anticipating God's answer for the destructive curse of Satan in the Garden of Eden. The Old Testament is not merely a repository of Israel's historical and poetic literature (although it does contain much of ancient Israel's history and tremendous literature). It is a text that bears an overarching message, the message of the coming Deliverer!

It is important to understand that the title "Messiah" comes from the Hebrew word *mashiach* and literally means "an anointed one." The Greek word for "an anointed one" is *christos*, from which we derive the English word "Christ." Everywhere you read "Christ" in the New Testament, you could just as easily and legitimately substitute the word "Messiah."[13] For modern English speakers, using the term "Christ" tends to obscure the Jewishness of Jesus.

MESSIANIC PROPHECY IN SCRIPTURE

The Scriptures are full of prophecies about the coming Messiah.[14] The promise of the Seed of a woman that was made in the Garden (Gen 3:15), we are later told, would be fulfilled in a descendant of Abraham, Isaac,

---

12. Postell, "Typology in the Old Testament," 166.

13. The concept of a coming Deliverer is found very early in Genesis, long before the word "Messiah" was used of him. We will be tracing the development of the promises of Messiah, even though this word may not be used of him in the earliest portions of the Bible.

14. Michael Rydelnik and Edwin Blum have edited the most comprehensive and valuable work on messianic prophecy from the perspective of direct fulfillment: *The Moody Handbook of Messianic Prophecy*.

and Jacob.[15] As we continue through Genesis and on to 2 Samuel, we are told that this Seed, or Deliverer, would be of the lineage of Judah and then of David. Eventually the prophet Isaiah would be told that the Deliverer would be born of a pregnant virgin. He would literally be the seed (or descendant) of a woman, just as was prophesied in the Garden of Eden.

The Bible presents many details about the coming Messiah, and it portrays him in a variety of ways. The Hebrew Scriptures present him as a poor, suffering, and humble martyr, whose death provides atonement for sin.[16] But it also paints him as a victorious conqueror, who judges righteously, restores justice, and utterly defeats his enemies.[17] David, Isaiah, and others portray him as the Servant of the Lord, the Son of God, and as God himself. Most importantly for our purposes, he is a specific prophet, a specific priest, and a specific king. These last three are his messianic offices.[18] He is the Anointed One, and these are the offices that require an anointing. Understanding these three offices will prove to be crucial in understanding the New Testament and the Messianic Kingdom.

MESSIANIC PROPHECY IN CHRISTIAN SCHOLARSHIP

Yet messianic prophecy is suffering at the hands of some contemporary biblical scholars who have lost confidence in the messianic significance of the Old Testament.[19] For example, Mark Boda says, "For an Old Testament scholar to venture into a study of Messiah is a daring act indeed."

---

15. For a defense of the futuristic and messianic interpretation of Genesis 3:15, see August, "The Messianic Hope of Genesis," 46–62; Postell, "Genesis 3:15," 239–50; and M. Rydelnik, *The Messianic Hope*, 129–45.

16. Cf., e.g., Ps 22; Isa 53; Zech 9:9–10.

17. Cf., e.g., Ps 89:24–37; Isa 42:1–4; 59:17–20; Zech 2:10–13.

18. They are often referred to by the Latin term *munis triplex*, the threefold office or employment. Eusebius (d. AD 339) first refers to them in his *Ecclesiastical History* (1.3.8). More than twelve hundred years later, Calvin (AD 1559) also wrote about these offices. See his *Institutes of the Christian Religion*, 2:15. In contemporary Reformed circles this threefold office is sometimes called the "Triple Cure," for all three roles provide the remedies we need in our sinful and fallen condition. For more on this, see Appendix 1.

19. For a historical survey of the rise of this non-messianic interpretation, see Provan, "The Messiah in the Books of Kings," 68–71. See also McConville, "Messianic Interpretation of the Old Testament," 2. Also addressing this skepticism, see Porter and Dyer, *Origins of New Testament Christology*, 135–36.

Modern Old Testament scholarship is reluctant to accept that messianic prophecy is legitimate.[20]

It appears some of these scholars do not believe the Bible to be the authoritative and inerrant Word of God. They seem to be saying the authors of the New Testament didn't know what they were talking about when they interpreted an Old Testament passage of the Messiah. James Hamilton addresses this type of scholar to make a valid point:

> We then set aside the possibility that ancient people were stupid, which seems to be an implicit assumption of a good deal of modern scholarship. . . . Since the authors of these [New Testament] texts are presumably seeking to be persuasive to their contemporaries, it seems to me unlikely that their contemporaries would grant the imposition of new meanings onto these texts.[21]

More than that, if the authors of the Gospels were wrong about messianic prophecy, the Gospels they wrote are unreliable, because according to these accounts, Jesus also claimed that the Old Testament spoke of him. In John 5, Jesus said to the religious leaders, "You search the Scriptures, because you think that in them you have eternal life; it is these that testify about Me; and you are unwilling to come to Me, so that you may have life" (vv. 39–40).[22]

He concludes by saying (vv. 45–47), "Do not think that I will accuse you before the Father; the one who accuses you is Moses, in whom you have set your hope. For if you believed Moses, you would believe Me; for he wrote about Me. But if you do not believe his writings, how will you believe My words?" They had misunderstood the Pentateuch, because they saw it as presenting the law as the ultimate goal and the way of salvation. Instead, the Pentateuch pointed forward to the coming Messiah who alone could provide salvation.[23] The Law was important, but preparatory (Gal 3:24). Messiah was the goal.

Due to the generally negative view of messianic prophecy, many Christians have never really been exposed to what the Old Testament says about the coming Messiah. It is important for us to hear the voices

---

20. Boda, "Figuring the Future," 35.
21. J. Hamilton, "The Skull Crushing Seed of the Woman," 44, n. 5.
22. See Matt 26:24; Mark 9:12; Luke 24:25, 27.
23. We see the same perspective on several other occasions in the Gospels. See, for example, John 1:43; 9:24–33; Luke 24:27. See also Chen, *The Messianic Vision*, 1–5.

of Moses, David, Isaiah, and others as they write what God had revealed to them.

THE CANONICAL APPROACH TO THE OLD TESTAMENT

Since the early 1990s, a revolution has occurred in Old Testament studies. There are certainly roots that go back earlier,[24] but with the writings of the late John Sailhamer and other scholars, the messianic message of the Old Testament has become more apparent. They give attention to the literary structure of the biblical books and to the way later texts quote directly from and refer to the earlier texts. This is called a "canonical" approach, and Sailhamer describes it as seeing "not only the content of the OT, but also its form, as theologically relevant."[25]

Sailhamer claims that the messianic message of the Old Testament is not limited to the various messianic prophecies scattered throughout the text; furthermore, it doesn't become apparent only after the resurrection. Instead, the Old Testament is "a single work with a single purpose,"[26] and it does not merely prophesy the coming of the Messiah but describes and identifies him. The Old Testament pre-interprets itself even before we get to the New Testament. In other words, the Old Testament is "both text and commentary."[27] It is self-explanatory.

People have taken different approaches to studying God's Word. Some look for verses that can be taken out of context and applied as sentiments to their lives. Others take the Bible more seriously, but it is little more than a narrative of events that took place thousands of years ago. The canonical approach, also called a compositional approach, prevents

---

24. Cf., e.g., Childs, *Introduction to the Old Testament as Scripture* and Wilson, *The Editing of the Hebrew Psalter*. The roots can even be traced back to Muilenburg, "Form Criticism and Beyond," 1–18.

25. Sailhamer, "The Canonical Approach to the OT," 307. Among Sailhamer's most important works are *The Pentateuch as Narrative*; *Introduction to Old Testament Theology*; and *The Meaning of the Pentateuch*. J. Hamilton points out that intertextuality may not be limited simply to verbal connections. See his article "The Skull Crushing Seed of the Woman." Among others, scholars who take the same general approach include M. Rydelnik, *The Messianic Hope*; Postell, Bar, and Soref, *Reading Moses, Seeing Jesus*; and most recently, the authors of essays in *Moody Handbook of Messianic Prophecy*, eds. M. Rydelnik and Blum.

26. Sailhamer, "Messiah and the Hebrew Bible," 48.

27. Sailhamer, "Messiah and the Hebrew Bible," 49.

us from taking verses out of context.[28] Instead, it is by studying the context that we can identify the verses that the text itself considers the most significant from the author's perspective.

Growing numbers of scholars have gone deeper into the text and discovered for themselves that the Bible is intricately structured, with a purposeful use of key words, connecting passages, and literary forms (such as poems) that reveal the author's main point. Rather than only seeking individual passages that explicitly speak of the Messiah, we need to give attention to the context and how these passages fit within the overall organizational (or canonical) strategy of the book.

Scholars who approach the text from this perspective have shown that the very structures of the books of the Pentateuch, as well as Psalms and Isaiah, are all designed to point to the Messiah. Even the way the three divisions of the Hebrew Bible—the Law, the Prophets, and the Writings—are connected to one another reveals this messianic theme.

This network of verbal connections in the Old Testament is overlooked by many. This makes our journey through the Old Testament a bit more interesting. We've already likened it to a hike. Now let's consider it an expedition through a jungle.

As a child, I loved watching Tarzan movies. Raised in the jungle by apes, Tarzan seemed to be intimately familiar with the trees and vines of the jungle, so that he could swing from one tree to another, and the vine was never too weak or too short to reach the next tree. What looked at first to be random growth had some kind of order to it.

I want to point out some of the individual "vines" and "trees" of the Old Testament, so that you can see how they are connected and actually carry the portrait of Messiah through the Scriptures. When we "swing" into the New Testament, I hope you find a new sense of adventure and the joy of discovery.

Although the Kingdom will be very important, the focus of Scripture is not so much on the Kingdom as it is on the Messiah. The Old Testament as a whole, as well as in its individual parts, can best be understood as a textbook about the Messiah.[29] As James Hamilton puts it, "The OT is a messianic document, written from a messianic perspective,

---

28. This approach is adopted to some extent by Israeli scholars, such as Garsiel, *From Earth to Heaven*, 6; Grossman, *Esther*; and Zakovitch, *Jacob*. These authors refer to their approach as the "Close Reading" method.

29. Cf., M. Rydelnik, *The Messianic Hope*, 7–12.

to sustain a messianic hope."[30] Understanding what the Old Testament says about him can only enrich our understanding of the New Testament witness. So, following a brief word about the messianic offices, we will turn to the Hebrew Scriptures of the Old Testament.

THE MESSIANIC OFFICES OF PROPHET, PRIEST, AND KING

God dealt with Israel in the Old Testament as a microcosm of humanity in order to bring salvation to the nations. Ultimately, the Messiah, or the Anointed One, would reveal God's authoritative Word and his will to Israel. But until his appearance, it would be revealed through prophets, priests, and kings. These Old Testament offices find their fulfillment in the Messiah. The Hebrew Scriptures present him as the Prophet like Moses (Deut 18:15–19), the Priest like Melchizedek (Ps 110:4), and the King like David (2 Sam 7:12–13, 16). These are three distinct offices which the Messiah is to occupy; nevertheless, in the Old Testament, the characteristics of these offices may not always be quite as distinct. For example, sometimes a king may do priestly things, but he is not actually ever a priest.

The Messiah's role as the Prophet like Moses is most neglected, and this has tremendous implications. This role is crucially important in understanding Jesus's earthly ministry. Likewise, his role as the Priest like Melchizedek does not receive the attention it deserves. Some authors, and many other Christians, completely ignore these offices and their distinctions in their discussion of messianic prophecy and the establishment of the Messianic Kingdom.[31]

The characteristics and offices of prophet, priest, and king are applied to Messiah throughout the Hebrew Scriptures. As we turn to the first five books of Scripture, we will look at several passages but focus primarily on only seven key texts: two that relate to his role as Prophet, two that relate to his role as Priest, and three that relate to his role as King. These will be the points of departure for our journeys through the remainder of Scripture. We will begin with the office of the prophet.

---

30. J. Hamilton, "The Skull Crushing Seed of the Woman," 30.

31. A notable exception is Arnold G. Fruchtenbaum, who says of Messiah, "He does not function in all three offices contemporaneously or simultaneously, but rather chronologically." See his *The Footsteps of the Messiah*, 18. I agree that these roles are inaugurated sequentially, but I also believe Scripture teaches these roles are in some sense cumulative as well.

Part 1

The Messiah in the Pentateuch

1

The Prophet Like Moses

MANY HAVE NOTED SIMILARITIES between Moses and the Messiah. One commonality is a humble birth. Moses was born into an Israelite family of slaves (Exod 2:1–2). He was born under the shadow of death (Exod 1:15–22). Nevertheless, not only was his life preserved, but he seemed destined for royalty. He was adopted by Pharaoh's daughter (Exod 2:10) and is referred to as a "prince" in Exodus 2:14.[1]

Likewise, the Messiah would be of humble birth, as he would be like a "root out of parched ground" (Isa 53:2). Messiah would also be born under the shadow of death (Jer 31:15–17; Matt 2:17–18). Nevertheless, his life would be preserved, and he would be destined for royalty (Gen 49:10) and would be referred to as a Prince (Dan 9:25).

The undercover Messiah humbled himself and took on the roles of Prophet and Priest before assuming his role as our King. But before this would unfold, God ordained Moses to prefigure the Messiah as an "undercover" redeemer—reared in Pharaoh's court to be a king, reduced to an exiled shepherd in the wilderness, until raised by God to greatness as a deliverer of millions.

---

1. Gerard Van Groningen claims, "It can be said, with good evidence, that the name *Moses* is derived from the Egyptian term *mesi*, meaning 'to bear.'" He continues, "The Egyptian princess thus indicated that the child she found was to be considered as of royal or noble birth." See his *Messianic Revelation in the Old Testament*, 200.

MOSES AS THE MASTER PROPHET

Most Christians are familiar with the great prophets of the Old Testament. You may not have given much thought to Moses as a prophet, but he was the "master prophet"—all the other prophets served Moses and the Law. One scholar has written, "Moses had a unique position in regard to the prophets: he is placed before them and 'over them in advance.'"[2] Moses delivered the Law, and the subsequent prophets called Israel back to the Law. In a sense, they were servants of Moses, the great prophet.

More than that, however, God gave Moses and Israel the revelation of a future Prophet yet to come—one who would be like Moses, only greater. Sailhamer says, "The mediator Moses becomes one of the central narrative vehicles for depicting the messianic hope."[3] In other words, Moses was, in many respects, a picture of what Messiah would be like. More than any other character in the Old Testament, Moses was a redeemer. If this is true, then Moses might be a key to a better understanding of the Gospels.

With that as a prelude, allow me to introduce you to the "Cinderella" of messianic prophecy;[4] that is to say, to one of the most significant messianic prophecies in Scripture—and, like Cinderella, one of the most neglected. I am speaking of Deuteronomy 18:15–19. Although Abraham is called a prophet in Genesis 20:7, and there are other early references to prophets, Sailhamer points out that this passage in Deuteronomy 18 "is the first to discuss the office of the prophet. The historical basis for the office of prophet is Israel's request for a mediator at Sinai."[5]

---

2. Geehardus Vos, as cited by Van Groningen, *Messianic Revelation in the Old Testament*, 197.

3. Sailhamer, *The Pentateuch as Narrative*, 245.

4. Much of the following material has been adapted from Jim R. Sibley, "Deuteronomy 18:15–19." See also, his adaptation, "The 'Cinderella' of Messianic Prophecy."

5. Sailhamer, *The Pentateuch as Narrative*, 456. He cites Exodus 19:16–19 and 20:19–21. For a defense of a directly messianic interpretation of this passage, see Sailhamer, *The Meaning of the Pentateuch*, 18; M. Rydelnik, *The Messianic Hope*, 56–64; and Sibley, "Deuteronomy 18:15–19." For a recent non-messianic interpretation, cf. Gary Edward Schnittjer, *Old Testament Use of Old Testament*, 130–31.

THE PROPHECY: DEUTERONOMY 18:15-19

In the preceding verses of Deuteronomy 18 (vv. 9–14), Moses had warned the people of Israel against "the detestable things"[6] they would encounter when they engaged with the inhabitants of Canaan, and especially against the evil practices of spiritism and necromancy (vv. 9, 12). Then, in contrast to these Satanic and unreliable sources of truth, Moses looked farther into the future and relayed the Lord's promise of an absolutely reliable source of truth, greater even than that which Moses himself could provide. Listen as Moses addresses the nation on the plains of Moab with this remarkable prophecy:

> The LORD your God will raise up for you a prophet like me from among you, from your countrymen, you shall listen to him. This is according to all that you asked of the LORD your God in Horeb on the day of the assembly, saying, "Let me not hear again the voice of the LORD my God, let me not see this great fire anymore, or I will die." The LORD said to me, "They have spoken well. I will raise up a prophet from among their countrymen like you, and I will put My words in his mouth, and he shall speak to them all that I command him. It shall come about that whoever will not listen to My words which he shall speak in My name, I Myself will require *it* of him." (Deut 18:15–19)[7]

Some Christian interpreters believe this passage is only pointing to a succession of prophets that God would raise up in the future. Others go further and claim that God is pointing to a prophetic aspect in the ministry of the coming Messiah. In other words, they are claiming the passage teaches that when Messiah would come, he would have a teaching ministry—he would reveal truth. But the passage says, both in verse 15 and again in verse 18, that God would raise up neither a succession of prophets nor a prophetic aspect, but a Prophet. This Prophet would be "like me [i.e., Moses]," "from among you [i.e., a person]," and "from your countrymen [i.e., an Israelite]." If words mean anything, God is promising to raise up an individual prophet from among the chosen people.

---

6. התועבת, *hato'avoth*.

7. For a discussion of the Hebrew verbal form used here for "raise up" and the intimation of resurrection from the dead, see Chen, *The Messianic Vision of the Pentateuch*, 124–30. He also demonstrates the connection between Genesis 49:10 and Deuteronomy 18:15, 18.

Chen says, "There is likely a sense in which the 'prophet like Moses' is the climax of this section of Deuteronomy."[8]

It is important to note that he will speak the very words of God, and therefore, what he says will carry the highest degree of authority. This divine authority with which he will speak results from the unique and close relationship he would have with the Father. In fact, the warning in Deuteronomy 18:19 is similar to that found in Genesis 2:17. God warned Adam against eating from the tree of the knowledge of good and evil, "for in the day that you eat from it you will surely die." Here, God warns those who will not heed his words, "I Myself will require it of him."

Moses's unique relationship with God is brought out clearly in Exodus 3, with his calling by God to deliver Israel from the oppression of Egypt. In Deuteronomy 18, as we have seen, God specifically calls Moses a prophet, and his unique relationship to God is described in Numbers 12:6–8, following the rebellion of Aaron and Miriam:

> [God] said, "Hear now My words: If there is a prophet among you, I, the LORD, shall make Myself known to him in a vision. I shall speak with him in a dream. Not so, with My servant Moses, He is faithful in all My household; with him I speak mouth to mouth, even openly, and not in dark sayings, and he beholds the form of the LORD. Why then were you not afraid to speak against My servant, against Moses?"

In this, God sets Moses apart from other prophets and accentuates the closeness of their communication. This coming Prophet would have an even closer, more intimate, relationship with the Father than any other. Because he would speak with God's authority, his message would carry the greatest possible measure of accountability. In fact, "servant" (Num 12:7) is the most frequently used title for Moses in the Hebrew Bible.[9] This fact will become more significant in the inspired thought of the prophet Isaiah.

There is evidence that Moses was anointed with the Holy Spirit, although Scripture is not explicit. In Numbers 11, when Moses selected seventy of the elders of Israel, God told him that he would "take of the

---

8. Chen, *The Messianic Vision of the Pentateuch*, 227.

9. Postell, "Typology in the Old Testament," 169. See p. 53, n. 48 below for a listing of references.

Spirit who is upon you [i.e., Moses], and will put *Him* upon them" (v. 17). The effect was that these seventy elders "prophesied" (v. 25).[10]

The very nature of a prophet was that he was to represent God to the nation. He would speak God's words—God's message—to the people, and, as we will see later, he would represent the nation before God. In the first verse of this key passage in Deuteronomy 18, Moses says, "You shall listen to him" (v. 15). In the final verse, God says, "It shall come about that whoever will not listen to My words which he shall speak in My name, I Myself will require *it* of him" (v. 19).

Although this particular prophecy does not specifically mention more than this essential point—that he will speak with the authority of God himself—it does say (twice) that the coming Prophet would be "like" Moses. His divine authority would manifest itself, not only in the messages he would proclaim, but also in supernatural signs or miracles. Moses's life was characterized by miracles, such as the plagues of Egypt, the dividing of the Red Sea, the provision of water and food in the wilderness, and healing from the bites of the serpents. The anticipated Prophet would also come with authenticating miracles. The clear implication is that they would be much more amazing, even jaw-dropping miracles. Moses also prophesied events in the future.[11] The coming Prophet, like Moses, would also reveal the future.

Yet these miracles and prophecies, like those of Moses, would not have the desired effect on the majority of the people. In Moses's day, the people were always grumbling and rebelling against God. In response, Moses functioned as a mediator between Israel and God. In Exodus 32, we read of the incident involving the worship of a golden calf and of God's threat to destroy the people. Verses 11–13 record Moses's intercessory prayer on behalf of the people of Israel. Following the death of about three thousand men of Israel in the ensuing judgment, Moses pled with God again on behalf of his people. Acknowledging the sin of the people, he said, "But now, if You will, forgive their sin—and if not, please blot me out from Your book which You have written!" (v. 32).

Later, in the incident of the rebellion of Korah and others, 14,770 people were killed in a plague from the Lord. On this occasion, Moses assumed, once again, an intercessory role. He directed Aaron to take his stand between the living and the dead, and he burned incense to atone

---

10. In this connection, it is interesting to note that "the Spirit of God came upon" Balaam as he prophesied over Israel in Numbers 24:2.

11. E.g., cf., Deut 4:22, 25–31; 30:1–10; 31:3–5, 29.

for the people and to stop the plague (Num 16:46–48). Later still, when the Israelites rebelled against Moses's leadership, God sent "fiery," or poisonous, snakes among the people. Once more, Moses interceded for the people (Num 21:7).

Yet, in spite of his intercession and his signs of divine authority, Moses was opposed by many of the Israelites, who on two separate occasions threatened to kill him.[12] The coming Prophet would also encounter the same kind of rebellion against God and opposition from the people. As with Moses, this Prophet's ministry would also be characterized by the suffering he would experience at the hands of his countrymen.

These major characteristics of Moses, which will be true in a greater sense with the future Prophet, can be expressed as a mnemonic device, an acronym. Although the letters do not form an actual word, this may help you remember them:

> **R**elationship with God
> **A**uthority of God
> **M**iracles from God
> **P**rophecy of the future
> **I**ntercession with God
> **O**pposition from Israel

THE CONCLUSION: DEUTERONOMY 34:10

In chapter 34, the last chapter of Deuteronomy, we find another reference to this Prophet. In this chapter we read of the death of Moses, so it is safe to say that Moses didn't write this last chapter. Most likely it was written and added to Deuteronomy by Ezra under the inspiration of the Holy Spirit at the end of the Old Testament period. Here, we read: "Since that time no prophet has risen in Israel like Moses, whom the Lord knew face to face" (v. 10).

Sailhamer and others have argued that Deuteronomy 34:10 has not been translated properly. It should be, "Never again did there arise in Israel a prophet like Moses, whom the Lord knew face to face."[13] Rather than simply saying that none of the subsequent prophets ever fulfilled the prophecy of the Prophet like Moses, the verse is emphasizing that the

---

12. Exod 17:4; Num 14:10.

13. Author's translation. See Sailhamer, *The Meaning of the Pentateuch*, 18; see NJPS. See also, Anderson and Giles, *Tradition*, 34.

Prophet like Moses had not come, and the door of the Old Testament has been closed. The implication is that he is yet to come.

Sailhamer continues by saying, "Thus by the time the last verses of Deuteronomy were attached to the Pentateuch, these verses in Deuteronomy 18 were already being understood eschatologically and messianically."[14] In other words, they pointed to the distant future, when Messiah would come. If so, the Old Testament period ends with the anticipation of the arrival of this ultimate Prophet.

Like Moses, he would be recognized by the characteristics we listed above ("RAMPIO"). Like Moses, he would also bring deliverance. Like Moses, he would initiate a covenant with Israel. Yet in all this, he would be much greater than Moses. Did Moses understand what he was writing? Jesus told his contemporaries, "If you believed Moses, you would believe Me, for he wrote about Me" (John 5:46). Yes, Moses understood.

Generally speaking, rabbinic tradition does not recognize the passages about the Prophet like Moses as messianic;[15] however, a famous scholar of the Middle Ages, Gershonides does make this connection.[16] Gershonides is significant because: (1) He links Deuteronomy 18:15–19 with 34:10. (2) He says that this prophet must have a ministry not just to Israel, but also to the nations. (3) He takes the prophecy as referring to the Messiah rather than to a succession of prophets, even citing Isaiah 11, a tremendously messianic passage. He refers to the nations, which may be an allusion to Isaiah 11:10, which says, "Then in that day the *nations* will resort to the root of Jesse, who will stand as a signal for the peoples; and His resting place will be glorious." (4) He says that the coming prophet

---

14. Sailhamer, *The Pentateuch as Narrative*, 456. See also Chen, *The Messianic Vision of the Pentateuch*, 241.

15. It is often claimed that rabbinic tradition never considers this passage to be messianic. H. L. Ellison comments: "If Moses's promise of 'a prophet like me' is never referred to the Messiah in rabbinic literature, if indeed it is seldom referred to at all, then it can mean only that the rabbis saw in the Christian interpretation something so dangerous that every reference to it had to be suppressed." See Ellison, *The Centrality of the Messianic Idea*, 16. Maimonides (Rabbi Moses ben Maimon, 1138–1204) may be an exception. He wrote, "The Messiah will be a very great Prophet, greater than all the prophets with the exception of Moses our Teacher . . . His status will be higher than that of the 19 prophets and more honorable, Moses alone excepted. The Creator, blessed be He, will single him out with features wherewith He had not singled out Moses" (Abraham Cohen, *The Teachings of Maimonides*, 121).

16. Rabbi Levi ben Gershon (also known as RaLBaG), 1288–1344.

must have greater signs and wonders than Moses, including possibly resurrection from the dead![17]

The Prophet whom God promised to raise up in Deuteronomy 18:15 can be none other than the ultimate Deliverer from sin, later to be known as the Messiah. He would be identified with even greater signs and wonders and would have an even closer relationship with God. Judgment would come to any who failed to heed his authoritative word. Messiah would be a Prophet like Moses. Now we will turn to consider the roles of priest and king.

---

17. For an English translation of this passage, see Sibley, "Deuteronomy 18:15–19," 326. Gershonides is known to be a non-conformist in his interpretations.

2

The Alternative Priesthood

HAVING TRACED THE OFFICE of the prophet through the Torah, we now want to consider the office of the priest. It might be helpful to highlight the distinction between prophets and priests. Although both are mediators, the prophets focused on spiritual and moral holiness, while the focus of the priests was primarily ritual purity. Priests were to guard the purity and holiness of God. Prophets called the people to repentance and faith in the Lord, while holding before them the messianic hope. Priests sanctified those who had heeded the message of the prophets.

First, we will examine a prophecy that the nation itself would become a priestly nation. Along the way, we want to consider the Aaronic priesthood as it would develop in Moses's day. Then we will consider an alternative priesthood—that of Melchizedek, which actually predates the Aaronic priesthood.[1]

---

1. Technically, the first-born sons of Israel were considered as consecrated to God, and thus like priests. They were set apart, for the Lord had "passed over" them, sparing them from death in Egypt. They belonged to the Lord. This provides the rationale for the ceremony of the redemption of the firstborn. This ceremony is observed by the Jewish people to this day.

THE PROMISE OF A PRIESTLY NATION: EXODUS 19:5-6

God told Moses when he first ascended Mount Sinai to tell the people: "Now then, if you will indeed obey My voice and keep My covenant, then you shall be My own possession[2] among all the peoples, for all the earth is Mine; and you shall be to Me a kingdom of priests and a holy nation" (Exod 19:5-6). These verses are usually understood to be a commission given to Israel, introduced with a condition. In other words, "*If* you obey My voice and keep My covenant, *then* you will have a special relationship to Me and an honored role." Many books and teachers point to this passage and say something like, "This was Israel's mission, but they failed, so the church has now taken over their mission."[3]

There are several reasons why this interpretation cannot be correct. First, regarding the status of the people, it had been previously established. They were by now already God's covenant people. God had reaffirmed his covenant with Abram, to his son, Isaac, and grandson, Jacob, to establish Israel as his covenant people.[4] God told Abram, "As for Me, behold, My covenant is with you, and you will be the father of a multitude of nations" (Gen 17:4). In Exodus 6:6-7, God told Moses to say to the sons of Israel, "I will bring you out from under the burdens of the Egyptians, and I will deliver you from their bondage.... Then I will take you for My people, and I will be your God; and you shall know that I am the LORD your God, who brought you out from under the burdens of the Egyptians." In fact, in Exodus 19:4 God says, "You yourselves have seen what I did to the Egyptians, and how I bore you on eagles' wings, and brought you to Myself."

This status of the people is also borne out later, before the Israelites entered the Promised Land, in Deuteronomy 7:6: "For you are a holy people to the LORD your God; the LORD your God has chosen you to be a people for His own possession."[5] Here he uses the same word as in Exodus 19:5. So, the status of Israel was not in doubt.

---

2. Heb., סגלה, *segullah*.

3. Cf., e.g., Goheen, *A Light to the Nations*, 37-40, 160; Moreau, Corwin, and McGee, *Introducing World Missions*, 36, 67; and Beale, *A New Testament Biblical Theology*, 651-65.

4. See Gen 12:1-3; 15; 22:18; 26:4; 28:14.

5. סגלה, *segullah* is relatively rare. It is found eight times in the Masoretic Text. Twice it refers to the king's personal treasury (1 Chr 29:3; Eccl 2:8). Six times it is used to designate Israel as God's treasure (Exod 19:5; Deut 7:6; 14:2; 26:18; Ps 135:4; Mal 3:17). Finally, in Malachi, it is used of the faithful remnant (3:6).

Second, at this point in God's dealings with Israel, they were incapable of meeting the conditions outlined in Exodus 19:5: "if you will indeed obey My voice and keep My covenant." Before they entered the Land, Moses told the Israelites of God's judgment: "Yet to this day, the Lord has not given you a heart to know, nor eyes to see, nor ears to hear" (Deut 29:4). This judgment of spiritual blindness lasted for the forty years of their wilderness wanderings (Deut 29:4–5). It was inflicted on the nation at Massah and Meribah (Exod 17:1–7; Heb 3:8–11) in the Wilderness of Sinai, prior to Moses's ascent of the mountain.

Third, Exodus 19:6 promises that Israel will be to God "a kingdom of priests and a holy nation." This promise is given here in the future tense, and it is also in the future in other passages in the Old Testament.[6] For example, in Isaiah 61:6 the Servant says of Israel, "But you will be called the priests of the Lord; you will be spoken of as ministers of our God." The phrase found in Exodus 19:6, that Israel would be "a kingdom of priests and a holy nation," is found in the New Testament in the present tense, suggesting at least the partial fulfillment of this verse. Since this is the case, it was not a hypothetical possibility for the Israelites in the wilderness, but more of a promise or a prophecy regarding their future.

This leaves us with a problem: How are we to understand the conditional conjunction, "if," in Exodus 19:5? As Terence E. Fretheim says:

> The force of the "if" and the conditionality of the covenant have to be carefully stated. The issue is not how they might become God's people; Israel is the elect people already. There is no interest in warning Israel that its status as God's people will be taken away if it is disobedient.[7]

There are two related possibilities. Since (1) Israel's status is not in question, (2) since this condition could not have been met by Israel during most of its history due to the judgment of spiritual blindness, and (3) since it has a future reality, it is possible that the conditional conjunction that is translated "if" must express another type of condition.

Since Israel's spiritual blindness will be lifted in the future, this conjunction may best be translated "when."[8] That is to say, "*When* you obey

---

6. Cf., e.g., Jer 31:33; Ezek 37:24.

7. Fretheim, *Exodus*, 213. Likewise, see Kaiser, "Exodus," 415; and V. Hamilton, *Exodus*, 301. These and other commentators struggle with the fact that Israel is already God's special and elect nation, and they conclude that the text is suggesting a new level of intimacy with God.

8. When אם, "if," is used with an imperfect, as here (תשמעו, *tishmᵉ'u*, you will hear

and keep My covenant, *then* you will have a relationship to Me that is much closer as well as an honored role." Or perhaps the Lord is saying that when they would obey his voice and keep his covenant, then they would *truly* be living as his own possession among all the peoples.

In either case, the issue is not *if* they would be God's covenant people, but *when* they would be able to live up to his purposes for them—namely, when they would become "a kingdom of priests and a holy nation." New Testament references to this passage indicate a partial fulfillment in the present tense among Jewish believers in Jesus.[9]

THE INAUGURATION OF ISRAEL'S PRIESTHOOD: EXODUS 19:10-24

Until that time, Israel would need a priesthood. A few verses later, in Exodus 19, we have the account of Moses, when he ascended Mount Sinai three times, and God told him to come up a fourth time.[10] God summoned the people to Mount Sinai (19:13b), but they were too fearful and remained in the camp (v. 16). Sailhamer tells the story:

> As the display of God's glorious power on the mountain grows stronger and louder, the people are able to listen as Moses converses with God. Moses speaks from the foot of the mountain, and God answers him from the top (Ex 19:19). Given the importance of this narrative, we might expect their conversation to center on the Ten Commandments. That was not the case, however.... The conversation here centers on access to God on the mountain. It is a conversation that lays the groundwork for the priesthood and tabernacle (Ex 19:20-24).[11]

Here, God told Moses not to let the people gaze upon him, lest they perish, and to have the priests consecrate themselves. The issue was the holiness of God.

The order of priests from the family of Aaron was soon inaugurated (Lev 8). Exodus 28-29 set out the liturgical requirements for these priests. Others from the Tribe of Levi were brought in to assist the

---

or obey) it can suggest an as yet unrealized condition. See *BDB*, 50. See also Waltke and O'Connor, *An Introduction to Biblical Hebrew Syntax*, 562 (§32.2.1).

9. Cf., e.g., 1 Pet 2:9-10. For a defense of Jewish believers in Jesus as the recipients of 1 Peter, see Sibley, "You Talkin' to Me?" 59-75.

10. Exod 19:3, 8, 20, 24.

11. Sailhamer, *The Meaning of the Pentateuch*, 384.

Aaronic priests. These Levites were responsible for moving the tabernacle while in the wilderness and later served as musicians and treasurers in the temple. They were set apart "to carry the ark of the covenant of the LORD, to stand before the LORD to serve Him and to bless in His name" (Deut 10:8). Now, let's go back to the time of Abram, some five hundred years earlier.

MELCHIZEDEK AND THE ALTERNATIVE PRIESTHOOD: GENESIS 14:18–20

The first priest mentioned in the Bible is Melchizedek, who was a priest of God Most High, and who served as a priest for Abram. In a fascinating major study of this passage, Joshua Mathews claims, "There is a textually recognizable and demonstrably distinct priestly succession—an order of Melchizedek—intended in the composition of the Pentateuch and continuing throughout the OT canon."[12] He goes on to say, "This priesthood of Melchizedek, which includes a royal aspect, is presented as an alternative order to the priesthood of Aaron."[13]

Following Abram's victory over the coalition of four kings and the rescue of his nephew Lot Abram went to Salem, which is almost universally identified as Jerusalem. Here, he was met by "Melchizedek, king of Salem," who was also "a priest of God Most High" (Gen 14:18). Genesis 14:19–20 completes the account of Melchizedek: "He blessed him and said, 'Blessed be Abram of God Most High, possessor of heaven and earth; and blessed be God Most High, who has delivered your enemies into your hand.'"

The phrases "Melchizedek, king of Salem" and "priest of God Most High" are full of significance. "Melchizedek," as a name, literally means "king of righteousness." "Salem" is most often related to the Hebrew word *shalom*, which means "peace." This king of righteousness and peace, however, is also a priest of God Most High. This can refer to none other than the God of Abram, for Abram uses the same name for God (Gen 14:22). The fact that Melchizedek's priesthood is connected to his role as a king is significant, as it points to Messiah's identity as one who fulfills both roles. This "alternative" priest is also a major theme of the Pentateuch.

---

12. Mathews, *Melchizedek's Alternative Priestly Order*, 2–3.
13. Mathews, *Melchizedek's Alternative Priestly Order*, 3.

In the following chapter of Genesis, it seems more than coincidental that Abram's faith is credited to him as "righteousness" (Gen 15:6). In 14:20, Melchizedek notes that God had "delivered" (Heb., *migen*) Abram's enemies into his hand. In 15:1, God told Abram that he would be a "shield" (Heb., *magen*) to him. In chapter 14, we are introduced to the king of righteousness, and in chapter 15, righteousness is credited to Abram.

Mathews makes this comment: "The blessing of the king of righteousness must be understood, it seems, in light of Yahweh's attribution of righteousness to Abram for believing his promise of a coming seed."[14] This seed, of course, is the coming Deliverer, the Messiah. At the very least, the account of Melchizedek gives additional information about this future Deliverer. He will not only be of the lineage of Abram, but he will be a priest-king, characterized by righteousness and peace. Most importantly, he will be able to attribute righteousness to sinful humans.

Mathews suggests that another, who we are to understand to be a successor to Melchizedek, is Jethro.[15] Notice these parallels: We meet Melchizedek, the Jebusite priest, in connection with a miraculous defeat of God's enemies, the coalition of four kings. Likewise, we meet Moses's father-in-law, Jethro, the Midianite priest, in connection with the miraculous defeat of God's enemies, Pharaoh and the gods of Egypt. He is a priest whose ministry is affirmed by Moses, just as Melchizedek's was affirmed by Abraham, but they both come from gentile backgrounds. Does this not arouse some curiosity?

How does this alternative priesthood of Melchizedek and Jethro compare to the Aaronic priesthood? When God told Moses to go to Egypt and speak to Pharaoh to bring the Israelites out of Egypt, Moses demonstrates a lack of faith.[16] Miraculous signs are given to him to bolster his faith, but he still doubts.[17] At this point, God provides Aaron to Moses as a concession for his lack of faith.[18] This is Aaron's introduction

---

14. Mathews, *Melchizedek's Alternative Priestly Order*, 71. For helpful articles on the interpretation of "seed," see Collins, "A Syntactical Note (Genesis 3:15)," 139–48; and Alexander, "Further Observations on the Term 'Seed' in Genesis," 363–67. Yahweh is the covenant name of God, sometimes anglicized as Jehovah.

15. Others have also been suggested. Chen, for example, suggests that Bezalel (Exod 31:1–6; 36–39) may also have functioned as a priest of this alternative order. See Chen, *The Messianic Vision of the Pentateuch*, 168–87. This is unlikely, for the Mosaic Covenant was functioning at that time.

16. Exod 3:11, 13.

17. Exod 4:1–10, 13.

18. Exod 4:14–16. See Mathews, *Melchizedek's Alternative Priestly Order*, 82.

in the record of Scripture—"as a concession, like the signs that Moses was given at the beginning of the chapter in response to Moses's weak faith and disobedience to God's call."[19]

The following chapters clarify that although neither Aaron nor Moses are completely obedient, "Aaron is at the center of these departures and deviations" from God's will.[20] The point is not to paint Aaron in an entirely negative light, but to demonstrate that he is somewhat of a disappointment. Aaron and his priesthood "are presented as accommodations necessitated by disobedience and lack of faith."[21]

Aaron was of the Tribe of Levi. It is also interesting to note that Levi had a shameful past. He and his brother, Simeon, had killed the men of Shechem and plundered their goods, following the rape of their sister, Dinah (Gen 34). This led to their father, Jacob, uttering a deathbed curse against them (Gen 49:5–7). As we have seen, the descendants of Levi, that is, the Levites of Moses's day, through their obedience to Moses in the incident of the rebellion of Korah, partially atoned for the shame of their ancestor (Exod 32:28).[22] Nevertheless, they were not allotted a portion in the Land. The point is that neither Levi nor his descendant Aaron is portrayed as an ideal model for the priesthood.

It is interesting to note here that there is a distinction between Moses and Aaron. Psalm 99:6 says, "Moses and Aaron were among His priests." The psalmist does not hesitate to refer to Moses as a priest, although he was not an Aaronic priest, like Aaron, but adopted some priestly functions. There is no record of Moses ever being anointed with oil, even though he made the oil with which Aaron was anointed (Exod 30:30; Lev 8:12).

JETHRO AND THE ALTERNATIVE PRIESTHOOD: EXODUS 18:8–12

In contrast to Aaron, consider Moses's father-in-law, Jethro, who was a priest of Midian. We read of him functioning as a priest for Moses in

---

19. Mathews, *Melchizedek's Alternative Priestly Order*, 85.
20. Mathews, *Melchizedek's Alternative Priestly Order*, 89.
21. Mathews, *Melchizedek's Alternative Priestly Order*, 96.
22. See Zakovitch, *Jacob*, 122–29. Also, Kissling, "The Testament of Jacob and the Blessing of Moses," 1–15, and especially 5.

Exodus 18:8–12. He is first mentioned in Exodus 2, and in chapter 4 he encourages Moses to be obedient to God's call.

In working through the relevant texts of Scripture in great detail, Mathews concludes that the Scripture intends for the reader to make a comparison between Aaron and Jethro. He demonstrates that a comparison between these two priests, their legal systems and their priesthoods, reveals Jethro as a representative of an alternative and superior priesthood—similar to that of Melchizedek, back in Abram's time.[23]

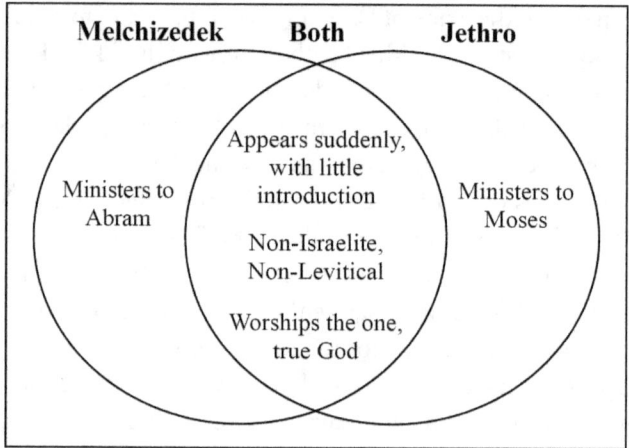

The Alternative Priesthood

What are some of the connections between Jethro and Melchizedek? Like Melchizedek, Jethro is a non-Levitical priest who arrives unannounced and with minimal introduction. Both worship the one true God, the God of Israel. Melchizedek ministers to Abram, and Jethro ministers to Moses. Unlike the Aaronic priesthood, the order of Melchizedek does not follow a genealogical lineage. Nevertheless, "Jethro is meant to be portrayed as continuing Melchizedek's priesthood, which is notably distinct from Aaron's."[24] Unlike the Aaronic priesthood, there is no record of either Melchizedek or of Jethro ever having been anointed with oil.

---

23. Mathews, *Melchizedek's Alternative Priestly Order*, 97–109. For example, compare Exod 4:14, 27 and 18:5, 7.

24. Mathews, *Melchizedek's Alternative Priestly Order*, 5. See also 109.

CONCLUSION

In addition to the Prophet like Moses, we are also to anticipate a Priest like Melchizedek and Jethro. The focus of the prophet was on the moral and spiritual purity of the nation, whereas the focus of the priest was on its ceremonial purity. Both were essential. Nevertheless, the ministry of the prophet was foundational for that of the priest, for the offerings and sacrifices were meaningless without repentance and faith.

We have noted the divine authority with which the coming Prophet will speak and act. We should also know, however, that the priest carried a similar authority. In Deuteronomy 17:12 we read, "The man who acts presumptuously by not listening to the priest who stands there to serve the Lord your God, nor to the judge, that man shall die; thus you shall purge the evil from Israel." If the Aaronic priest had such authority, how much more the Great Priest to come?

3

The Coming King

THE PATTERN IN THE POEMS

MESSIAH WAS NOT ONLY to be a prophet and a priest, but also a king. This kingship is also portrayed in the Pentateuch, primarily in the poems that form its overall structure. The books of Torah are arranged in chronological order, but they also use a poetic framework that ties them together as a unit. A long narrative section is followed by a poetic section, which is followed by an epilogue.[1]

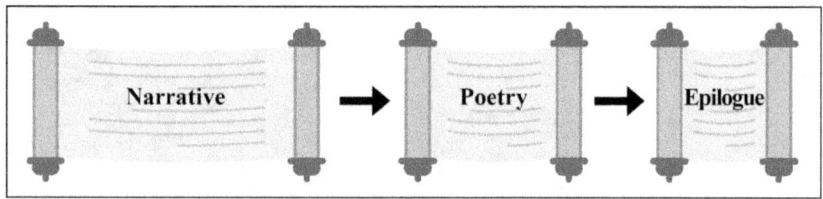

The Pattern of the Pentateuch

At this point, I need to say a word about Hebrew poetry. It is not like Western poetry, which is characterized by meter and rhyme (e.g., "The thunder roared, the lightning flashed, the tree was split, the frog was

---

1. Sailhamer notes that this pattern is common in smaller units in the Pentateuch as well as in the macrostructure. Cf., Sailhamer, *The Pentateuch as Narrative*, 35. See, e.g., Gen 1—2:22 (narrative); 2:23 (poetry); 2:24 (epilogue).

smashed!").[2] Hebrew poetry uses alliteration, couplets (i.e., parallelism), puns, cadence, and other features, most of which are completely lost in English translation. Alliteration, where words beginning with the same or similar sounds are used together, may also be found in some psalms, like Ps 119, when the first word of each line begins with the same letter (in Hebrew).

Hebrew poetry is most often characterized by parallelism (either synonymous or antithetic). A good example is from Isaiah 1:3: "An ox knows its owner, and a donkey its master's manger." In these two lines, "ox" is parallel to "donkey," and "owner" is parallel to "its master's manger." This is parallelism. The two lines that comprise the rest of the verse are also a synonymous parallel: "But Israel does not know, My people do not understand." These phrases basically say the same thing. However, the first two lines form an antithetical parallelism with the last two lines, for they highlight the contrast between farm animals and Israel. Later, we will see good examples of parallelism when we consider Genesis 49:10–12 and Numbers 24:17–19.

Puns are also a major feature of Hebrew poetry. In Isaiah 5:7, in the "Song of the Vineyard," Isaiah says that the Lord "looked for justice (*mishpat*), but behold bloodshed (*mispach*), for righteousness (*ts'dakah*), but behold a cry of distress (*ts'akah*)." In Genesis 49:8, we read, "Judah (*Yehudah*), your brothers shall praise you (*yoduka*)." These features are not apparent in English. Most modern translations indent poetic sections of Scripture as an aid to the reader. We can recognize it as poetry even if we miss out on the word play.

The major poems of the Pentateuch and their introductions help us understand the overall purpose of the author. There are four major poems at key junctures in the text that give cohesion to the entire Pentateuch. We want to focus on three of them.[3] In each case, (1) the main character

---

2. Source unknown.

3. Chen says of the second such poem, Exodus 15:1–18, that it "does not have the same emphasis on the Messiah and does not refer to the 'end of days'" (Chen, *The Messianic Vision of the Pentateuch*, 100). He continues, "Israel's exodus from Egypt, as essential as it is to the overall divine plan, was never intended to be their ultimate salvation. Moses was not from the line of Judah, but a future prophet like Moses would be" (146). He suggests that its major significance is in establishing the pattern of the Exodus for the future eschatological "second exodus" that centers on the Messiah (156). The first exodus required a Moses; the next will require the Prophet like Moses.

(2) calls an audience together and (3) proclaims what will happen in the last days.[4]

In Genesis 49, the main character is Jacob, and he calls an audience together and proclaims what will happen in the last days. Genesis 49:1 says, "Then [1] Jacob summoned his sons and said, [2] 'Assemble yourselves that I may tell you [3] what will befall you in the days to come.'"

In Numbers 23 and 24, we have poetic oracles of Balaam. He has been hired by Balak, the king of Moab, to curse Israel, but God only puts words of blessing in his mouth. This happens four times, and just before the last words of (1) Balaam, (2) he summons Balak and all the leaders of Moab and proclaims, (3) "Come, and I will advise you what this people [i.e., Israel] will do to your people in the days to come" (Num 24:14).

In Deuteronomy 32, we find the "song of Moses," but immediately preceding it, in Deuteronomy 31:28–29, we read that (1) Moses, just as Jacob and Balaam, is (2) assembling an audience and (3) proclaiming what will happen in the last days.

The earliest portion of Genesis looks back to tell us about the creation of the heavens and earth and of mankind. These earliest Scriptures also tell us about the origin of sin and of the evil that pervades God's good creation. But beginning with Genesis 3:15, the focus is no longer on the past, but on the future—the focus is on the coming Deliverer who will redeem the created universe and mankind from both the effects and presence of sin and evil. This is the futuristic orientation of the Pentateuch.

As we study the verses that introduce these poetic sections, we will find this same focus on the future. They point to "the last days." So do the poetic sections themselves. They specifically focus on a coming king of Israel who will also bring peace and blessing to the nations in the Messianic Age.[5] This is what the Old Testament commentator Michael Shepherd concludes on the use of the phrase "the latter days": "Its sparse and strategic use always occurs in passages that speak of the messianic kingdom."[6]

In these poems we find key words, phrases, and imagery that are repeated by the later poems and tie them together. Sailhamer says, "Each poem is linked to the others by a network of cross-referencing. . . . The intent of this cross-referencing to other poems in the Pentateuch is to connect each of the images in these poems to the single picture of a future

---

4. See Sailhamer, *The Pentateuch as Narrative*, 35–37.
5. Gen 49:8–12; Num 24:5–9; Deut 33:4–7.
6. Shepherd, *A Commentary on the Book of the Twelve*, 53.

king."⁷ In another place, he says, "On all three occasions the subject matter introduced by the phrase 'in the last days' is that of God's future deliverance of his chosen people. At the center of that deliverance stands a king."⁸

It would be worthwhile to examine each of these passages in more detail. These passages structurally carry the messianic theme of the Pentateuch through the words they use.

JACOB: GENESIS 49:8–12⁹

Kevin Chen claims that Genesis 49:8–12 is "the longest continuous Messianic prophecy in the Pentateuch." He argues that it is "an exclusively Messianic prophecy."¹⁰

Jacob gathers his sons together in order to prophesy over them. When he turns to Judah, he tells him that his brothers will praise him, for he will not only be able to exert authority over his enemies, but that even his brothers will bow down to him. He compares Judah to a young lion; in fact, in verse 8 alone, three different words for "lion" are used. Of course, the lion is a common symbol for a king, and this king is associated with the house of Judah. This lion became a symbol for the Tribe of Judah and for the Messiah. In this passage the lion "crouches," patiently waiting to spring into action.

In verse 10, Jacob says Judah will rule and bear a king's scepter.¹¹ Judah will evidently have a dynasty, for the right and authority to reign "will not depart from Judah" until "Shiloh comes." This literally means, until "He to whom it [i.e., the scepter] belongs" will come. This was the understanding of those who followed in the line of Old Testament prophets.¹²

Judah is told that the reign of his descendant will extend to all "the peoples." The following verses (vv. 11–12) are also important. They prophesy that when this descendant comes, the abundance of the Garden

---

7. Sailhamer, *The Meaning of the Pentateuch*, 467.
8. Sailhamer, "Genesis," 275.
9. See M. Rydelnik, *The Messianic Hope*, 47–52; Merrill, "Genesis 49:8–12," 271–84.
10. Chen, *The Messianic Vision of the Pentateuch*, 108.
11. This "scepter" reappears often as a figure of speech (metonymy) of Messiah's authority to rule (see Deut 33:21; Judg 5:15; 2 Sam 7:7; Ps 45:6; 76:1–2; 78:68–70). See Merrill, "Genesis 49:8–12," 271–84.
12. Ezek 21:27; Mic 7:14; see also Ps 78:67–68.

of Eden will be restored in the Messianic Kingdom.[13] Now, hold on to this passage, and let's "swing" to the next poetic section.[14]

BALAAM: NUMBERS 24:5–9, 17–19

The second of the poetic sections is found in Numbers.[15] Chen claims that this section contains "some of the most extensive description of the Messiah in the Pentateuch."[16] Balaam was a pagan prophet who was hired by the king of Moab to curse Israel. However, whenever Balaam attempts to curse Israel, he utters a blessing instead. Balaam's third oracle describes Jacob and the king mentioned in Genesis 49. Sailhamer observes that the oracle "begins with a vision of the restoration of the Lord's garden and the rise of a future king."[17]

The king of this passage is specifically identified by means of a quotation from Genesis 49:9. In Numbers 24:9 we read: "He couches, he lies down as a lion, and as a lion, who dares rouse him? Blessed is everyone who blesses you, and cursed is everyone who curses you." This verse is composed of an allusion to Genesis 49:9 and a direct reference to Genesis 12:3. Sailhamer comments:

> Balaam quotes these words to describe the king of his vision . . . to show to Balak, that, according to words addressed by Jehovah to the Israelites through their own tribe-father [i.e., Jacob], they were to overcome their foes so thoroughly, that none of them should venture to rise up against them again.[18]

---

13. Likewise, Solomon, in Ecclesiastes 2:5, speaks of his efforts to beautify the palace in Jerusalem by planting "all kinds of fruit trees" and making "gardens." The word for "gardens" was translated by the Septuagint as *"paradeisous,"* a word also used of the Garden of Eden in Genesis 2:8. The use of this word in combination with the reference to "all kinds of fruit trees" (cf., Gen 2:9: "every tree that is pleasing to the sight and good for food") may imply that Solomon was trying to restore the Garden of Eden in Jerusalem through human effort, which he finally concluded was all "vanity and striving after wind" (Eccl 2:11).

14. Sailhamer, *The Meaning of the Pentateuch*, 469.

15. See M. Rydelnik, *The Messianic Hope*, 102–3, 143–44; Postell, "Numbers 24:5–9, 15–19," 285–308.

16. Chen, *The Messianic Vision of the Pentateuch*, 199.

17. Sailhamer, *The Meaning of the Pentateuch*, 469. Sailhamer brings out fascinating parallels between Pharaoh and Balak and between Exodus 1 and Numbers 23–24 (Sailhamer, *The Pentateuch as Narrative*, 405–9).

18. Sailhamer, *The Meaning of the Pentateuch*, 469.

The king in question, of course, is the coming Messianic Deliverer. In his final oracle (Num 24:17–19), Balaam says, "I see him, but not now; I behold him, but not near; a star shall come forth from Jacob, a scepter shall rise from Israel, and shall crush through the forehead of Moab, and tear down all the sons of Sheth" (v. 17).

Once again, the Lion of the Tribe of Judah is associated with a ruler's scepter and is said to rise from Israel. A miraculous star would announce his arrival. The Seed of woman, who was promised in the Garden, would be dominant over the serpent and crush his skull (as in Gen 3:15). Here, in Numbers 24, we find a coming skull-crushing king, this time crushing the forehead of Moab (v. 17).[19] Postell concludes his excellent study of this passage by saying:

> The Balaam narrative with its discourses provides the interpretive key for connecting the dots between the creation mandate [Gen 1:28], God's promises to Abraham [Gen 12:1–3], and the coming Messianic King [Gen 49:8–12]. God's plan for humanity through Adam, and through Abraham, will be fully and completely realized through the Messiah's rule in the last days.[20]

MOSES: DEUTERONOMY 33:4–7

In Deuteronomy 32, we find the "Song of Moses." In the introduction just preceding it we read:

> Assemble to me all the elders of your tribes and your officers, that I may speak these words in their hearing and call the heavens and the earth to witness against them. For I know that after my death you will act corruptly and turn from the way which I have commanded you; and evil will befall you *in the latter days*, for you will do that which is evil in the sight of the Lord, provoking Him to anger with the work of your hands. (Deut 31:28–29, emphasis added)

Here, it is Moses assembling an audience and proclaiming what will happen in the last days.

---

19. The language and/or imagery of the crushing of a skull may sometimes be an echo of Genesis 3:15. See Num 24:17; Judg 4:21–22; 9:53. See also J. Hamilton, "The Skull Crushing Seed of the Woman," 30–54.

20. Postell, "Numbers 24:5–9, 15–19," 305.

Following the Song of Moses in Deuteronomy 32, we come to our third poem, in chapter 33. Here, Moses blesses Israel shortly before his death. Moses speaks of loyal subjects—the tribes of Israel, gathered around their king. Moses then turns attention to Judah and prays:

"Hear, O LORD, the voice of Judah, and bring him to his people. With his hands he contended for them, and may You be a help against his adversaries" (v. 7).

When he says, "bring him to his people," he is referring back to Genesis 49:10, to the coming Deliverer, the Lion of the Tribe of Judah. The prayer is that this deliverer will indeed come to "his people," i.e., the people of Judah and all of Israel. Just as the Israelites needed a leader to bring them out of Egypt, so they will need a "Moses-like" king to lead them to salvation. Who will this king be? Him to whom the right belongs, Shiloh.[21]

CONCLUSION

In this first portion of the book, we identified several passages in the Pentateuch that are most important for carrying the revelation of the roles of Messiah. They will continue to be significant as we move through the rest of Scripture. The key passages that speak of the Prophet like Moses are Deuteronomy 18:15–19 and 34:10; the key passages that speak of the Priest-King, after the order of Melchizedek, are Genesis 14:18–20 and Exodus 18:8–12; and the key passages that speak of Messiah as the King are the poems of Genesis 49:8–12; Numbers 24:5–9; and Deuteronomy 33:4–7.

These foundational passages are all found in the Torah, the Book of Moses. They introduce Messiah's offices that we will trace through the Scriptures. We should all become familiar with these crucial passages—ancient words that still live and are still being fulfilled. What a wonderful Savior; what an awesome plan of redemption.

The Pentateuch graphically portrays the sin that emanated from the Garden and that has affected all of God's creation. God indicated right away that sin could not ultimately be tolerated and that he already had a plan to deal with it. The sin of man caused an alienation from God that

---

21. For an excellent discussion of ways in which Genesis 14:18–20 (the Melchizedek passage) is linguistically connected both to the Abrahamic Covenant and to these major poems in the Pentateuch, see Mathews, *Melchizedek's Alternative Priestly Order*, 70–78.

would be addressed by a Prophet who had an intimate relationship with God. If Moses spoke to God face to face, this Prophet like Moses would have an even greater intimacy with God. The sin of man brought guilt, shame, and brokenness, but the Priest like Melchizedek would present an atoning sacrifice and offer forgiveness, comfort, and transformation. The sin of man produced rebellion, confusion, and violence, but when the son of Judah comes again, the one whose right it is to hold ultimate authority, he will govern with righteousness and establish peace.

The Torah—by presenting the Hope of Israel as a prophet, a priest, and a king—is not pointing to three deliverers, but to the one divine Savior who will bear each of these three identities and fulfill each of these roles in God's great plan of redemption. Jesus said, "If you believed Moses, you would believe Me; for he wrote of Me" (John 5:46). Now we turn to the Prophets and Writings of the Old Testament.

Part 2

The Messiah in the Prophets and Writings

In the Pentateuch, Messiah is portrayed as prophet, priest, and king. If we want a truly biblical understanding of the Messiah, we cannot overlook any one of these three offices. Messiah, the Son of God, is all three.

4

Messiah as the Prophet Like Moses

IN THE PROPHETS AND Writings, when Messiah is presented in his role as the Prophet like Moses, he is primarily portrayed from three angles: as the Servant of the Lord, as the Shepherd of Israel, and as the one who suffers. We will look at each of these characteristics. For the sake of brevity, we will limit ourselves to Psalms, Isaiah, and Ezekiel.

DAVID'S PSALMS

God used several people to write the psalms: Moses, David, Solomon, Asaph, and others. The psalms of David are those attributed to him, usually in the superscription to the psalm. Those that give a historical setting are found in five groupings in the Book of Psalms: 3–31, 51–72 (plus 86), 101–3, 108–10, and 138–45. Peter Ho writes that these psalms "first trace the establishment of the Davidic kingship, followed by his downfall. Then, remarkably, the Davidic characterization shifts to a . . . figure, who is blameless, victorious, and juridically condemned. The final Davidic collection reveals a community of people supplicating patiently before the arrival of a blissful and just society."[1] This pattern clearly lends itself to a messianic interpretation. These psalms portray the Messiah as the Servant, as the Shepherd, and as the one who suffers and dies for others.

---

1. Ho, "The Shape of Davidic Psalms as Messianic," 515.

DAVID'S FOCUS

David's final testimony, in 2 Samuel 23:1–5, is very significant for our purposes. These were not the last words he uttered before death, but, as Michael Rydelnik says, "They should be viewed as David's final and formal statement about his writings and kingship."[2] Verse 1 provides the introduction: "Now these are the last words of David. David the son of Jesse declares, the man who was raised on high[3] declares, the anointed of the God of Jacob, and the sweet psalmist of Israel." The way this is translated, all these descriptions could be seen as applying to David. But there is another way to understand this verse.

Of course, this was written in Hebrew, with no vowels. The vowel markings we find today above and below the lines of text were not there originally; they were added by Jewish scribes in the Middle Ages. By slightly changing only one of those vowel marks, you get a dramatically different translation.

The word is 'al (עָל, which, or concerning)—depending upon the vowel—can be translated "on high" or "concerning." Michael Rydelnik translates the last sentence: "The oracle of David son of Jesse the oracle of the man raised up *concerning* (עַל, 'al) the Anointed (Messiah) of the God of Jacob the Delightful One of the songs of Israel."[4] As Sailhamer puts the question, "Is David the 'Anointed of the God of Jacob' . . . or did David himself write about the Anointed of the God of Jacob?"[5]

An oracle is a message from God. The one to whom this oracle has been given is referred to twice. He is "David the son of Jesse," and he is "the man who was raised up." David was very aware that God had raised him up from the sheepfolds; "from the care of the ewes with suckling lambs He brought him to shepherd Jacob His people, and Israel His inheritance" (Ps 78:71).

Not only is the one to whom this message has been given mentioned twice, but the subject is also given twice. David's subject is "the anointed one [Messiah] of the God of Jacob" and "the delightful one of the songs

---

2. M. Rydelnik, "2 Samuel 23:1–7," 400.

3. עַל, 'al.

4. For exegetical support for this claim, see M. Rydelnik, "2 Samuel 23:1–7," 401–2; M. Rydelnik, *The Messianic Hope*, 39–41; Sailhamer, *Introduction to Old Testament Theology*, 221.

5. Sailhamer, *Introduction to Old Testament Theology*, 204.

of Israel."⁶ This says that the "songs of Israel" were about "the Delightful One." When you translate the verse this way and understand it to be pointing to the Messiah, this changes the way you read the psalms.⁷

In these last words, David indicated his favorite subject in the psalms was the Messiah. The psalms are much more messianic than we may have thought. In fact, there is so much messianic material in Psalms that we can only scratch the surface. But as we look for evidence that David saw Messiah as the Prophet like Moses, we must realize that David saw patterns in Scripture. The experiences of Moses were, to a greater extent, to be experienced by the Messiah. As Moses was rejected and opposed by Israel, so also were the prophets who followed him. Most were persecuted, and some of them actually were killed.⁸ The sufferings and opposition in David's life allowed him to identify with the sufferings of the men of God throughout the history of Israel, but preeminently with the coming Messiah, who would be born of his lineage.

Though we primarily think of David as king, David was also a prophet who faced opposition and persecution. In this passage in 2 Samuel 23:1, David twice uses the word, "oracle,"⁹ which is usually reserved for the revelation a prophet would receive from God. In the next verse (v. 2), he says, "The Spirit of the LORD spoke by me, and His word was on my tongue." Again, David prophesied as the Holy Spirit gave him the words to speak and write.

Messiah as the Servant. Several verses from Psalm 69 are quoted in the New Testament as having been fulfilled by Jesus. When verse 17 says, "Do not hide Your face from Your servant," the reference is not to David himself, but to his descendant, the Messiah. In this psalm, the Messianic Servant is obedient in the face of distress (v. 17), reproach, and shame (v. 19). He is offered gall with vinegar to drink (v. 21) yet is obedient unto death.

In a similar vein, Psalm 86 speaks of the universal worship of Messiah (v. 9, as also Ps 72:11). Here again, this worship occurs following persecution, suffering, and death. It is very interesting that David quotes Exodus

---

6. It is interesting to observe that the word translated "delightful" (נעים, *na'im*) is found in 2 Samuel 1:23 and also here in 2 Samuel 23:1.

7. Not only is this the case in light of 2 Samuel 23:1, but also the very structure of the Psalms. See Sailhamer, *NIV Compact Bible Commentary*, 315; D. Mitchell, *The Message of the Psalter*. See also Postell, "Messianism in the Psalms," 457–75.

8. E.g., cf., 1 Kgs 18:4, 13; 19:10, 14; Jer 11:21; 38:4–6; Neh 9:26.

9. נאם, *ne'um*.

34:6 in verse 15. Robert Cole says this "has the effect of casting the speaker as another Moses."[10] Indeed, "Thy servant," that familiar descriptor for Moses, occurs three times in this messianic psalm (vv. 2, 4, and 16).

Messiah as the Shepherd. Not only is the Messiah presented as the Servant of the Lord in Psalms, but he is also pictured as the Shepherd of Israel. Psalm 23 will be given more attention below, but in Psalm 28:9 David writes, "Save Your people, and bless Your inheritance; be their shepherd also, and carry them forever." In Psalm 80:1, he prays, "Oh, give ear, Shepherd of Israel, You who lead Joseph like a flock; You who are enthroned above the cherubim, shine forth!"

Messiah as the Sufferer. In these psalms, as we have seen, David portrays the sufferings and death of the Messiah, which would be utterly unique and go far beyond the experience of Moses or of David himself. Messiah would be rejected, despised, mocked, and be given gall and vinegar to drink (Ps 22:6–8; 69:19–21); he would be estranged from his people and be reproached (Ps 69:20); he would be forsaken by God and suffer disgust, mocking, tremendous thirst, weakness, the piercing of his hands and feet, and the distribution of his garments, presumably because he would have no use for them in death (Ps 22:1–2, 14–18). Even so, his bones would not be broken (Ps 34:20). Even in death his body would not suffer decay, but he would be raised from the dead (Ps 16:10). Another prophecy of his resurrection is found in Psalm 3.[11] Because of prophecies like these, Peter had no problem referring to David as a prophet in his sermon on the Day of Pentecost (Acts 2:30–31).

Just as Moses before him and the prophets who would follow, David knew opposition and suffering. King Saul spent at least ten years pursuing David with murderous intent! Later, as king, David experienced attempted coups—one led by his son, Absalom, and another by Sheba.[12] He saw his suffering as characteristic of the sufferings of Messiah. Yet in these psalms of David, the suffering of Messiah is followed by resurrection and victory.

Of all of David's psalms, Psalm 23 is probably the most famous and one of the best loved. It has brought comfort and strength to believers in times of trials and death. But many have never considered it a messianic psalm.[13]

10. Cole, "Psalms 86–88," 620.
11. Cole, "Psalm 3," 491–502. See also Cole, "Psalm 3," 137–48.
12. 2 Sam 15; 17:21—18:33; 20.
13. This judgment is subjective, but in a review of five commonly used (though

When considered in its context in Psalms, its messianic message becomes more obvious. Psalm 22 pictures the crucifixion and abandonment by God. Jesus quoted from this psalm when he was on the cross. Psalm 24 is sometimes known as the Psalm of the King of Glory. It describes the coronation of the Messiah and his entrance into Jerusalem and the establishment of the Messianic Kingdom.

In between is Psalm 23. Sailhamer says that it "is centered on the theme of God's presence in the face of death." If God's abandonment characterizes Psalm 22, his presence characterizes Psalm 23. The sheep can follow this Shepherd through the valley of the shadow of death with confidence because he has already conquered death. Contrary to some popular treatments of Psalm 23, the "green pastures" (v. 2) are not the hills of the Judean wilderness with their sparse vegetation, but "flourishing pastures (*deshe'*), a description that parallels the paradise of Gn 1."[14] Sailhamer adds, "The psalm is about the 'anointed' one who enjoys God's presence forever (v. 6)."[15] With this, the Anointed One looks forward to his return to the temple.[16] Turning from the psalms of David to the "psalms of individual lament,"[17] we find the same themes. These are psalms in which the devout and guiltless man of God suffers the hatred and opposition of the people. Moses suffered opposition, and so did the prophets who followed. Therefore, so also would the Messiah suffer opposition, as the Prophet like Moses.

The psalms of individual lament, contrary to the prevailing views of the past, are not primarily about David and his suffering. David's trials are only springboards to direct our thoughts to the future sufferings of Messiah.[18] Randall McKinion says, "His words are spoken as one to

---

diverse) commentaries on Psalms, not one took Psalm 23 as a messianic psalm. Those consulted are Craigie, *Psalms 1–50*; Dahood, *Psalms I, 1–50*; Kidner, *Psalms 1–72*; and Grogan, *Psalms*; VanGemeren, "Psalms."

14. Cole, "Psalm 23," 551. Cole's article is excellent in locating Psalm 23 in the larger context of Psalms.

15. Sailhamer, *NIV Compact Bible Commentary*, 320.

16. Psalm 22 has in view the Prophet as the Suffering Servant, Psalm 23 his priestly ministry as our Shepherd, and Psalm 24 his return as our great King.

17. Categories such as "lament" are subjective and most often ignore the overall structure of Psalms. Nevertheless, the psalms that are usually identified as psalms of individual lament are 3, 5, 6, 7, 13, 17, 22, 25, 26–28, 39, 42, 43, 54–57, 59, 61, 64, 70, 71, 86, 141, and 142. For evidence that David saw himself as a prophet, see M. Rydelnik, "2 Samuel 23:1–7," 402–3.

18. See Bolen, "A Case for a Messianic Reading of Psalm 18," 48–64; McKinion, "Psalm 69," 592–603; Spencer, "Psalm 72," 605–15; Cole, "Psalms 86–88," 617–30; Cole,

whom the covenant was made but also as a prophet, on behalf of the King of Ps 2, who is called Son."[19] In other words, they were spoken by David, but with regard to the Messiah.

ISAIAH AND THE MESSIAH

There has been speculation about who truly fulfills the prophecy of the Prophet like Moses (Deut 18:15-19). Some have thought that Joshua fulfilled this role, but there is no mention of Joshua ever being called a prophet. Some have proposed Ezekiel and Elijah as fulfillments of this prophecy. Although a number of Old Testament prophets resembled Moses in a variety of ways,[20] the only individual presented in the Hebrew Scriptures as truly "like Moses" is the Servant of the Lord in the book of Isaiah.[21] It is also worth noting that the passage in Deuteronomy 34:10—probably added at the conclusion of the Old Testament period—eliminates any other Old Testament prophet from consideration as a fulfillment of this prophecy. Israel was still anticipating his arrival.

We may wonder about the use of servant, rather than prophet, in Isaiah, but Matthew Harmon claims that "no other individual in Scripture is referred to as the servant of Yahweh more often than Moses."[22] Since Moses was known as the servant of the Lord, the coming Prophet like Moses would be the preeminent Servant of the Lord.

Scholar G. P. Hugenberger, after evaluating other attempts to identify the Servant in these texts, says, "What is proposed here is that this dominant and unifying image [i.e., the image of the Servant] is that of a second Moses figure. In other words, the servant is the 'prophet like Moses' promised in Deuteronomy 18:15ff. and 34:10ff."[23] Although others, such

---

"Psalm 90," 645–61; Cook, "Psalm 109," 663–71; and Snearly, "Psalm 118," 693–700.

19. McKinion, "Psalm 69," 592.

20. For an evaluation of the position that this prophecy was fulfilled by one or a number of the prophets of Israel, see Allison, *The New Moses*, 11–95. See also Sibley, "Deuteronomy 18:15–19," 325–41.

21. See Isa 42:1–4; 49:1–6; 50:4–9; 52:13—53:12; perhaps 61:1–3.

22. Harmon, *The Servant of the Lord and His Servant People*, 43. J. Hamilton suggests that when we read in Isaiah 41:8; 42:1; 44:1; and 52:13 of the servant who may appear to be the nation or an individual, the individual (i.e., the Messiah) may be seen as one "standing in place of the nation." See his, "The Skull Crushing Seed of the Woman," 32.

23. Hugenberger, "The Servant of the Lord," 119. Far from a novel view, it may be found even in the Talmud (*b. Sota* 14a). Other evidence, both ancient and modern, of this view may be found in Hugenberger, "The Servant of the Lord," 119–20. See also

as Jacob, Isaiah, and David, are also referred to as God's "servant," it was Moses who was primarily thought of as the servant of the Lord.

Hugenberger's conclusion that the Servant of the Lord in Isaiah 40–55 is the Prophet like Moses is based on the context of the servant songs in Isaiah.[24] These chapters use language that suggests a future, second exodus, similar in some ways to the Exodus from Egypt. If Israel needed deliverance from Egyptian bondage, how much more does Israel (and the nations) need an exodus from sin and rebellion? Hugenberger says that "the controlling and sustained theme of these chs. is that of a second exodus."[25] Postell notes that "the promise of the second exodus is grounded in the reality of the first exodus (see Isa 51:9–10)." This second exodus of the future reveals the Servant as the Prophet like Moses in four ways: in the deliverance he brings, in the relationship he has with God, in the covenant he mediates, and in the suffering he endures.[26]

SECOND EXODUS IMAGERY AND MIRACULOUS DELIVERANCE

As Gerard Van Groningen says, "The exodus from Egypt was a redemptive event at the dawn of Israel's history, comparable to no other subsequently recorded event in the Scriptures."[27] The Exodus from Egyptian slavery was such a significant event that the imagery and vocabulary of the Exodus is used centuries later to describe the return from the Babylonian Exile. Just as God delivered the people from Egypt in the past, so he would deliver them from Babylon. Both Moses and Cyrus were raised up for the purpose of providing deliverance for Israel.

This imagery and vocabulary are not only used of the "exodus" from Babylon, but of a future "exodus" or deliverance of the Jewish people from their scattering in the nations of the earth, as God calls Israel, His

---

Allison, *The New Moses*, 142, and Lindsey, *The Servant Songs*, 64.

24. The "servant songs" are four poetic passages that speak of the Messiah as the Servant of the Lord in Isaiah 40–55. They are Isaiah 42:1–9; 49:1–13; 50:4–11; and 52:13—53:12.

25. Hugenberger, "The Servant of the Lord," 122. See also, Pao, *Acts and the Isaianic New Exodus*.

26. Wong Yee-cheung suggests that the servant of "the Lord of Hosts is Moses (Isa 63:11), David (Isa 37:35), Isaiah (Isa 20:3), Jacob (Isa 44:1; 45:4; 48:20), Israel (Isa 41:8), and above all, the Servant (Isa 42:1; 49:3, 5, 6; 52:13; 53:11)." See Yee-cheung, *A Text-Centered Approach to Old Testament Exegesis*, 278–79.

27. Van Groningen, *Messianic Revelation in the Old Testament*, 202.

first-born son, back to the Land of Israel. Any time this kind of imagery is used, it is called a "second exodus," even if it is the third "exodus."

More importantly, second exodus imagery is used to describe a spiritual return to the Lord and to salvation. Van Groningen notes, "The first Exodus was a necessary preliminary event which set the stage for the new, full, and complete exodus."[28] This is found in each of the servant songs of Isaiah; in fact, Hugenberger says it is "almost omnipresent" in them.[29] He points out that they begin and end with second exodus language (40:1–11 and 55:12–13), and the parallel is clear. God would raise up the Servant, just as he had raised up Moses, to provide deliverance. A new exodus requires a new Moses. In Isaiah, the new exodus becomes the way to a new creation. It is the way back through sea and desert to the Land of promise, which is expressed in the language of Eden. For example, we read in Isaiah 43:16–21:

> Thus says the LORD, who makes a way through the sea and a path through the mighty waters, who brings forth the chariot and the horse, the army and the mighty man (they will lie down together and not rise again; they have been quenched and extinguished like a wick): "Do not call to mind the former things, or ponder things of the past. Behold, I will do something new, now it will spring forth; will you not be aware of it? I will even make a roadway in the wilderness, rivers in the desert. The beasts of the field will glorify Me; the jackals and the ostriches; because I have given waters in the wilderness and rivers in the desert, to give drink to My chosen people. The people whom I formed for Myself, will declare my praise."

Here, the Lord brings the people out of bondage, through the wilderness, back to the Land, which is as Eden, in which nature is transformed, and the Servant of the Lord is the new Moses.[30] In Isaiah 53:1, the saving work of the Servant is described as the arm of the Lord being revealed. Moses refers to the saving work of the Exodus as the Lord bringing the people out of Egypt "with a mighty hand and an outstretched arm" (Deut 26:8).

28. Van Groningen, *Messianic Revelation in the Old Testament*, 203.

29. Hugenberger, "The Servant of the Lord," 122.

30. See also Isa 43:3–5. Isaiah 40 also contains new exodus language, and the Lord is likened to a shepherd tending His flock (v. 11). In Numbers 27:15–17, Moses prays for a successor who will shepherd God's people, even as he has. The Lord responded with the choice of Joshua, but the implication is that ultimately the Prophet like Moses will be that Shepherd.

In Isaiah, sometimes the Servant seems to be the people of Israel, and sometimes he seems to be an individual. Israel and Messiah may be considered the two major trajectories in the Hebrew Scriptures. Both Messiah and Israel are mentioned in similar ways in Scripture. For example, both are referred to as the seed of Abraham,[31] both bear the name, "My servant" (in reference to God),[32] and both are given priestly functions.[33] This tension between a corporate understanding of the Servant and an individual interpretation is resolved if the Servant is identified as the Prophet like Moses. He is never seen as replacing Israel, but he serves as the epitome of Israel.[34]

As Hugenberger says, "The servant is the representative of and model for his people: they share a common calling to be the servant of Yahweh, a light to the nations, etc."[35] Nevertheless, as David Pao says, "Just as the Law of Moses came from Sinai, so now the [Torah] will go out from Zion."[36] So, we see second exodus language used of the Servant that makes us think of the Prophet like Moses. This one who is both Servant and Prophet will bring deliverance. More than that, if the second exodus is from captivity to sin and death, it is the ultimate deliverance, far greater than the first exodus. Therefore, the Prophet like Moses must be infinitely greater than Moses.

THE SERVANT'S INTIMATE RELATIONSHIP WITH THE FATHER

The Servant, who we have determined to be the Prophet like Moses, has a specific relationship with God. God says he is the one "in whom My soul delights" (Isa 42:1). In Isaiah 50:4 the Servant says, "The Lord GOD has given Me the tongue of disciples, that I may know how to sustain the weary one with a word. He awakens Me morning by morning, He awakens My ear to listen as a disciple." This indicates that the Servant listens directly to God daily, so that he can communicate God's message

---

31. E.g., see Ps 105:6; Gal 3:16, 19.
32. E.g., see Isa 41:8–9; 42:1.
33. E.g., see Exod 19:6; Ps 110:4.
34. Hugenberger, "The Servant of the Lord," 131.
35. 129Hugenberger, "The Servant of the Lord," 131.
36. Pao, *Acts and the Isaianic New Exodus*, 158.

effectively. F. Duane Lindsey says, "Thus the Servant asserts claim to a disciple's ear in preparation for His exercise of a disciple's tongue."[37]

Having listened to the Lord, the Servant only speaks what he has been told. This description confirms our understanding, as it is exactly like the description of the Prophet like Moses in Deuteronomy 18:18: "I will raise up a prophet from among their countrymen like you, and I will put My words in his mouth, and he shall speak to them all that I command him." This is similar to Jesus's statement in John 12:49–50: "For I did not speak on My own initiative, but the Father Himself who sent Me has given Me commandment, what to say and what to speak. . . . The things I speak, I speak just as the Father has told Me."

In Isaiah 42:9 we read, "Behold, the former things have come to pass, now I declare new things; before they spring forth I proclaim *them* to you." This verse makes it very clear that the Servant's ministry will involve proclamation and prophecy, and the Messiah's proclamation of the future authenticates his Word (Isa 43:12; see Deut 18:22). He has been "anointed . . . to bring good news . . . to proclaim liberty to captives, and freedom to prisoners; to proclaim the favorable year of the LORD" (Isa 61:1–2). The relationship Isaiah's Servant has with the Father clarifies his identity. The Servant is the Messiah—the Prophet like Moses.

THE SERVANT AS THE MEDIATOR OF AN ETERNAL COVENANT

As Moses was the mediator of the covenant at Sinai, the Servant also will inaugurate a new covenant. In Isaiah 42:6c God says, "I will appoint You as a covenant to the people." Based on this verse, Lindsey makes a compelling argument that the Servant "is the mediator of the New Covenant with Israel, elaborated in Jeremiah 31:31–34 and referred to in numerous other prophetic texts."[38] In support of this reading, Isaiah refers to an eternal covenant to be established by Messiah in 24:5 and 61:8. This new covenant of the Servant would fulfill and replace that of Moses. Another parallel not to be missed is that even as Moses and the prophets interceded for Israel, so also the Servant intercedes for Israel.[39]

---

37. Lindsey, "The Commitment of the Servant in Isaiah 50:4–11," 220.
38. Lindsey, "The Call of the Servant in Isaiah 42:1–9," 25.
39. Exod 32:30–32; Isa 53:12.

THE PROPHET AS THE SHEPHERD IN EZEKIEL

The Prophet like Moses is not only identified with the Servant of the Lord in Isaiah, but he is also portrayed as the Shepherd by Ezekiel. This makes sense, for Moses was a shepherd for forty years.[40] As seen with David, the imagery of a shepherd was used of prophets as well as kings.

Moses as a shepherd. At the beginning of his ministry, Moses was called from shepherding Jethro's flocks to shepherd Israel instead. At the burning bush, Moses was shown that his shepherd's staff would become "the staff of God" (Exod 4:20). It would be used in the performance of supernatural signs and plagues in Egypt,[41] in the miraculous parting of the Red Sea,[42] in the miraculous provision of water in the wilderness,[43] and in miraculous victory over enemies.[44] Under God's leadership and with God's authority, Moses shepherded Israel in the way they should go, and he protected them from enemies.[45]

Near the end of his life, Moses, the great Prophet of God, prayed to the Lord for a successor who could continue his ministry to the people of Israel. He asked the Lord for a leader "who will go out and come in before them, and who will lead them out and bring them in, so that the congregation of the LORD will not be like sheep which have no shepherd" (Num 27:17). This great prophet, Moses, saw himself as a shepherd for the people of Israel, and he recognized the need for a divine Shepherd who would succeed him to care for the people of Israel.

The Shepherd behind the shepherd. In Psalm 78:52–53 we read, "He led forth His own people like sheep, and guided them in the wilderness like a flock; He led them safely, so that they did not fear; but the sea engulfed their enemies." Of whom does the psalmist write? Moses? No, the Lord. The entire psalm is about what the Lord has done. Listen to the first verse of Psalm 80: "Oh, give ear, Shepherd of Israel, You who lead Joseph like a flock; You who are enthroned above the cherubim, shine forth!" Moses was a shepherd (as was David), but the real Shepherd of Israel is the Lord, the coming Messiah.

---

40. As seen with David, the imagery of a shepherd was used of prophets as well as kings.
41. Exod 4:1–3, 16; 7:9–10, 19–20; 8:5, 16; 9:23; 10:13.
42. Exod 14:6.
43. Exod 17:5–7.
44. Exod 17:8–13.
45. See Exod 15:13; Ps 77:19–20.

Among the many messianic passages in Scripture, I want to call attention to Ezekiel 34:23-24, which may at first be misunderstood. Here, the Lord says, "Then I will set over them one shepherd, My servant David, and he will feed them; he will feed them himself and be their shepherd. And I, the Lord, will be their God, and My servant David will be prince among them; I the Lord have spoken."

There are several observations worth noting. First, the shepherd for whom Moses prayed seems to be identified here as God's servant "David." However, this was written long after David had died and speaks of the Shepherd who is to come, who will feed them and be prince among them. Ezekiel is not actually speaking of David, then, but rather about David's promised heir—the Son of David, the Messiah.

Second, by referring to the covenant God made with David, the Lord is giving assurance that his promises will not be forsaken. In 2 Samuel 7, the word translated "everlasting" or "forever" is used eight times.[46] David was promised an eternal house, throne, and kingdom. Although in Ezekiel's day it may have looked as though all was lost, as the kingdom had ceased, and the people had been removed to Babylon, God had not forsaken his promises.

Third, the shepherding role of this Coming One is presented emphatically. Twice it is stated that "he will feed them," and twice it is stated that he will be their "shepherd."

Fourth, there will not be more than one shepherd. At the time Ezekiel wrote, it seemed as though the nation was hopelessly divided. But this promise underscores there would not be two shepherds, one for Israel and another for Judah, but only one.[47] This prophecy suggests that the tribes of Israel will once again be unified under Messiah.

Fifth, this shepherd is also called the "Servant" of the Lord. As we have seen, Isaiah had already prophesied about this coming Servant of the Lord, and he has been presented as the fulfillment of the prophecy of the Prophet like Moses.[48]

---

46. עוֹלָם, 'olam.

47. Block, "Bringing Back David, 173-77.

48. Block is one who does not recognize the prophecy of Deuteronomy 18:15-19 as messianic. See his article, "My Servant David," 26-27. Consequently, when commenting on this messianic passage (i.e., Ezek 34:23-24), he does not make reference to Moses. In this otherwise excellent article, the "shepherd" who will be the "servant" of the Lord is understood only as a descendant of David. It is obviously true that there are two references here to "My servant David;" however, this "Servant" will be the fulfillment of the prophecies of both Moses and of David. Both Moses and David are figures

Sixth, he is here presented not only as a shepherd and as the Lord's Servant, but also presented as their "prince." As the heir of the Davidic promises, he certainly has the right to reign, but at this time, his ministry is pastoral; it is feeding and shepherding the people. Here, he is the "Prince of Peace" (Isa 9:6) and "Messiah the Prince" (Dan 9:25). Daniel Block points out that "both his status as shepherd among sheep and the expression 'prince over them' suggest authority as well as identification."[49] These are also primary characteristics of the Prophet like Moses. He will be "from among you" (Deut 18:15), and he will speak God's authoritative words (Deut 18:15, 19).

As such, this prophecy appears to point to the earthly ministry of the Messiah, "the great Shepherd of the sheep" (Heb 13:20).[50] He was born in Bethlehem, the City of David, and he was often referred to as the "Son of David." Matthew's Gospel emphasizes this more than the others. Will Varner says, "The closest title to Matthew's 'Son of David' is the unlikely title 'Shepherd' which is mentioned as much if not more than the title 'Messiah.' . . . To Matthew, Jesus is the Davidic Shepherd who leads the lost sheep of Israel in a new exodus marked by forgiveness, healing, and restoration."[51]

THE REJECTED PROPHET, SERVANT, AND SHEPHERD

The coming Prophet, the Servant of Isaiah 40–55, and the Shepherd of Israel are all portrayed as God's servants, so any opposition to them is opposition to the God they serve (Exod 16:8 and Isa 53:1[52]). These three

---

of authority, and both are servants and shepherds.

Both Moses and David were shepherds of Israel. Both were also quintessential "servants" of the Lord. "My servant" is used of David thirty-one times in the Old Testament, and Moses is referred to as the Lord's servant thirty-three times (Num 12:7, 8; Josh 1:1, 2, 7, 13, 15; 8:31, 33; 9:24; 11:12, 15; 12:6; 13:8; 14:7; 18:7; 22:2, 4, 5; 1 Kgs 8:53, 56; 2 Kgs 18:12; 21:8; 1 Chr 6:49; 2 Chr 1:3; 24:6, 9; Neh 8:1; 9:14; 10:29; Ps 105:26; Dan 9:11; Mal 4:4).

49. Block, "Bringing Back David," 176.

50. See also John 10:11–16; 1 Pet 2:25; 5:2, 4; Rev 7:17.

51. Varner, *Messiah's Ministry*, 54.

52. The plural ("Who has believed our message?"), long an interpretive conundrum, is best explained as the Lord and the Servant, whose message is not believed by the nation. It relates to 52:14 ("Just as many were astonished at you, *My people*," where NASB95 supplies "My people," but the words are not in the Hebrew. Franz Delitzsch rejects the view that Israel (or "My People") is the referent of "you" and points out the obvious fact that "you" is singular. Delitzsch, "Isaiah," 5:343. E. J. Young also understands

figures are all portrayals of the one Messiah. Because he will speak with God's authority, it should not be surprising that he will be a lightning rod for rebellion against God. He would engender hostility and be opposed by the majority of the people of Israel, his very own people. Yet there was a minority who were trusting in God's promises. To spurn this righteous remnant was to spurn the Lord.

We see the same dynamic in the New Testament. When the Lord confronted Saul on the road to Damascus, he said, "Saul, Saul, why are you persecuting Me?" (Acts 9:4). In persecuting Jewish disciples of Jesus, Saul was actually persecuting him. In light of the opposition against God, his people, and his servants (such as Moses and the prophets), it makes sense that Messiah would also face this same level of opposition and violence, even to death.

Isaiah prophesies that one of the identifying characteristics of the Servant would be rejection by his own people. Isaiah 53:3 says, "He was despised and forsaken of men, a man of sorrows and acquainted with grief; and like one from whom men hide their face He was despised, and we [i.e., the people of Israel] did not esteem Him." Of course, as we have seen, this is consistent with the psalms of lament and the prophecies of Messiah's sufferings.

In this, there is one very significant difference. Though the opposition to Moses was intense, it never actually resulted in his death. Furthermore, unlike Moses, the Servant is completely innocent. But in both cases, this opposition was associated with the judgment of spiritual blindness. It characterized the opposition and rejection of Moses by the majority of the Israelites in the wilderness (Deut 29:4). Likewise, a judgment of spiritual blindness was enacted upon the majority of the Jewish people in Isaiah's day (Isa 6:9–10). This spiritual blindness is explicitly connected to the suffering of the Servant (Isa 53:1, 3).[53]

The Suffering Servant of Isaiah bears all the marks of the Prophet like Moses. This leads Hugenberger to say: "A felicitous consequence of the present approach to the servant songs is the substantial support it

---

that the object of astonishment is the Servant, not Israel. Young, *The Book of Isaiah*, 3:336. See also the discussion in *The Moody Bible Commentary*, eds. M. Rydelnik and Vanlaningham, *ad passim*. In 52:13–15, Yhwh introduces the Servant, addresses him, and describes him. Indeed, "the arm of Yhwh" is revealed in the experience of his Servant (53:1), and this is the content of the "message." Therefore, the "our" of 53:1 must have reference to the Lord and the Servant, whose message is not being heard by any but a small remnant.

53. See the use of verse 1 in John 12:38. Compare Numbers 14:11c with John 12:37.

offers for the New Testament's Messianic interpretation without presupposing that interpretation." Certainly, if the Prophet like Moses is the Servant of the Lord, and if the Servant is to be identified as the Messiah, then Moses was directly prophesying about the Messiah, whom God would raise up. The Servant, even as the Prophet, was rejected by the majority of his own people

If both the Prophet and the Servant were to experience opposition from the nation, so also would the Shepherd of Israel. Zechariah 13:7–9 speaks of the Shepherd being struck. It says he will suffer, and his disciples (his "sheep") are to be scattered. Notice, however, that there are "sheep" that belong to the Shepherd. This speaks of the faithful remnant. Jesus said that he was this anticipated Shepherd: "I am the good shepherd; the good shepherd lays down His life for the sheep" (John 10:11). Deuteronomy presents the Prophet; Isaiah presents the Prophet as the Suffering Servant of the Lord; and Psalms, Ezekiel, and Zechariah present the same Deliverer as the Shepherd of Israel.

5

Messiah as the Priest Like Melchizedek

WE WERE INTRODUCED TO Melchizedek in Genesis 14, and we compared his priestly ministry with Jethro's in Exodus 18. Messiah was to be a priest after the order of Melchizedek—an alternative priesthood to that of Aaron. Now we will look at other passages in the Hebrew Scriptures that carry this imagery further.

THE PERMANENTLY FAITHFUL PRIEST: 1 SAMUEL 2:35

Beginning in 1 Samuel 2:27, Eli the priest is confronted by a prophet of God who pronounces judgment on his lineage for his unfaithfulness and for the wickedness of his sons. The sons of Eli treated the offerings of the Lord with contempt (1 Sam 2:17). They slept with the women who served at the tabernacle (2:22). The judgment pronounced on the house of Eli is found in 1 Samuel 2:30–34. One author points out that "the books of Samuel begin not with a crisis over the absence of a king, but with the failure of the priesthood. The promise of 1 Sam 2:35 is designed to address this problem."[1] So, let's look at this promise.

According to most of our translations, God prophesied through an unnamed prophet, "But I will raise up for Myself a faithful priest who will

---

1. Karl Deenick, "Priest and King or Priest-King," 325–39. His argument is based on grammatical, contextual, and literary evidence. A similar solution is offered by Kaiser, *The Messiah in the Old Testament*, 74–76.

do according to what is in My heart and in My soul; and I will build him an enduring house, and he will walk before My anointed always" (1 Sam 2:35). However, there are very persuasive reasons this last phrase should be translated, "and my anointed one will walk before me always."[2]

The first thing to notice is that just as God had promised in Deuteronomy 18:18, "I will raise up a prophet," so here God promises, "I will raise up for Myself a faithful priest." Later, in 2 Samuel 7:12, we will find that God says to David, "I will raise up your descendant after you . . . and I will establish his kingdom." In each case, God raises up his Anointed One.[3]

Secondly, it is worth comparing what is said of this future priest with what was said to Moses of the future prophet. Regarding the prophet, we read, "I will put My words in his mouth, and he shall speak to them all that I command him" (Deut 18:18). Regarding the priest, he will be "a faithful priest who will do according to what is in My heart and in My soul" (1 Sam 2:35).

We must then ask of whom does the Lord speak? The priesthood of Eli would end, but this verse does not tell us more about this alternative, eternal priesthood. It cannot be Samuel, for he is established as a prophet, rather than a priest (1 Sam 3:20). Some scholars say this future priest is Zadok, and that priestly authority is being transferred from the lineage of Eli to that of Zadok.[4] Even though Zadok and his descendants do, in fact, replace the sons of Eli, the remainder of 1 and 2 Samuel does not present them as the fulfillment of this prophecy.

Ronald Youngblood makes the observation that "the issue is not simply an issue of replacing one Aaronic priestly line with another . . . but of replacing the Aaronic priesthood in general."[5] God's judgment is not simply addressed to the house of Eli, but "to the house of [his] father" (1 Sam 2:27–28; see also vv. 30, 31). The prophecy does not declare the utter destruction of the Aaronic priesthood, but the destruction of its strength.

---

2. Deenick, "Priest and King or Priest-King," 327.

3. In Deut 18:18, "I will raise up," אקים, *akim*; in 1 Sam 2:35, "I will raise up," הקימתי, *hakimoti*; and also in 2 Sam 7:12, "I will raise up," הקימתי, *hakimoti*. Jeremiah 30:8–9 records God's promise: "'It shall come about on that day,' declares the LORD of hosts, 'that I will break his yoke from off their neck and will tear off their bonds; and strangers will no longer make them their slaves. But they shall serve the LORD their God and David their king, whom I will raise up [אקים, *akim*] for them.'" See also, Ezek 34:23–24. For other references to Messiah as "David," see Hos 3:5; Ezek 3:24–25.

4. For example, see, Youngblood, "1, 2 Samuel," 588.

5. Youngblood, "1, 2 Samuel," 328. Here, Deenick is referring to the commentary by Keil and Delitzsch.

In 1 Samuel 2:35, what is promised is not merely a "faithful priest" and an "enduring house," but more. The same Hebrew word is used to describe both the priest and his house. Of the priest it is translated "faithful," but of his house it is said to be "enduring." The word carries both nuances, so it could be translated: "But I will raise up for Myself a permanently faithful priest who will do according to what is in My heart and in My soul; and I will build Him a permanently faithful house, and My Anointed One will walk before Me always."[6]

This same word is also used of the royal lineage promised to David in 2 Samuel 7:16. So, using the same adjective that applies to the royal lineage promised to David, God promised there would also be a permanent, or faithful, priesthood. Scripture is whispering to the attentive reader that this alternative priest will come through the lineage of David. The future, permanently faithful priest will be the Son of David!

There is one final issue which still needs to be addressed. What is the meaning of the "permanently faithful house"? This cannot refer to physical descendants of the Messiah, so it must have reference to the priests and leaders of the people who will serve under his direction, as well as to all his disciples. In Exodus 19, God said he would make of the entire nation of Israel "a kingdom of priests." We are later told in the New Testament that the remnant of Israel today forms that priesthood (1 Pet 2:9–10).[7] Addressing Jewish disciples of Jesus, Hebrews 3:6 says, "Messiah was faithful as a Son over His house—whose house we are." Of course, as gentile believers have been made partakers of the spiritual promises to Israel, they too comprise his "house."

DAVID AND THE PRIESTHOOD

Though we primarily think of David as a forerunner of the Messianic King, he also seems to have functioned as both a prophet (as we discussed previously) and as a priest on some occasions. When David brought the ark of the covenant to Jerusalem, he wore a linen ephod, like a priest

---

6. The Hebrew word translated "faithful" or "enduring" is נאמן, ne'man. This word is also used in 2 Samuel 7:16, where it is translated "shall endure." This word carries the meanings "faithful," "permanent," or "enduring." See *HALOT*; Deenick, "Priest and King or Priest-King," 327. The royal Davidic lineage will be as enduring as the promise of this Messianic Priest.

7. First Peter was written to Jewish believers in Jesus (1 Pet 1:1). For a defense of the conclusion that the recipients of 1 Peter were Jewish, see Sibley, "You Talkin' to Me?"

(2 Sam 6:14). He led the procession with frequent sacrifices to "the tent which David had pitched for [the ark]" (2 Sam 6:13–17). He then "blessed the people in the name of the LORD of hosts" (v. 18). This blessing was likely the Aaronic benediction of Numbers 6:24–26, the priestly blessing.

In 2 Samuel 24, following David's disobedience in taking a census, seventy thousand people died of a pestilence until he built an altar and offered sacrifices. Significantly, the temple would later be built on the same location (2 Chr 3:1).

These verses describe David acting as a priest. He was not a priest in the proper sense, and he could not be one according to the Law of Moses. The priests had to be from the lineage of Aaron. David was from the Tribe of Judah. Only on exceptional occasions such as these did he act "priestly," by wearing an ephod or offering sacrifices. It would only be his Seed who could truly serve as a priest, indeed, as the ultimate High Priest.

THE PRIEST LIKE MELCHIZEDEK: PSALM 110

Most likely David wrote Psalm 110 after God revealed to him that his heir would be the Messianic King. Furthermore, God revealed to David that this Messianic King would also be a Priest like Melchizedek. He would occupy both offices, king and priest, even as Melchizedek had. David likely understood this priestly aspect from his careful study of the Torah, and perhaps also because of God's revelations through Samuel.

Psalm 110 is in the center of a literary unit of seven psalms. The three psalms that precede it (Pss 107–9) contain pleas for deliverance, and the three that follow (Pss 111–13) are composed of praises for deliverance. Michael Rydelnik says, "Psalm 110 is central to the thoughts of these psalms since it reveals the Messiah as King, Priest, and Warrior, who, as the answer to God's people's supplications for rescue, is the reason for their praises to God."[8]

Psalm 110:1 is quoted in the New Testament more than any other Old Testament passage. Other than Genesis 14:18, Psalm 110:4 is the only other direct reference to Melchizedek in the Hebrew Scriptures. Psalm 110 begins:

---

8. M. Rydelnik, "Psalm 110," 678. Herbert W. Bateman IV, Eugene Merrill, and others reject a direct messianic fulfillment. See Bateman, "Psalm 110:1 and the New Testament," 452–53; and Merrill, "Royal Priesthood," 50–61.

> The LORD says to my Lord: "Sit at My right hand, until I make Your enemies a footstool for Your feet." The LORD will stretch forth Your strong scepter from Zion, *saying*, "Rule in the midst of Your enemies." Your people will volunteer freely in the day of Your power; in holy array, from the womb of the dawn, Your youth are to You as the dew. The LORD has sworn and will not change His mind, "You are a priest forever according to the order of Melchizedek." (vv. 1–4)

According to this psalm, Messiah is a priest because God has declared it. But he will be a unique sort of priest—one like Melchizedek, both a priest and a king. Although he does not serve as a king, the only other priest who fits this role as a non-Levitical priest is Jethro. Melchizedek and Jethro point to a future priesthood—one that is not based on Levitical lineage and that is far superior, led by the Messianic High Priest. In other words, Psalm 110 is connecting three dots: Melchizedek, Jethro, and the Messiah. This psalm also becomes the foundation for later prophecies

THE PRIEST IN ISAIAH

Following the Exodus from Egypt, God established the Aaronic priesthood. As mentioned before, exodus language is also used to describe deliverance from captivity to sin and death. This second exodus—the spiritual exodus brought about when the Servant offered himself "like a lamb ... and like a sheep" (Isa 53:7)—ushers in the ultimate priesthood, that of Messiah.

Isaiah 53:10b says that the Servant "render[ed] Himself as a guilt offering." But the guilt and sin offerings of the Mosaic Law required a bull (Lev 4:3, 14) or a goat (Lev 4:23, 28). Sometimes the sacrifice was for the nation; at other times it was for an individual. The sacrifices under the Mosaic Covenant only provided temporary atonement, for they had to be repeated periodically.[9]

In contrast, the sacrifice of Messiah would provide ultimate atonement. This atonement would be for individuals who put their trust in

---

9. Hebrews 9:11–14 have been taken by some as an indication that the sacrificial system of the Mosaic Covenant did not provide atonement for sin. But Leviticus 17:11 is clear that the sacrificial system was given by God for the purpose of making atonement. In light of this, this passage in Hebrews is emphasizing that these sacrifices provided only a temporary atonement for sin, for they had to be repeated. How much better is the permanent atonement of Messiah!

him. Initially, it would apply to the remnant of Israel, then to the nations, and finally, at his return, to all Israel.[10] He is never portrayed as a bull or as a goat, but as the Passover Lamb, without spot or blemish (Isa 53:6–7). The Apostle Peter said that we were not redeemed with perishable things, "but with precious blood, as of a lamb unblemished and spotless, the blood of Messiah" (1 Pet 1:19). It is in providing final atonement for sin that the Servant of the Lord would be qualified to serve as the Priest like Melchizedek (Isa 53:11–12).[11]

Just as in other Scriptures, here in Isaiah we find once more that the entire nation will be a priesthood. In Isaiah 61:6, the Servant says of Israel, "But you will be called the priests of the LORD; you will be spoken of as ministers of our God." This indicates that Israel as a nation is to be a priest to the other nations of the earth. The implication is that the future priesthood will not be that of Aaron, governed by a genealogical relationship, but of Melchizedek, governed by a spiritual relationship.

THE PRIEST IN EZEKIEL 21:25–27

We move now from David, at the high point of Israel's history, to Ezekiel, at the nation's low point, when Israel was in a time of judgment. Yet, in the midst of this crisis, the prophet delivered a promise that pointed to this coming Priest.

Ezekiel had already been exiled to Babylon in one of the first groups to be forced from its homeland. The temple and the city of Jerusalem would be destroyed within five years. These events would bring to an end the offices of priest and king as Israel had known them. Some might have wondered if God would actually carry out such severe judgment against his people; perhaps he would give them victory over the Babylonians at the last minute, even as he had with the Assyrians. It was not to be.

After the Babylonian siege of Jerusalem in 597 BC, King Jeconiah was deposed, and his uncle Zedekiah was installed as the last king of Judah (2 Kgs 24:17). Jeremiah was Zedekiah's counselor, but Zedekiah rejected Jeremiah's counsel, and his epitaph reads, ". . . he did evil in the

---

10. See, e.g., Zech 12:10; 13:1; Jer 50:20; Rom 11:26.

11. Chen (*The Messianic Vision of the Pentateuch*, 152) calls our attention to the fact that in Exodus 12:3–5, the word "lamb" is repeated five times, and in Isaiah 53, the Messiah is referred to five times using the word "he." These references in Exodus and in Isaiah provide the answer to the five references to "the serpent" in Genesis 3 (vv. 1, 2, 4, 13, 14).

sight of the LORD" (2 Kgs 24:19–20; Jer 52:2–3). He reigned from c. 597 BC until 586 BC, when Jerusalem was destroyed. He saw his sons put to death. Then his eyes were put out, and he was loaded with chains and taken captive to Babylon. This was the end of the Davidic line of kings in Judah, until "He to whom it belonged" would come.

Sadly, Israel's sin was so persistent and the rebellion so strong that there would be no hesitation in visiting upon them the resulting judgment (Ezek 20:1–33). Ezekiel 21:1–17 speaks of the sword of God's wrath being unsheathed against the nation and people of Judah. Judgment would be inevitable, not only because of the sin of the people, but also because of the wickedness of King Zedekiah. When you know the meaning of his name, you can appreciate the irony—Zedekiah means "Yahweh is righteous."[12]

Abner Chou asks: "Since Israel's leadership is headed to inevitable judgment, what will become of them? Can and will God save Israel? If so, how will He do that?"[13] Here is God's answer:

> "And, you, O slain, wicked one, the prince of Israel, whose day has come, in the time of the punishment of the end," thus says the Lord GOD, "Remove the turban, and take off the crown; this[14] will be no more the same. Exalt that which is low, and abase that which is high. A ruin, a ruin, a ruin, I will make it. This also will be no more, until He comes whose right it is; and I will give it to Him." (Ezek 21:25–27)

The "prince" refers to King Zedekiah, who is being judged. When the text says, "This will be no more the same," the phrase has to do with "how the turban and crown will be no more until a particular person comes."[15] The leadership of the nation: the priest (i.e., "turban") and king (i.e., "crown"), will come to an utter ruin and will not be restored "until He comes whose right it is." Embedded in this prophetic utterance is a divine "until." Paul Wilkerson says "until" is "an underwhelming English word that conveys an overwhelming Hebrew promise."[16]

Eugene Merrill says that here, despite the destruction of the leadership, this passage "includes the promise that this devastation is only

---

12. McKinion calls attention to the irony in "Jeremiah 33:14–26," 1053.
13. Chou, "Ezekiel 21:25–27," 1077.
14. Regarding the interpretation of "this," see Kaiser, "Until Messiah Comes," 160.
15. Chou, "Ezekiel 21:25–27," 1075.
16. Wilkinson, *Israel*, 115.

temporary. It will last only 'until He comes whose right it is,' a direct allusion to Gn 49:10."[17] When Ezekiel says, "Exalt that which is low, and abase that which is high," he is saying that the king and priests, and perhaps the aristocracy associated with them, will be on the same level as the common people. They will be treated alike in captivity.

God had promised the Seed of woman who would defeat the serpent. In Genesis 49:10, we were told that this one—obviously a king, for he would have a scepter—would come from the Tribe of Judah. He was called Shiloh, which means, "him-to-whom-it-belongs." This means deliverance must await the Seed of a woman, who would come from the Tribe of Judah, and who had the right, the qualifications, and the authority to rule.

In 2 Samuel 7, we are told this Coming One would be a descendant of David. We are also told the covenant God made with David was irrevocable and that this future descendant would not only be a king but also a priest. David wrote of this in Psalm 110; Messiah would be a priest after the order of Melchizedek, a Priest-King, not an Aaronic priest.

Judah, however, had become presumptuous because of God's irrevocable covenant with David and because of the promise of the Messianic King (Gen 49:10).[18] But now, was all of this coming to an end? How could it be? Were God's promises failing? Would there be no Deliverer after all?

Notice the end of Ezekiel 21:27: It "will be no more, *until He comes whose right it is.*" With the mention of the turban and crown in verse 26, Ezekiel "brings out the theology of Psalm 110," as Chou says, "to show the only way for the collapse[d] Davidic dynasty to be repaired. Another Davidic monarch cannot fix this. Only the individual of Ps 110, the culmination of king and a new priestly order, can make both leadership and Israel right."[19] Both the turban and the crown were being removed until he (sing.) comes—the one who would have the right to be both king and priest.

Although the offices of priest and king will be brought to an end for many years, it is worth noting that prophets would continue to function for a century and a half. Both Ezekiel and Daniel were prophets of God

---

17. Wilkinson, *Israel*, 282.

18. See Ezek 21:10b, 12 (NIV): "Shall we rejoice in the scepter of my royal son [Judah]? The sword despises every such stick.... Testing will surely come. And what if even the scepter [of Judah], which the sword despises, does not continue? Declares the Sovereign LORD."

19. Chou, "Ezekiel 21:25–27," 1077.

during the period of the Exile. Prophets also served in Israel following the Exile: Haggai, Zechariah, and Malachi. Following Malachi, the voice of prophecy would be silenced as well. Ultimate fulfillment would await the arrival of him whose right it is to pick them up once more. In any case, this passage is important for our understanding of two passages in Zechariah.

THE PRIEST IN ZECHARIAH

Sixty-five years later, the prophet Zechariah also speaks of Messiah as a priest. In one very significant night in c. 520 BC, the prophet was given a series of eight visions, which were followed by a symbolic action. The third vision is especially significant for our purposes, as is the symbolic act that occurs in the morning. This third vision is found in Zechariah 3, and the following episode is recorded in Zechariah 6:9–15.

Zechariah 3:1–10. The vision in Zechariah 3 is of Joshua, the high priest, "standing before the angel of the LORD, and Satan standing at his right hand to accuse him" (Zech 3:1). This priest was supposed to be ritually clean and clothed in pure white linen robes. But verse 3 says that his garments were filthy, and the suggestion is that they were filthy with excrement.[20] But before Satan can speak one word of accusation, we read (v. 2), "the LORD said to Satan, 'The LORD rebuke you, Satan!'"

Then, the angel of the Lord says, "'Remove the filthy garments from him.' Again, he said to him, 'See I have taken your iniquity away from you and will clothe you with festal robes'" (v. 4). Joshua was then clothed with clean, festal robes and with a turban on his head (3:1–5). The angel then tells Joshua that if he walks in the ways of the Lord and performs his will, then he will govern God's house and have charge of his courts (3:6–7).

In this vision, the text indicates that Joshua is a symbol for the Messiah, who is called "My servant the Branch" (v. 8). The Branch is a very significant title for the Messiah.[21] If this is all true, how could Joshua have been clothed with filthy garments? This only makes sense if we understand this in relation to his bearing the sin of the nation. In verse 9, God says, "I will remove the iniquity of that land in one day." Isaiah 53 had

---

20. In Hebrew, "The filthy garments" is הבגדים הצאים (*habᵉgadim hatso'im*). For צאי, ("filthy"), see *HOL*, 302.

21. Isa 4:2, 11:1; Jer 23:5.

already taught that Messiah would bear the sin of the nation.[22] So the coming of Messiah is clearly in mind.

But more should be noted here. In verse 7 God says, "If you will walk in My ways and if you will perform My service, then you will also govern My house and also have charge of My courts." Here, the Messiah is to be given authority over the temple ("My house") and its courts. This imagery will be continued in chapter 6.

Zechariah 6:9–15. Mathews says, "This anticipation of a time of peace, under the leadership of the high priest Joshua, or a figure like him, is picked up in chapter 6 with more explicit echoes of the Melchizedek order."[23] The episode is recorded in Zechariah 6:9–15.

> The word of the LORD also came to me, saying, "Take an offering from the exiles, from Heldai, Tobijah, and Jedaiah; and you go the same day and enter the house of Josiah the son of Zephaniah, where they have arrived from Babylon. Take silver and gold, make an ornate crown and set it on the head of Joshua the son of Jehozadak, the high priest. (vv. 9–11)

Most likely, the previous evening, when Zechariah had begun to receive these visions, three prominent men arrived in Jerusalem from exile in Babylon. Since the Jewish people consider a day as beginning with sunset, if they had arrived after the sun had set, the following morning would have been considered the same day.[24] They had brought with them an offering of silver and gold for the temple, which was then under construction.

Zechariah, who was a priest as well as a prophet, was told to go to the home where they were staying and receive the gifts of gold and silver. Then, he was immediately to make a crown using both metals and to place the crown on the head of Joshua, the high priest (whose name is given as Yeshua in 1 Chr 6:15). In verse 11, "crowns" is used, but in this case the plural is used to indicate an ornate crown as the NASB95 translation reflects.[25]

Having placed this ornate crown of gold and silver on the head of the high priest, Zechariah was to deliver the following message:

---

22. See also 2 Cor 5:21.
23. Mathews, *Melchizedek's Alternative Priestly Order*, 123.
24. Unger, *Zechariah*, 109.
25. As also in Job 31:36.

> Then say to him, "Thus says the LORD of hosts, 'Behold, a man whose name is Branch, for He will branch out from where He is; and He will build the temple of the LORD. Yes, it is He who will build the temple of the LORD, and He who will bear the honor and sit and rule on His throne. Thus, He will be a priest on His throne, and the counsel of peace will be between the two offices.'" (Zech 6:12–13)

The Messiah, who is referred to as "Branch," "will be a priest on His throne." Once again, the high priest is clearly only playing a role. We know this because, at this time, both the roles of king and priest had been destroyed (Ezek 21:25–27). Also, no priest of Israel could wear a crown or sit and rule upon a throne, since, under the Mosaic and Davidic Covenants, the priesthood and royalty were assigned to different tribes.[26]

Many evangelical scholars agree that these prophecies from Ezekiel and Zechariah are interrelated. Michael Brown concludes, "The Branch, clearly identified as the Davidic Messiah in Jeremiah 23:5 and 33:15 will combine the offices of high priest and king as one."[27] Michael Rydelnik says, "This passage relates a role-play wherein Joshua the high priest is crowned as a representative of the Messiah, who will unite the offices of priest and king and be named 'Branch.'"[28] A respected British scholar declares, "Nowhere else in the Old Testament is it made so plain that the coming Davidic king will also be a priest."[29] The obvious point is that this king, as a priest-king, is none other than the priest after the order of Melchizedek.

Interestingly, centuries later, three other men would also come from the East bearing precious gifts, but for the Messiah, not the temple. Both of these delegations from the East are precursors of the vast numbers of Gentiles in the future who are to bring treasures to build the Millennial Temple.[30]

---

26. Baron, *The Visions and Prophecies of Zechariah*, 192.

27. M. Brown, "Zechariah 6:9–15," 1254.

28. M. Rydelnik, *The Messianic Hope*, 126.

29. Baldwin, *Haggai, Zechariah, and Malachi*, 137. See also M. Rydelnik, *The Messianic Hope*, 126–28.

30. Isa 2:2–3; Mic 4:1–2. See Munck, *Paul and the Salvation of Mankind*, 303–4. See also, Auler, "More Than a Gift," 143–60.

THE PRIEST IN EZRA

The Babylonians invaded Judah in 605 BC, and in 586 BC, they destroyed Jerusalem and the temple. They took the people into captivity in waves, the first of which was in 605 BC, and the last in 586 BC. Babylon then fell to the Persians in 539 BC, and a series of rulers allowed Jewish people to return: first, Cyrus, then Darius, and finally, Artaxerxes. The temple was rebuilt in 515 BC, seventy years after its destruction.

However, many Jewish people remained in Babylon. In about 458 BC, Ezra (a scribe who was living in Babylon), made his way to Susa, the capital of Persia. There he appealed to Artaxerxes I for permission to lead more of his people back to Jerusalem. Both Ezra and Nehemiah are significant for our purposes here, but for the sake of brevity, I will only deal with Ezra.

Artaxerxes issued a decree, recorded in Ezra 7:11–26, and it contained all Ezra could have wanted. In response, Ezra said, "Blessed be the LORD, the God of our fathers, who has put such a thing as this in the king's heart, to adorn the house of the LORD which is in Jerusalem" (Ezra 7:27). He first blesses "the God of our fathers," and he follows this with gratitude for what he has done, "putting such a thing as this in the king's heart."

This is similar to the blessing of Melchizedek. When he met Abram, he said, "Blessed be Abram of God Most High, Possessor of heaven and earth; and blessed be God Most High, who has delivered your enemies into your hand" (Gen 14:19–20). Jethro also blessed Moses in Exodus 18:10 by saying, "Blessed be the LORD who delivered you from the hand of the Egyptians and from the hand of Pharaoh, and who delivered the people from under the hand of the Egyptians." As Sailhamer puts it, "Melchizedek was to Abraham what Jethro was to Moses, and, in a similar way, Cyrus and Artaxerxes were to Ezra."[31]

By way of summary, Melchizedek and Jethro clearly seem to form "the order of Melchizedek." Joshua, Cyrus, and Artaxerxes all bear enough similarities to serve as reminders, or "echoes," of this alternative priesthood. These reminders gave reassurance and kept the promise of the Priest like Melchizedek on the minds of the Jewish people.

The priesthood had ended. It would resume with the rebuilt Second Temple (until its destruction in AD 70), but these priests would prove

---

31. Sailhamer, *The Meaning of the Pentateuch*, 372. For a good comparison of the evidence in Zechariah for Melchizedek with what is found in Ezra and Nehemiah, see Mathews, *Melchizedek's Alternative Priestly Order*, 134.

to be false shepherds. With the crucifixion, even the last vestige of their usefulness would be removed. The sacrifices would no longer provide atonement for the nation. At the ascension, a new and different priesthood would emerge—that of the order of Melchizedek. As Melchizedek and Jethro were not of the people of Israel, so the coming Priest would not be of the tribe of Aaron, but of Judah.

As we move through the Scriptures and survey passages relating to the Messiah, we recognize that doubtless there were questions that puzzled godly Israelites. The Messiah would be a man, yet he would be God. He would be born of a virgin, yet he would be killed. He would be a prophet, yet he would also be a priest! Not only that, but he would be a king! As Gavin Ortlund says, "In short, all of God's promises from Genesis-Malachi converge upon one person. A thousand parallel streams gradually merge into one massive river."[32]

---

32. G. Ortlund, "Resurrected as Messiah," 757–58. See n. 11.

6

Messiah as the King Like David

To this point, we have examined the roles of prophet and priest in the Prophets and Writings of the Old Testament. Messiah would be the Prophet like Moses and the Priest after the order of Melchizedek. Now, we want to give attention to what the Prophets and Writings say specifically about the Messiah as king.

God spoke to David through the prophet Nathan in 2 Samuel 7 and established a covenant with him (the Davidic Covenant). At this time, God promised: "I will raise up your descendant after you, who will come forth from you, and I will establish his kingdom. . . . Your house and your kingdom shall endure before Me forever" (2 Sam 7:12, 16).[1] In the book of Isaiah, we see that the central message has to do with how the blindness of Israel will lead to the rejection and atoning death of Messiah and the eventual establishment of his kingdom.[2] The Messiah will be king—a king from the lineage of David.

---

1. For a full discussion of the messianic significance of this passage from 2 Samuel 7, see M. Rydelnik, "The Davidic Covenant as Messianic Prophecy," 175–86, and Kaiser, "2 Samuel 7," 385–97.

2. For the theme of blindness see also Abernethy, *The Book of Isaiah and God's Kingdom*; Evans, *To See and Not Perceive*; and Sibley, "The Blindness of Israel and the Mission of the Church."

THE LORD IN ISAIAH 6

Isaiah reports, "In the year of King Uzziah's death I saw the Lord sitting on a throne, lofty and exalted [רָם וְנִשָּׂא, *ram vᵉnisa*], with the train of His robe filling the temple" (Isa 6:1). With this, the chapter begins in which Isaiah receives his prophetic commission. A strong case can be made that the Lord whom he saw was none other than the pre-incarnate Messiah.[3]

Only one other passage in Isaiah calls someone "lofty and exalted." Isaiah 52:13 refers to the Servant of the Lord, the Messiah, and says, "Behold, My servant will prosper, He will be high and lifted up [יָרוּם וְנִשָּׂא, *yarum vᵉnisa*] and greatly exalted." This is a king like no other, for unlike any other king, this king reigns as the divine Priest-King, whose throne is in the very temple in Jerusalem.

Isaiah is given a commission to pronounce a judgment from God of spiritual blindness on the majority of the people of Israel. Isaiah 6:9–10 is the foundational text for the teaching about the blindness of Israel. Not only do we find this theme of spiritual blindness in the first verses of Isaiah and in the call of Isaiah, but we also see it reappear throughout the book.[4] What connection is there between this judgment of spiritual blindness that afflicts the majority of the people and the Messiah's role as king?

We have seen how the Suffering Servant in Isaiah fulfills the role of the Prophet like Moses, but the Servant is also related to Messiah's role as king.[5] Richard Schultz of Wheaton College claims that the theme of spiritual blindness makes it clear. He says that Isaiah is told that the people's dulled senses will prevent them from understanding and repenting until the future king reigns in righteousness (Isa 32:3–4). In fact, he points out that the Servant is sent "to open eyes that are blind" (42:7).[6] In Isaiah 35, we are told that this eye-opening will occur at the return of the Lord when he establishes his Kingdom. Here we read, "Behold, your God will come with vengeance; the recompense of God will come, but He will save you. Then the eyes of the blind will be opened, and the ears of the deaf

---

3. See, for example, Dekker, "The High and Lofty One," 475–91.

4. See Isa 1:2–4; 6:9–10; 29:9–12, 17–18; 30:10–11; 32:3–4; 33:23; 35:5–6; 42:7, 18–20; 43:8; 44:18; 59:10.

5. As mentioned earlier (p. 53, n. 48), the word for "servant" (עֶבֶד, *eved*) is used of Moses thirty-three times, and of David thirty-one times. So the figure of the Servant of the Lord most often refers to the Prophet like Moses, but it may also refer to the King like David.

6. Schultz, "The King in the Book of Isaiah," 156.

will be unstopped. Then the lame will leap like a deer, and the tongue of the mute will shout for joy" (35:4b–6a).

THE KING IN ISAIAH 24, 32, AND 33

In Isaiah 24:23, Isaiah prophesies, "For the LORD of hosts will reign on Mount Zion and in Jerusalem." Later, he writes, "Behold, a king will reign righteously and princes will rule justly" (Isa 32:1). Eva Rydelnik points out that "Isaiah frequently identified the Messiah as the King who is righteous or rules righteously."[7]

In another messianic passage in Isaiah 33:17 we read, "Your eyes will see the King in His beauty." Eva Rydelnik says, "This King is described as beautiful (*yofi*). The same root word is used as a verb in describing the Messianic King in Ps 45:3."[8] So Isaiah presents the Messiah as a king who will reign with righteousness and justice, so that his reign will be like a breath of fresh air. This King and his government will be a marvel of beauty and joy, even in his destruction of all the forces of evil that would oppose his people. Here is a realm in which there is no terror, no plague, no threat, and no deceit.

Psalm 2:6–9 carries this thought as well:

> But as for Me, I have installed My King upon Zion, My holy mountain. I will surely tell of the decree of the LORD: He said to Me, "You are My Son, today I have begotten You. Ask of Me, and I will surely give the nations as Your inheritance, and the *very ends* of the earth as Your possession. You shall break them with a rod of iron, You shall shatter them like earthenware."

Notice the following points made in this psalm: (1) Messiah will be King, (2) he will rule from Mount Zion, (3) he will be God's Son, and (4) he will judge and rule the nations. What is true in this well-known psalm is also found in other psalms.[9] The presentation of the Messiah as the King like David is found repeatedly.

---

7. E. Rydelnik, "Isaiah 32:1–8; 33:17–24," 898. She cites the following: Isa 9:1–7; 11:1–16; 16:4–5; 24:21–25; 32:1–8; 33:17–24.

8. E. Rydelnik, "Isaiah 32:1–8; 33:17–24," 903. Ps 45:3 is verse 2 in English Bibles, "You are fairer."

9. The psalms generally considered to be "royal psalms" are Pss 2, 18, 20–21, 28, 45, 61, 72, 89, 101, 110, and 132.

THE BRANCH-KING IN JEREMIAH

What is true of Isaiah is also true of other biblical prophets who often refer to Messiah as King. Sailhamer says we should see how the promise of Genesis 22:18 was interpreted in Jeremiah. Following the word order of the Hebrew, Genesis 22:18 literally says, "All the nations of the earth in your seed will be blessed." Likewise, Jeremiah 4:2b reads, "The nations in him will be blessed." Sailhamer points out that "Jeremiah has replaced the word 'seed' with the singular pronoun 'him,' giving the sense that 'the nations of the earth will be blessed in him.'"[10] He goes on to say:

> Here in the book of Jeremiah the "seed" is also identified as an individual king from the house of Judah and is identified . . . as the Davidic "righteous branch" whose name is "the LORD is our righteousness.". . . A central thesis of the book of Jeremiah is the demonstration that the "seed" of Abraham is to be understood as an individual king from the house of David who is the focus of Jeremiah's hope in the LORD.[11]

The prophet Jeremiah recorded, "'Behold, *the* days are coming,' declares the LORD, 'When I will raise up for David a righteous Branch; and He will reign as king and act wisely and do justice and righteousness in the land'" (Jer 23:5). In the passage in Zechariah 6:12–13, where the Branch was seen to be a priest, Zechariah adds that he will reign as a king—not only as a king over Israel, but also over all the earth. It should be noted that according to this passage, the Branch will sit and rule upon his throne after the Millennial Temple is built.[12]

THE GLORY OF GOD IN EZEKIEL

As the Priest-King, his throne will be in the temple (Ezek 43:7). Ezekiel 43 also indicates that this Priest-King, the Messiah, is "the glory of the God of Israel"!

---

10. Sailhamer, *The Meaning of the Pentateuch*, 481.

11. Sailhamer, *The Meaning of the Pentateuch*, 486.

12. Answering those who claim that Zerubbabel is the "Branch," Mathews calls attention to an observation by James VanderKam: "If Branch in [Zech] 3:8 is an epithet for Zerubbabel, the text contains a puzzling feature: The LORD says that he is bringing or will bring Branch. Zerubbabel, however, had been in Jerusalem for years, according to Ezra 2–5. It does seem peculiar that . . . he will be brought to a place where he has been for eighteen to nineteen years." See Mathews, *Melchizedek's Alternative Priestly Order*, 127–28, n. 47.

> Then he led me to the gate, the gate facing toward the east; and behold, the glory of the God of Israel was coming from the way of the east. And His voice was like the sound of many waters; and the earth shone with His glory. And *it was* like the appearance of the vision which I saw, like the vision which I saw when He came to destroy the city. And the visions *were* like the vision which I saw by the river Chebar; and I fell on my face. And the glory of the Lord came into the house by the way of the gate facing toward the east. And the Spirit lifted me up and brought me into the inner court; and behold, the glory of the Lord filled the house. (vv. 1–5)

The glory of the God of Israel is sitting on Messiah's throne, the throne of David, in the temple on Mount Zion.[13] Furthermore, when he reigns as King, neither his throne nor his name will be defiled any longer. He told Ezekiel, "Son of man, this is the place of My throne, and the place of the soles of My feet, where I will dwell among the children of Israel forever. And the house of Israel will not again defile My holy name" (Ezek 43:6–7).

THE PRINCE OF PRINCES IN DANIEL

It is also important for us to consider the testimony of Daniel. Twice Daniel refers to Messiah as a "prince,"[14] using two synonymous words in the original Hebrew. It is true that these words may be applied to a leader in general, but, as in modern usage, they can also convey the meaning of a "king-in-waiting."

In Daniel 8:25, the prophet is prophesying about Antiochus Epiphanes, who is often seen as a prototype of the Antichrist. Daniel says that this insolent king (v. 23) will "destroy many while they are at ease. He will even oppose the Prince of princes, but he will be broken without human agency." In the next chapter, Daniel tells us who this "Prince of princes" is: "Messiah the Prince" (Dan 9:25). He is not yet functioning as King, for he is to be "cut off" or killed before the destruction of the temple and of Jerusalem (v. 26), which, of course took place in AD 70.

Following a survey of Messiah as prophet, priest, and king in the Old Testament, Gavin Ortlund asks: "What is the picture that emerges

---

13. "Zion" can be used metaphorically, or by extension, of Mount Moriah (see Isa 2:2–4; 8:18; Mic 4:1–5; Jer 31:6).

14. שר, *sar*, 8:25 and נגיד, *nagid*, 9:25.

from the OT of this Davidic King's rule?"[15] He then summarizes and lists Scripture passages under each of these headings: (1) his rule is universal; (2) his rule is everlasting; (3) God's enemies are subdued and destroyed during his rule; (4) God's people are delivered and protected under his rule, and 5) righteousness, peace, and a saving knowledge of God is spread to all nations during his rule.[16]

CONCLUSION

God's plan to deal with the sin of man would be worked out through the Jewish people, and specifically through Judah. The Davidic Covenant reveals that the hope has narrowed to David's lineage.

In the Old Testament, and particularly in Isaiah, we see that the Prophet like Moses is identified with the Servant of the Lord, who supernaturally leads his people in a new exodus. As the Prophet, he has a close, intimate relationship with God, and he receives an authoritative message, which consists of God's very words. This message would be proclaimed to Israel and accompanied with miraculous signs.

Both the message and the messenger, however, would be rejected and suffer such strong opposition that he would be "cut off out of the land of the living" (Isa 53:8). This is inconceivable: If this one—this Prophet like Moses, the Servant of the Lord—is killed, is there any hope? Has God's plan failed? Yet perhaps unexpectedly, his death leads to his exaltation (Isa 52:13), for through his death, he "will justify the many, as He will bear their iniquities" (Isa 53:11).

This leads to his office of high priest, for following his provision of full and final atonement for sin, "He will see His offspring" and "prolong His days" (Isa 53:10). It is because of his ministry as the Prophet, that he can assume his role as our High Priest. He survives death so he can serve the sinful. Most importantly, it is as High Priest that he conveys God's blessings. As we see in the later prophets and in the psalms, he is a priest with royal authority and a king who governs with purity, truth, and righteousness. It is significant to observe that since this King is from the Tribe of Judah and of the lineage of David, this must also be true of the Prophet and Priest.

---

15. G. Ortlund, "Resurrected as Messiah," 758.
16. G. Ortlund, "Resurrected as Messiah," 758–59.

With the Babylonian Exile, the offices of priest and king were destroyed in Israel. Priests would again function following the rebuilding of the temple, but the next and ultimate Davidic King would be the Messiah. The voice of prophecy was silenced by approximately 400 BC. God promised that Messiah would be a Prophet like Moses, a Priest like Melchizedek, and a King like David. Would these offices actually be restored? This coming Deliverer would somehow fulfill these different roles in his identity as the Branch of the Lord, the Seed of David, and Immanuel. King Messiah will come and will one day rule from Jerusalem, over Israel and over the nations. The different messianic roles doubtless caused some confusion.

Following the resurrection, Jesus spoke into the despair and confusion in the lives of two of his disciples: "Then beginning with Moses and with all the prophets, He explained to them the things concerning Himself in all the Scriptures" (Luke 24:27). Jesus would come as a prophet, priest, and king, each in their order. But before he comes as a Lion in judgment, we need him as a Lamb. In reflecting on this, the hymn writer wrote these words:

> Come not in terror, as the King of kings,
> But kind and good, with healing in Thy wings;
> Tears for all woes, a heart for every plea.
> Come, Friend of sinners, thus abide with me.[17]

---

17. Lyte, "Abide with Me."

Part 3

The Messiah in the New Testament

# 7

Jesus as the Prophet in the New Testament

Pope Sixtus IV built the Sistine Chapel as a part of the Vatican in Rome, and it was completed in about 1481. Its walls were decorated with frescoes painted by some of the most gifted artists of the time. There were originally sixteen panels, each ten feet tall, on the side walls of the chapel. Together, they make up one of the most significant works of art in the world.

Over the centuries, however, they were almost completely hidden beneath a dark layer of the waxy grime of candle smoke and pollution from the city streets. Because they were so covered with grime that the colors and even the figures were hard to make out, they were often overlooked.

Their restoration between 1981 and 1994 was one of the most significant restoration projects of all time. Breathtaking colors and details that had not been seen for centuries were revealed. It is clear now that these frescoes depict parallels between Moses, on the left wall, and Jesus, on the right wall. In a similar way, we need to restore the biblical picture of Jesus as the Prophet like Moses.

As we begin our study of Jesus as the Prophet like Moses, it is crucially important that we make a distinction between identity and function.[1] For example, Tiger Woods's identity is that of a professional golfer,

---

1. It may also be possible to speak of "essential identity" and "functional identity."

but he is only functioning as a professional golfer when he is playing in a professional golf tournament.

Jesus's identity is always that of the Anointed One, the Messiah, and he is always the Messianic Prophet, Priest, and King. But he functions in these roles at different times.[2] He was the Prophet like Moses; he is the great High Priest; and he will return as the King of Israel. His activities at any given time reveal the role in which he is functioning.

MESSIAH AS SUPERMAN

The most common Jewish view of Messiah is that he will be a mere mortal, but one, nonetheless, who will deliver Israel from her enemies; perhaps he will be superhuman, though not divine. In this light, the Jewish origin of Superman (and indeed of most superheroes of comic book and movie fame) is of interest. Superman was born in 1938, so he's getting up in age by now! His creators were Jerry Siegel and Joe Shuster, the children of Jewish immigrants to the United States.[3] Some have quipped that, because of his Jewish origin, instead of "Up, up, and away," the cry of the "Man of Steel" should have been more Jewish—perhaps, "Up, up, and *oy veh*!" This is a Yiddish exclamation like saying, "Aw, man!"

The story of Superman also reveals how Jewish people perceive the Christian view of Messiah. One of Israel's major newspapers, *Yediot Ahronot*, reviewed the movie "Superman Returns," which was released in 2006. The author compares the "saviour role" of Superman with Jesus. She says, "Christians have a reason to smile again, their saviour is back on screen."

She continues, "Instead of a white sheet, he is wearing a red cloak, boots instead of biblical sandals and he flies through the air instead of walking on water. . . . All this is secondary" because "the main thing is that he is here for truth, justice and the American way." The author also says, "For many Christians in the USA there are parallels; a Father who sent his only son to save the world" and "the fact that Yeshu[4] was born by

---

2. We will examine the Messianic Kingdom and its distinction from God's universal kingdom in a later chapter.

3. Goldstein, "Superman Is Jewish." See also, Kaplan, "Supermensch!" 93–94.

4. Yeshu is a traditional way to express Jesus's name in Hebrew. Most Jewish people today are unaware that it is an ancient rabbinic acronym for the pronouncement, "May his name and memory be blotted out." His true name, Yeshua, means "salvation," as it is the masculine form of the word for salvation (*yeshuáh*). Against those who claim that

immaculate conception and that Superman landed on a childless couple speaks for itself."[5]

A mistake most Jewish people make (and unfortunately, also many Christians) is that the Messiah is *only* a king or a superhero who comes with power to rescue the righteous and destroy the wicked—a Superman. Sometimes, Superman was the mild-mannered journalist, Clark Kent, and at other times, he was the "man of steel." Actually, according to the story, the name he was given at birth on the planet Krypton was Kal-El. Kal-El is Hebrew and could be translated "lightweight god."

In stark contrast, the real Messiah is not a "lightweight god." He is a mighty God, the Creator God of Scripture. For this reason, it is extremely important for us to fully appreciate all three roles of Messiah as outlined in the Hebrew Scriptures. It's time to clean up and restore the biblical picture of Messiah. We have allowed Jesus's identity as King to obscure his especially important roles as Prophet and Priest. God's ways are not our ways, and a Superman messiah would indeed be a lightweight god. Instead, Messiah first had to come in humility to suffer and die.

THE AUTHORITY OF MESSIAH

All agree that a major characteristic of Jesus was his authority. Many automatically want to associate that authority with the role of a king. But authority is manifested in each of his different roles. Who can read of the Prophet of Deuteronomy 18 and fail to see that he speaks and acts under the direct authority of God himself? Who can read Psalm 110 and fail to see the authority of this great Priest who is seated next to the Almighty? Of course, when he comes as King, "EVERY KNEE WILL BOW . . . and every tongue will confess" him to be Lord, but he has always been Lord (Phil 2:10–11)! His earthly ministry as God's ultimate Prophet was characterized by authority as well.

---

his name was Joshua and that Jesus is a shortened form, his name was given to Joseph by an angel (Matt 1:21), "for it is He who will save His people from their sins."

5. Mannhardt, *Yediot Ahronot*, July 7, 2006. Of course, the author has switched the original (i.e., the truth of the incarnation) with the caricature (the story of Superman).

THE SEQUENTIAL NATURE OF MESSIAH'S ROLES

Philip Ryken, the president of Wheaton College, wrote a very interesting book that deals with the major characters in J. R. R. Tolkien's work *The Lord of the Rings*.[6] He suggests that Tolkien, whether consciously or not, has presented his major characters as messianic figures. Gandalf, he suggests, represents the prophetic role of Messiah; Frodo represents the priestly role of Messiah; and Aragorn represents the royal role of Messiah. In *The Lord of the Rings*, as well as in the Old Testament, the three roles are seen operating somewhat concurrently. But in the New Testament, the roles are initiated sequentially and exercised cumulatively. That is to say, Messiah is first the Prophet like Moses, then he begins to function also as the Priest like Melchizedek, and finally, he will also reign as the King like David. While his identity does not change, his role does. For example, he was born a king, but he was not ruling as a king from the manger. The importance of the distinction between identity and function cannot be stated strongly enough.

When we read Hebrews 9:24–28, we should pay attention to the ways Jesus is said to be revealed to us. The author uses three different synonyms that are usually translated either "to appear" or "to be made manifest,"[7] but more importantly, he refers to the manifestations of Jesus in the present, in the past, and in the future.

> For Messiah did not enter a holy place made with hands, a mere copy of the true one, but into heaven itself, now to appear in the presence of God for us; nor was it that He would offer Himself often, as the high priest enters the holy place year by year with blood that is not his own. Otherwise, He would have needed to suffer often since the foundation of the world; but now once at the consummation of the ages He has been manifested to put away sin by the sacrifice of Himself. And inasmuch as it is appointed for men to die once and after this comes judgment, so Messiah also, having been offered once to bear the sins of many, will appear a second time for salvation without reference to sin, to those who eagerly await Him. (Heb 9:24–28)

Here, the ministry of the Messiah is presented in three phases. Jesus has been "revealed" or "made known" as our Priest at present (v. 24).

---

6. Ryken, *The Messiah Comes to Middle-Earth*.

7. The three Greek verbs are ἐμφανίζω ("reveal, make known"), φανερόω ("reveal, make clear"), and ὁράω ("see, become visible, appear").

Previously, he was "revealed" as the Prophet who suffered and died to put away sin (v. 26). In the future, he will "become visible" or "appear" to those who eagerly await him in his role as King. We see this also, though not as clearly, in John's description of the Messiah in Revelation 1:5: "and from Jesus the Messiah, the faithful witness [Prophet], the firstborn of the dead [Priest], and the ruler of the kings of the earth [King]."[8]

In his incarnation, Jesus retained his inherent authority but limited its *exercise*. This is a limitation he willingly took upon himself. Prior to his resurrection, Romans 6:9 says that death had mastery over him. This is what Paul was writing about in Philippians 2:5–8. Jesus took "the form of a bond-servant" and "became obedient to the point of death." This limitation marked his role as the Prophet.

In Luke 4:6, in connection with the temptations of Jesus, Satan said to him, "I will give You all this domain and its glory; for it has been handed over to me, and I give it to whomever I wish." At present, this world is under the dominion of Satan. This is the context in which Jesus functions as our Priest and advocate. But when he returns, all his enemies will have been put under his feet (Ps 110:1; Heb 1:13; 2:8).

Through this study, I hope to demonstrate that during his earthly ministry, Jesus functioned as the Prophet like Moses. With his ascension, he assumed his role as the Priest like Melchizedek. When he returns, he will rule as the King like David.

Some deny that these are distinct roles or offices and instead claim they are merely avenues in which he ministers to his disciples.[9] It is true that as the Prophet, he reconciles us to the Father; as the Priest, he reshapes us for the Father; and as the King, he reigns over us with the Father. Yet the emphasis of Scripture is that these functions are related to distinctly messianic roles, as we have seen. This will become even more evident as we survey the material in the New Testament.

JEWISH CONTEXT OF MESSIAH'S BIRTH

The coming of Messiah fulfilled many prophecies (more than can even be mentioned here) and connected many dots in the Hebrew Scriptures. Here is a small sampling:

---

8. I am grateful to William Varner for calling these passages to my attention in his "Messianic Theology of the Old and New Testaments," 92–93.

9. See Appendix 1.

- Messiah's birth was prophesied to be in Bethlehem (Mic 5:2), and it was.
- Messiah was to be born of the lineage of David (2 Sam 7:16), and He was.
- Messiah's birth was to be heralded by a miraculous star (Num 24:17), and it was.
- Messiah was to be born of a virgin (Isa 7:14), so he could also be the Seed of a woman (Gen 3:15), and he was.
- Messiah's birth was announced by angels on five occasions—the first appearances of angels in more than four hundred years.
- Messiah was placed in a manger as a sign pointing to Isaiah 1:3.

Jesus came as Israel's Messiah and Redeemer that he might also be the Savior of all. But there was little consensus as to the role of Messiah two thousand years ago among the Jewish people. There were two major perspectives. The majority of the people expected a powerful king. Against this majority stood a minority who constituted the faithful remnant. They were not certain of all that Messiah would be, but they knew he would bring redemption and provide atonement for sin.

THE MAJORITY'S VIEW OF MESSIAH

As we have seen, most of the Jewish people were in spiritual darkness. God commissioned the prophet Isaiah to pronounce a judgment of spiritual blindness over the majority of the people of Israel in Isaiah 6:9–10: "Go, and tell this people: 'Keep on listening, but do not perceive; keep on looking, but do not understand. Render the hearts of this people insensitive, their ears dull, and their eyes dim, otherwise they might see with their eyes, hear with their ears, understand with their hearts, and return and be healed.'"

Shortly thereafter, Isaiah describes the condition of the people: "They will pass through the land hard-pressed and famished, and it will turn out that when they are hungry, they will be enraged and curse their king and their God as they face upward. Then they will look to the earth, and behold, distress and darkness, the gloom of anguish; and they will be driven away into darkness" (8:21–22). For this reason, studies of the development in the understanding of the Messiah that include Jewish writings from the period between the Old and New Testaments are of little value. These writings are not inspired and reflect the views of this spiritually darkened majority.[10]

The popular view was that Messiah would come as a great leader, as a king, who would overthrow the oppression of Rome and restore the greatness of the kingdom to Israel. So, the majority of the people were primarily interested in a political leader who would make their lives more bearable. They may have known that Messiah was to be a prophet and a priest, but they were mostly looking for a king.

The same is true today. Among some of the very devout Jewish people, there is a group who believe that their former leader was the messiah and that he will return from the dead. They have posters up in Israel and in New York that proclaim him "King Messiah." It is interesting and instructive that they never describe him as a prophet like Moses or as a great high priest like Melchizedek, but only as a king. Many Christians make the same mistake. We are only looking for a king. Don't misunderstand, the King is coming, and we yearn for his coming, but he must first be our Redeemer.

THE MINORITY'S REPORT

On the other end of the spectrum, the faithful remnant was looking for the Messiah as their Redeemer, though they likely had many questions. Would he be a prophet, such as the one prophesied in Deuteronomy 18? Perhaps he would be a lowly and humble Messiah, such as the one prophesied in Zechariah 9:9, who would suffer for the people as in Isaiah 53. Of course, they recognized that Messiah would also be the great King. Apparently, they had fellowship with one another, for Anna spoke about Messiah "to all those who were looking for the redemption of Jerusalem" (Luke 2:38).

Their perspectives can best be discovered by looking at their testimonies, given before they had been influenced by the teaching and

---

10. For an example of one such study, see Bateman, Bock, and Johnston, *Jesus the Messiah*. This work does not recognize Deuteronomy 18:15–19 or 34:10 as messianic. It restricts the role of Messiah to that of a king. It gives great attention to intertestamental Jewish literature, produced by those who were spiritually blind, yet does not even consider the testimony of the remnant who were looking for the Hope of Israel (e.g., cf., Luke 2:38).

miracles of Jesus. So, we will look at the early chapters of the Gospels, which record his birth and the beginning of his ministry.

- Elizabeth saw this Messiah as her Lord, even though he was as yet unborn (Luke 1:43).
- Zacharias anticipated Messiah's arrival as "redemption" (Luke 1:68) and saw him as the Davidic "horn of salvation" (Luke 1:69) and "salvation from our enemies" (Luke 1:71). This salvation, however, was not just from enemies, but from sin. By preparing the way for Jesus, John would be giving Israel "the knowledge of salvation by the forgiveness of their sins" (Luke 1:77).
- Simeon was looking for "the consolation of Israel" (Luke 2:25), the Messiah (Luke 2:26), God's "salvation" (Luke 2:30), who would be "a light of revelation to the Gentiles, and the glory of Your people Israel" (Luke 2:32). But he also saw him as "a sign to be opposed" (Luke 2:34).

There were other testimonies as well.

- Anna saw him as "the redemption of Jerusalem" (Luke 2:38).
- When he began his public ministry, John the Baptist saw him as a righteous judge (Matt 3:12), but also as "the Lamb of God who takes away the sin of the world" (John 1:29) and as the "Son of God" (John 1:34, 36).

To summarize, the remnant's conception of the Messiah was strikingly consistent with what we have learned from the Old Testament.

Even the gentile wise men from the East understood Messiah in terms of Old Testament prophecy. They arrived in Jerusalem in response to the miraculous star, which they understood as the fulfillment of Numbers 24:17. They asked, "Where is He who has been born King of the Jews?" (Matt 2:2). The idea was obviously not that he was claiming the throne as an infant, but that he was born to become the King of Israel in the future.

A "king-in-waiting" is referred to as a prince. In Isaiah 9:6, Messiah is the "Prince of Peace;" in Daniel 9:25, he is "Messiah the Prince." In the previous chapter, we saw that he is called a prince in Ezekiel 34:24. In Acts 3:15, Peter boldly proclaimed Jesus as "the Prince of life, the one whom God raised from the dead." In Acts 5:31, Peter calls him "the one whom God exalted to His right hand as a Prince and a Savior." He was a prince who was destined to become king in the future. During his earthly ministry, however, the only crown he would wear would be made of thorns.

What were the concepts of Messiah held by the religious leadership before Jesus began his public ministry? It is interesting that when the priests and Levites from Jerusalem questioned John the Baptist, thinking that he might be a messianic pretender, they asked him if he was the Messiah. He denied it. "Are you Elijah?" Again, he denied it. Finally, they asked him, "Are you the Prophet?" Once more, John denied that he was more than "a voice of one crying in the wilderness" (John 1:20–23). In an attempt to identify John's ministry, they asked him if he was Messiah, Elijah (the forerunner of Messiah), or *the* Prophet (notice the definite article). He was not, but he pointed to one who was the Messiah and the Prophet.

THE PROPHET IN THE GOSPELS AND ACTS

The fulfillment of promises and prophecies of several millennia was wrapped in swaddling clothes and placed in a stone feeding trough, or manger, in Bethlehem. "The hopes and fears of all the years"[11] were met in him, the promised Seed of a woman. Serious engagement with the Old Testament is necessary to really appreciate the incarnation of the Son of God and the roles he would fulfill. For example, an understanding of the blindness of Israel and of the remnant that was being called to be his disciples is very important in really understanding the ministry of Jesus in his earthly ministry, as recorded in the Gospels. Equally important is an understanding of Jesus's role as the Messianic Prophet.

Jesus was proclaimed a king at his birth and at his death. When he rode a donkey into the city of Jerusalem, it was in fulfillment of Zechariah 9:9: "Behold, your king is coming to you; He is just and endowed with salvation, humble and mounted on a donkey, even on a colt, the foal of a donkey."

Even though his identity as king has honorable mentions, in actual fact, when attention is given to the way Jesus presents himself, it seems as though he studiously avoids presenting himself as a king; instead, he presents himself as the ultimate Prophet. That is to say, his role as king takes a back seat in the Gospels to his function as prophet. Andreas Stutz comments, "Thus the Synoptic Gospels mutually emphasize that Jesus did not want to be regarded as the Messiah according to the popular

---

11. Brooks, "O Little Town of Bethlehem," public domain.

understanding, but that he connected his messiahship with his atoning death."[12] He was functioning as the Servant of the Lord of whom Isaiah had spoken. Jesus deliberately steered away from self-identifying as a king during his earthly ministry, reserving his role as king for the future.

In the Gospels, there is no explicit quotation of the prophecy in Deuteronomy 18, nor is reference ever made to Jesus as "the Prophet like Moses." Yet his words and actions make it clear that he had come in fulfillment of this ancient prophecy. Postell says, "Events in the life of Jesus only make sense with reference to the story of Moses."[13] The Suffering Servant is the same as the Prophet like Moses promised in Deuteronomy 18:15–19 and 34:10.[14] Craig Evans concludes that "the evidence that Jesus saw himself as a prophet is compelling."[15]

This aspect of his ministry is often overlooked, even though it is the primary role he assumed during his earthly ministry. This is due in part to the references to Jesus's identity as King and as the Son of David; yet all the Gospels, and especially Matthew and John, emphasize his role as the Prophet like Moses. References to Jesus as "a prophet" or as "the prophet" are salted throughout the Gospel accounts. Since Scripture presents Jesus as the one and only Messiah, what is said of the coming King would also apply to the coming Prophet or Priest, since these three roles or offices are filled by the one and only Messiah. When Jesus is referred to as the Son of David in the Gospels, this speaks more to his identity than to the role he is fulfilling in his earthly ministry. He is the Son of David. As such, he is the promised Prophet, the promised Priest, and the promised King. In the Gospels, the Son of David functions as the Prophet.

The identity and office of Jesus as the promised Prophet is emphasized throughout the Gospels. Matthew even structures his Gospel after the five books of Moses. He organizes his material into alternating sections of stories and teachings. There is a section in which Jesus is active, followed by a long section of teaching. After each teaching section, Matthew repeats the same phrase, "when Jesus had finished these words." Matthew does this to mark the end of each teaching section.[16] There are a total of five blocks of teachings, even as there are five books in the Pentateuch.

---

12. Stutz, "Jesus as Messiah in the Synoptic Gospels," 149.

13. Postell, "Typology in the Old Testament," 167.

14. For an examination of this role by a Jewish believer of the 1800s, see Baron, *Rays of Messiah's Glory*, 180–221.

15. Evans, "Prophet, Sage, Healer, Messiah, and Martyr," 1219.

16. Matt 7:28; 11:1; 13:53; 19:1; 26:1.

Even more striking, however, are the ways in which the events of his life point to his role as the promised Prophet like Moses. One author comments, "It is clear that the idea of a coming prophet as a messianic figure was strong in Jewish belief based on Deut. 18:15, 18. . . . All four Gospels contain evidence that Jesus was regarded as a prophet during his lifetime, although all four evangelists recognize that Jesus is greater than a prophet."[17]

AN INTIMATE RELATIONSHIP WITH THE FATHER

Moses was known for the intimate relationship he enjoyed with God. To a much greater extent, Jesus has this kind of relationship with the Father. In many passages that carry a heavy emphasis on Jesus's identity as this Prophet like Moses, we find references to him as God's Son.[18] Of course, this relationship should not be surprising, for there are several references to Messiah as God's Son in the Hebrew Scriptures.[19]

In the Gospels, Jesus repeatedly refers to himself as the one sent from the Father. Although Matthew, Mark, and Luke have nine such references,[20] the Gospel of John has forty-one references to Jesus as the Sent One.[21] John summarizes, "For God so loved the world that He gave His only begotten Son [this speaks of His intimate relationship with the Father] that whoever believes in Him shall not perish, but have eternal life" (John 3:16). Here, the fateful choice is presented, even as in Deuteronomy 18:19: "Whoever will not listen to My words which he shall speak in My name, I Myself will require it of him." The claim that God "gave" or "sent" Jesus fills his words and actions with the full authority of the Father. Jesus only says and does what the Father wills, even as the prophesied Prophet like Moses.

---

17. Cho, *Jesus as Prophet in the Fourth Gospel*, 2–3.

18. Ps 2:7; Prov 30:4; Isa 7:14.

19. 2 Sam 7:14a; Ps 2:7, 12; Prov 30:4; Isa 7:14; 9:6; Dan 3:25.

20. Matt 10:40; 15:24; 23:37; Mark 9:37; Luke 4:18, 43; 9:48; 10:16; 13:34. Each of these uses some form of *apostellein*.

21. In the Gospel of John, Jesus uses the Greek verb *pempein* to refer to "the Father who sent Me" no fewer than twenty-four times. These focus on the Father, who authorizes and empowers the Son on his mission. In another seventeen passages, however, the verb *apostellein* is used to focus instead on Jesus, as the one who is sent. See also Moessner, *Lord of the Banquet*, 115.

John 4 records the encounter Jesus had with the woman at the well. At the beginning of this narrative, John says, "And He *had* to pass through Samaria" (v. 4).[22] Why was this necessary? One commentary suggests that "He may have wanted to defy popular prejudices against the Samaritans," or, it says, a "sufficient explanation" may simply be that "the way was shorter and more convenient."[23]

However, as the Prophet like Moses, who would only do or say what the Father directed, Jesus had to go through Samaria because the Father had directed him to go this way. This is borne out near the end of this episode when the disciples return with food and urge Jesus to eat. Jesus says, "My food is to do the will of Him who sent Me, and to accomplish His work" (John 4:34).

The intimacy of the relationship between Jesus and the Father is stated clearly in John 14:7–10:

> If you had known Me, you would have known My Father also; from now on you know Him, and have seen Him." Philip said to Him, "Lord, show us the Father, and it is enough for us." Jesus said to him, "Have I been so long with you, and yet you have not come to know Me, Philip? He who has seen Me has seen the Father; how do you say, 'Show us the Father'? Do you not believe that I am in the Father, and the Father is in Me? The words that I say to you I do not speak on My own initiative, but the Father abiding in Me does His works.

DIVINE AUTHORITY

The Prophet like Moses would carry in his person ultimate authority, which was derived from the intimate relationship he would have with God. His identity as God's Son is found so often in the New Testament passages that emphasize his likeness to Moses in order to emphasize both the authority with which he spoke and acted, as well as his superiority over Moses. As the author of Hebrews says,

> He [Jesus] was faithful to Him who appointed Him, as Moses also was in all His house. For He has been counted worthy of more glory than Moses, by just so much as the builder of the

---

22. Emphasis added. Greek, ἔδει, *edei*.

23. Turner and Mantey, *The Gospel According to John*, 105–6. See also, Harrison, *John*, 29; and Westcott, *The Gospel According to St. John*, 67.

house has more honor than the house. For every house is built by someone, but the builder of all things is God. Now Moses was faithful in all His house as a servant, for a testimony of those things which were to be spoken later; but Messiah *was faithful* as a Son over His house. (Heb 3:2–6a)

THE PROPHET AS AN INTERCESSOR

This role of this Prophet is also characterized by intercession. Although many automatically associate intercession with a priestly ministry, intercession was an important characteristic of Moses and the other prophets of the Old Testament. Even Pharaoh asked Moses to intercede for him.[24] One scholar lists intercession among the six characteristics of Old Testament prophets.[25] Moses probably interceded for Israel frequently, perhaps daily, and several of his prayers for his people are recorded in the Torah. In response to God's warning that he would destroy the people because of their sin of making and worshiping the golden calf, Moses prays:

> O Lord, why does Your anger burn against Your people whom You have brought out from the land of Egypt with great power and with a mighty hand? Why should the Egyptians speak, saying, "With evil intent He brought them out to kill them in the mountains and to destroy them from the face of the earth"? Turn from Your burning anger and change Your mind about doing harm to Your people. Remember Abraham, Isaac, and Israel, Your servants to whom You swore by Yourself, and said to them, "I will multiply your descendants as the stars of the heavens, and all this land of which I have spoken I will give to your descendants, and they shall inherit it forever." (Exod 32:11–13)

Later in this chapter, Moses offers to make atonement for the sin of the people by offering himself in their place (v. 30). He prays, "But now if You will, forgive their sin—and if not, please blot me out from Your book which You have written" (v. 32).

On another occasion, when the people refuse to trust the Lord in response to the report of the scouts who returned from searching out the Land, the Lord threatens to strike them with a plague and disown them (Num 14:12). But he does not follow through with this judgment

---

24. Exod 8:8, 28; 10:16–17.
25. Cho, *Jesus as Prophet in the Fourth Gospel*, 93.

because of Moses's intercession, recorded in verses 13–19. In verse 19 Moses prays, "Pardon, I pray, the iniquity of this people according to the greatness of Your lovingkindness, just as You also have forgiven this people, from Egypt even until now." The Old Testament also records other intercessory prayers for Israel (e.g., Deut 9:26–29 and Num 16:22).

Intercession also characterized other prophets of Israel. Perhaps ironically, it is the *prophet* Joel who urges the *priests* to join him in praying for the people (Joel 2:17)! Amos prays, "Lord GOD, please pardon! How can Jacob stand, for he is small? ... Lord God, please stop! How can Jacob stand, for he is small?" (Amos 7:2, 5). Micah prays for God to shepherd his people (Mic 7:14–20). Habakkuk pleads for God to show mercy and to revive his work, even in the midst of judgment (Hab 3:2).

Certainly, intercession characterized the ministry of Isaiah. At a time of national crisis, King Hezekiah sends his servants to specifically request intercessory prayers from the prophet (2 Kgs 19:1–7). Later, Isaiah intercedes for the king himself. Hezekiah had been stricken with a terminal illness, but God hears Hezekiah's prayer and says that fifteen years would be added to his life. The king, however, is still fearful, so Isaiah prays that the Lord would give a miraculous sign to strengthen the king's faith (2 Kgs 20:11). Isaiah prays once again for Israel in Isaiah 64–65. Intercessory prayer was a vital aspect of Isaiah's ministry.

Jeremiah indicated that prayer should characterize true prophets: "But if they are prophets, and if the word of the LORD is with them, let them now entreat the LORD of hosts" (Jer 27:18). He prays for the people of Judah in Jeremiah 10:23–25 and again in 14:7–9. Likewise, in the midst of God's judgment on the inhabitants of Jerusalem, Ezekiel cries out (Ezek 9:8), "Alas, Lord God! Are You destroying the whole remnant of Israel by pouring out Your wrath on Jerusalem?" Again, in Ezekiel 11:13 he cries out, "Alas, Lord God! Will You bring the remnant of Israel to a complete end?" In response, the Lord gives assurance of his preservation of the remnant, and he also gives a revelation of the future New Covenant (Ezek 11:16–20).

Daniel prays three times daily (Dan 6:10), and in Daniel 9:4–19, Daniel once again turns to the Lord. He confesses the sins of the nation and appeals to the Lord's compassion and righteousness to restore the people to the Land of Israel and to the temple. He concludes his prayer by saying: "We are not presenting our supplications before You on account of any merits of our own, but on account of Your great compassion. O Lord, hear! O Lord, forgive! O Lord, listen and take action! For Your own sake, O my God, do not delay, because Your city and Your people are called by Your name" (Dan 9:18b–19). There is evidence that the other prophets carried a prayer burden for Israel before the Lord as well.

In 1943, shortly after German bombs destroyed the Common Chamber of Parliament, Winston Churchill famously said, "We shape our buildings and afterwards, our buildings shape us." In a similar way, we form our expressions of biblical understanding, and then our expressions shape our biblical understanding. It is often claimed that prophets represented God to the nation and priests represented the nation to God.[26] This distinction needs to be challenged.

With reference to Moses, Van Groningen says that when God revealed the Ten Commandments to him, "The people, in response, trembled at the hearing of God's voice; they pleaded with Moses to be their mediator and spokesman (20:19)."[27] Clearly the prophets had a ministry of intercession and Moses represented the people before God. It seems it would be better to acknowledge that both prophets and priests were mediators between God and the nation, although their ministries differed in other respects.

MIRACULOUS SIGNS

The miracles of Jesus served several purposes. First, they identified Jesus as the Prophet like Moses whom God would raise up. He had been anticipated for centuries; now he had come.

Moses's role as God's designated leader was demonstrated by his miraculous signs. There were the plagues of Egypt, the parting of the Red Sea, miraculous feedings with manna and meat, water from the rock, and many more. The stupendous miracles of Moses authenticated his ministry as God's prophet. The even greater miracles of Jesus confirmed his identity as the Messiah. They underscored his role as the ultimate Prophet to whom Moses's life pointed. In contrast, miraculous signs are never associated as explicitly with Messiah as Priest or King.

Second, the miracles of Jesus incontrovertibly undergirded his identity by demonstrating that his power and authority were from God. As Nicodemus said, "Rabbi, we know that You have come from God as a

---

26. See, for example, Vos, "The Priesthood of Christ in the Epistle of Hebrews," 423–47; Treier, *Lord Jesus Christ*, 233.

27. Van Groningen, *Messianic Revelation in the Old Testament*, 211.

teacher, for no one can do these signs that You do unless God is with him" (John 3:2).

In an attempt to evade this conclusion, some of those who opposed Jesus claimed that his miraculous power was demonic. The account is found in Luke 11:20, after Jesus had cast a demon out of a man who had been mute. Jesus demonstrates the foolishness of their argument (vv. 17–18) and their hypocrisy in making the claim (v. 19). In verse 20 Jesus says, "But if I cast out demons by the finger of God, then the kingdom of God has come upon you."[28]

His reference to "the finger of God" was intentional and is only found this once in the New Testament. It points to Exodus 8:19.[29] Pharoah's magicians had duplicated the first two of the plagues of Moses, but the third was beyond their power, and they attributed it to "the finger of God." Jewish tradition in Jesus's day held that these magicians had demonic power.[30] Yet Pharoah's magicians confessed that the miracles of Moses were not of magic or of demonic power, but they were of God. Evans concludes, "If his power is 'by the finger of God,' then Jesus stands in the company of Moses and Aaron, not in the company of Pharoah's magicians."[31]

The third purpose of Jesus's miracles was to call out the remnant of the people who would become his disciples. Some would be drawn to Jesus because of the miracles, while others would be angered or offended by them. Near the end of his Gospel, John declares, "Therefore many other signs Jesus also performed in the presence of the disciples, which are not written in this book; but these have been written so that you may believe that Jesus is the Messiah, the Son of God; and that believing you may have life in His name" (John 20:30–31).

So, the purpose of the miracles was three-fold: 1) to authenticate the person and ministry of Jesus as the promised Prophet like Moses, 2) to prove his power and authority came from God, and 3) to attract those who had "ears to hear."[32] Yet, for most of the people in Jesus's day, the miracles did not have the desired effect any more than they had for

---

28. Regarding the last portion of the verse, "the kingdom of God has come upon you," this will be discussed later, in connection with the Kingdom.

29. The expression is also found with reference to the giving of the Ten Commandments in Exodus 31:18 and Deuteronomy 9:10; however, Evans (correctly, in my opinion) maintains that the allusion here is to the plagues in Exodus 8. See Evans, "Exodus in the New Testament," 443, n. 8.

30. Evans, "Exodus in the New Testament," 443–44.

31. Evans, "Exodus in the New Testament," 444.

32. Matt 11:1–15.

the Israelites in the wilderness—despite the fact that the miracles of Jesus were greater and more numerous than those of Moses.

OPPOSITION

Moses certainly experienced opposition. This opposition came not only from Egypt and the surrounding gentile nations, but also from his own people. This opposition, rejection, and persecution—even martyrdom—was also endured by the prophets who served Moses and the Law, the prophets of the Hebrew Scriptures. It was almost like a genetic trait passed from one generation to the next. With the coming of Jesus as the Prophet like Moses also comes the distinction between those who listen and obey him and those who don't. When Jesus speaks of his impending death in John 12:31, he says that with the cross, judgment is pronounced on the world and on Satan. But in verse 32, he says that with the cross, people will be drawn to him and to the salvation he offers.

We have discussed what it meant to be "like Moses." In this role, Messiah would have authority, have a ministry of intercession, have an intimate relationship with the Father, perform miraculous signs, be opposed, and suffer. Most Jewish people were not anticipating such a Messiah. But a careful study of the Old Testament shows us this is precisely what Messiah's earthly ministry would look like. As we begin to study Jesus's life more closely, we can search for these themes and see how Jesus is truly the Greater Moses.

8

The Arrival of Jesus, the Prophet Like Moses

WHEN WE LOOK AT the earthly life and ministry of Jesus as it is revealed in the Gospels, we see Jesus functioning as the Prophet of Deuteronomy and as the Suffering Servant of Isaiah. When Jesus gave two of his disciples the real significance behind the things they had witnessed in his ministry, he began with Moses (Luke 24:19). So, with the prophecy from Deuteronomy 18:15–19 in mind, we will look at a selection of incidents from Jesus's life.

THE BIRTH OF JESUS AND THE SLAUGHTER OF THE INNOCENTS

Jesus was born in Bethlehem, but having grown up in Nazareth, there was some confusion about his origins. When he was recognized by the multitudes as the Prophet like Moses or as the Messiah (Luke 7:40), they were perplexed as to where this Prophet was supposed to be born. In John 7:19–27 and 37–43, we read that no one knew where Jesus was from. This would also be true of the religious authorities in John 9. Nicodemus appealed to the Pharisees that they should investigate further before condemning him. In John 7:52, we read that the Pharisees rebuffed Nicodemus's appeal by saying, "*no prophet arises out of Galilee*" (emphasis added). However, the oldest existing copy of this verse (which dates to about AD 140) reads, "*the* prophet does not arise out of Galilee" (emphasis added).[1] Yet Isaiah 9:1 hints at his upbringing there: "But there will be no more gloom for her who was in anguish; in earlier times He treated the land of Zebulun and the land of Naphtali with contempt, but later on He shall make it glorious, by the way of the sea, on the other side of Jordan, Galilee of the Gentiles."[2]

Following the birth of Jesus in Bethlehem, his circumcision (eight days later), the arrival of the wise men, and his dedication as a first-born son at the temple (when forty days old), Matthew tells us that an angel warned Joseph that Herod would try to kill the child.[3] So, Joseph took Mary and Jesus and fled to Egypt—to the land of the pharaohs and the birthplace of Moses.

When Herod realized that the wise men were not returning to supply him with more information about this new-born king, he ordered the execution of all male children two years old and younger in Bethlehem and the surrounding area. In this, he displayed the same attitude as Pharaoh who had ordered all the male babies born to the Israelites in Egypt to be killed. Remember, Moses had been born at this time. Forty years later, the first-born sons of Egypt were to die in the judgment of the final plague.[4] But just as the infant Moses was delivered from Pharaoh's murderous intent, so also was the infant Jesus delivered from Herod's.

---

1. Reference is to the Bodmer papyri, P^{66}. Comfort and Barrett, eds., *The Complete Text of the Earliest New Testament Manuscripts*, 406. Lesser prophets who had arisen out of Galilee would include Micah, Elijah, Jonah, Nahum, and Hosea. But the Prophet was not to come from Galilee, but from Bethlehem. In John 9, the formerly blind man mocks the religious leaders because they do not know where this "prophet," Jesus (v. 17), is from (v. 30). Of course, John is emphasizing that Jesus ultimately was sent from the Father.

2. See Matt 4:12–16.

3. Rather than understand this to have been almost two years following his birth, it is better to see this as happening shortly after Jesus's dedication at the temple. Given Herod's paranoia and his lack of concern for human life, his parameters were broad, not narrow. He wanted to be certain the child had not been born a year or so before the arrival of the wise men.

4. It is interesting to observe that following the death of the first-born sons of Egypt, the Egyptians gave costly gifts to the Israelites, and following the birth of the first-born Son, men from the East gave costly gifts to Israel's Messiah. Through Moses, God formed a nation; through his Son, he formed a kingdom.

THE RETURN FROM EGYPT

Messiah's sonship can be seen in the account of Joseph and Mary's sojourn in Egypt with the infant Jesus. In speaking of their return from Egypt, Matthew (2:15) quotes from Hosea 11:1, "When Israel was a youth I loved him, and out of Egypt I called My Son." Many interpreters are perplexed by this quotation because it seems Matthew is not dealing with the text in a straightforward manner. They point to Exodus 4:22: "Israel is my son, my firstborn." So they object, "The text is speaking about Israel, and it was Israel that was called out of Egypt."

Let's look at this more closely. Matthew is quoting from Hosea, and Hosea is quoting from Numbers 24:8. Hosea understood the Exodus as a historical event, and so did Matthew. But it is important to understand that Hosea already knew that the Messiah would be born of the Tribe of Judah (Gen 49:10). When Judah, along with the other tribes, was brought out of Egypt, Messiah, though unconceived, also left Egypt. Hosea was also familiar with Numbers and the oracles of Balaam. To Balaam it was revealed that Messiah would not only come out of Egypt seminally, but geographically.

In Numbers 23:22 Balaam says, "God brings *them* out of Egypt." The plural refers to the people of Israel. This is the historical Exodus. In the next chapter (Num 24:8), he says, "God brings *him* out of Egypt."[5] Here, the singular refers to the Messianic Seed (24:7), who will defeat King Agag (or, perhaps, Gog),[6] and whose kingdom will be exalted. This is clearly a reference to the Messiah. Sailhamer says, "When Matthew sees a fulfillment of Hosea's words in the coming of the Christ and his own return out of Egypt (Matt 2:15), he was reading the book of Hosea as it had originally been intended."[7]

When this is understood, we see that Hosea is using this passage from Numbers to refer to the Messiah and to this ultimate deliverance. David Finkbeiner says, "Hosea may be hinting that the Messiah should be considered a prophet like Moses who leads his people out of exile."[8]

---

5. Emphasis has been added to both quotations above.

6. As in LXX, Samaritan Pentateuch, Aquila, Symmachus, and Theodotion. See M. Rydelnik, *The Messianic Hope*, 38–39; also, Chen, *The Messianic Vision of the Pentateuch*, 217. James Hamilton, however, sees significance in Saul's failure to kill Agag (1 Sam 15) and in Haman's identification as an Agagite (Esth 3:1). See "The Skull Crushing Seed of the Woman," 33.

7. Sailhamer, "Hosea 11:1 and Matthew 2:15," 88–97.

8. Finkbeiner, "Hosea 3:4–5," 1161.

Certainly, with the angelic summons of Joseph, Mary, and Jesus back to the Land of Israel, Matthew understands Numbers the same way Hosea did. The Messiah is being called out of Egypt! Jesus is unmistakably seen here as the Prophet like Moses.

HIS BAPTISM IN THE JORDAN

No one knows the exact spot where Jesus was baptized, but it is surely not without significance that Jesus was baptized in the same stretch of the Jordan River where the Israelites entered the Land.[9] The Jordan marked the limit beyond which Moses could not go. Jesus was greater than Moses and began his public ministry where Moses concluded his.

John the Baptist apparently recognized Jesus as both the Son of God and the Prophet like Moses, for he said of him, "He who believes in the Son has eternal life; but he who does not obey the Son shall not see life, but the wrath of God abides on him" (John 3:36). As we have seen, the same kind of warning was to accompany the appearance of the Prophet: "Whoever will not listen to My words which he shall speak in My name, I Myself will require it of him" (Deut 18:19).[10]

When Moses and the people of Israel were "baptized" in the Red Sea, they were united under his leadership (1 Cor 10:1–2). Jesus's baptism harkens back to the experience of Moses as the pattern by which his disciples are joined to him (Rom 6:3–7).

THE ANOINTING OF JESUS

We see Jesus's identity as the Prophet in his anointing. Since Jesus came as the Messiah, and since "Messiah" means "the anointed one," when was Jesus anointed? Our failure to recognize his identity as the Prophet like Moses may prevent us from understanding this. Kings and priests were anointed with olive oil, but we have no record of prophets being anointed

---

9. Perhaps it is worth noting that in this same area not far from Jericho, the "fords of the Jordan," Elijah the prophet struck the Jordan with his mantle, so that the waters parted, and he and Elisha crossed on dry land (2 Kgs 2:8). There was likely a "school of the prophets" in the same area (2 Kgs 6:1–7). Furthermore, John the Baptist came in the spirit of Elijah.

10. Brian J. Tabb and Steve Walton write, "John is the promised prophet like Elijah, who prepares the way for the Lord Jesus, in the fulfillment of God's new exodus program of judgment and salvation" ("Exodus in Luke-Acts," 66).

with oil. On the other hand, we know prophets were anointed, for in both Psalms and in Chronicles we read, "Do not touch My anointed ones; and do My prophets no harm" (Ps 105:15; 1 Chr 16:22). Here, the prophets were called "the anointed ones."

We need to understand that prophets were anointed with the Spirit. One example is Elisha. God commissioned Elijah to anoint Elisha, but there is no record of this taking place, at least not with oil (1 Kgs 19:16). Instead, we are told that Elisha received the Spirit. Second Kings 2:9 says that when Elijah and Elisha had crossed over the Jordan River, "Elijah said to Elisha, 'Ask what I shall do for you before I am taken from you.' And Elisha said, 'Please, let a double portion of your spirit be upon me.'" He received the prophet's anointing, an anointing with the Holy Spirit.

This is in keeping with other prophets who seem to have been anointed, not with oil, but with the Holy Spirit. For example, Saul had an experience with the Holy Spirit that called to mind God's anointing of prophets. We read, "When they came to the hill there, behold, a group of prophets met him; and the Spirit of God came upon him mightily, so that he prophesied among them" (1 Sam 10:10). Of course, Saul was anointed with oil by Samuel as well (1 Sam 10:1). But here it was the fact that "the Spirit of God came upon him mightily" that caused him to behave like a prophet.

In Joel 2:28, the outpouring of God's Spirit is associated with prophecy. God says, "It will come about after this that I will pour out My Spirit on all mankind; and your sons and daughters will prophesy." Perhaps more significantly, Isaiah prophesies, "Behold My Servant, whom I uphold; My chosen one in whom My soul delights. I have put My Spirit upon Him" (Isa 42:1; see also Matt 12:18).

Following his baptism, Jesus was anointed with the Holy Spirit. He was always the Son of God, but this was the moment he became the Messiah, or Anointed One. At Jesus's baptism, the Holy Spirit came down from heaven as a dove. This served as a visible sign of his anointment with the Spirit. As Peter would say, "You know of Jesus of Nazareth, how God anointed Him with the Holy Spirit and with power, and how He went about doing good and healing all who were oppressed by the devil, for God was with Him" (Acts 10:38).[11] Once we understand the significance of his anointment with the Holy Spirit as the Messianic Prophet

---

11. See also Acts 4:27; 10:38.

like Moses, we can understand his baptism as a ceremonial preparation for this anointing by the Spirit.

JESUS AS THE SON OF GOD

At this time, the voice from heaven said, "This is My beloved Son, in whom I am well-pleased" (Matt 3:17). So, God called his *Son* out of Egypt as an infant and at his baptism pronounced him his beloved *Son*. Both Israel and Jesus are referred to as God's Son, and both experienced a baptism of sorts.[12] Furthermore, as we have seen, Jesus's identity as God's Son is often associated with his role as the Prophet like Moses.[13]

When John objected to baptizing Jesus, Jesus said, "Permit it at this time; for in this way it is fitting for us to fulfill all righteousness" (Matt 3:15). David Turner says, "In Jesus' baptism he and John fulfill the Scriptures by introducing the Messiah to Israel. This baptism, as the inauguration of Jesus' ministry to Israel, leads immediately to biblical fulfillment in that the Spirit as a dove comes upon the Messiah ("the Spirit of the Lord will rest on Him," Isa 11:1–2) and the Father endorses his Son in the voice from heaven (Ps 2:7; Isa 42:1)."[14]

HIS TEMPTATIONS IN THE WILDERNESS

Jesus's public ministry was bracketed by two 40-day periods, one at its beginning and one at its conclusion. This first one was a time of testing; the last was a time of teaching. Both were expressions of Jesus's ministry as the ultimate, prophesied Prophet—the one to whom Israel must listen and obey.

Here we see more parallels between Jesus and Moses. Jesus fasted in the wilderness for "forty days and forty nights" (Matt 4:2), "and He ate nothing during those days" (Luke 4:2). Of Moses, the Scripture says, "So he was there with the LORD forty days and forty nights; he did not eat bread or drink water" (Exod 34:28).

---

12. Interestingly, in 1 Corinthians 10:1–5, Paul describes our baptism with the metaphor of the Israelites crossing the Red Sea.

13. In John 1:17, prior to John's account of the baptism, he says, "For the Law was given through Moses; grace and truth were realized through Jesus the Messiah." Even here, Moses is the point of comparison for Jesus.

14. D. Turner, *Matthew*, 119.

There are also parallels with the experience of Israel. As Israel entered the wilderness and was tested for forty years (see Deut 8:2), so Jesus was tested in the wilderness for forty days. The first temptation, to turn stones into bread, is reminiscent of the miraculous provision of manna pronounced by Moses during the wilderness experience of Israel. Jesus responded to this temptation with Deuteronomy 8:3, "Man does not live by bread alone, but man lives by everything that proceeds out of the mouth of the LORD." In its context, Moses makes mention of the manna God provided, not just to meet the physical needs of the people, but more importantly, to teach them to be dependent upon the Word of God.

Jesus's second temptation, to trust God to rescue him from a leap from the pinnacle of the temple, was answered with a quotation from Deuteronomy 6:16: "You shall not put the LORD your God to the test." This seems to point to the incident recorded in Exodus 17, where, in response to their thirst, the people were angry with both God and Moses. Here, Moses responded, "Why do you test the LORD?" (v. 2). Moses was warning the people against testing the Lord and his provision. In a similar way, Jesus did not need to test the Lord, for the Lord was testing him, revealing him to be the beloved Son in whom the Father was well-pleased (Matt 3:17).

The third temptation, offering Jesus the kingdoms of the world in exchange for his worshiping Satan, is met by a command for Satan to leave and a quotation based on Deuteronomy 6:13: "You shall worship the LORD your God, and serve Him only" (Matt 4:10). This passage also alludes to Exodus 23:24–25, where Moses warns against following foreign gods, and to Israel's worship of the golden calf (Exod 32). Notice also that in these testings, and in the midst of the failure and sin of the majority of Israel, Moses remained faithful—so also, would the Prophet like him.

Postell points to the larger picture:

> In Matthew 2, God brings Jesus out of Egypt. In Matthew 3, God brings Jesus through the waters of the Jordan. In Matthew 4, God brings Jesus to the wilderness to be tested. Matthew's three temptations follow the exact order of Israel's wilderness temptations, up to and including the sin of the Golden Calf, where Israel bows down and worships a false god, something Jesus refuses to do.[15]

---

15. Postell, "Abram as Israel, Israel as Abram," 33.

How are we to understand these temptations? In Scripture, Israel is presented as God's first-born son (Exod 4:22). Where God's son, Israel, failed, his Son, the Prophet like Moses, overcame. It is not that Jesus replaces Israel, but that Israel's experiences point to him.

THE TESTIMONY OF PHILIP AND THE FIRST MIRACLE

In John 1, we find the testimony of Philip. First, Jesus called two of the disciples of John the Baptist—Andrew and Simon Peter—to follow him. They followed on the basis of John's testimony. Next, Jesus called Philip (v. 43), and when Philip found Nathaniel, Philip told his friend, "We have found Him of whom Moses in the Law and *also* the Prophets wrote— Jesus of Nazareth, the son of Joseph" (v. 45). It seems Philip correctly identified the Prophet like Moses with the Messiah of the prophets, and certainly this coming Deliverer was none other than Jesus of Nazareth. Indeed, as Nathaniel would discover, he was "the Son of God; the King of Israel" (John 1:49).

Immediately following this account is the story of Jesus turning the water to wine in John 2. In verse 11, John specifically draws attention to the fact that this was Jesus's first miracle. There are many who explain the meaning of this miracle in terms of Christian superiority. Since the water in these pots was used in the purification rites spelled out in Leviticus 11 (especially v. 32), they claim that the water pots stand symbolically for the Mosaic Law that was being replaced by Jesus. Others see the pots as symbolic of Judaism that is being replaced with Christianity. For example, George Beasley-Murray says, "Most writers acknowledge that in the Johannine narrative there is an implicit contrast between water used for Jewish purificatory rites and the wine given by Jesus; the former is characteristic of the old order, the latter of the new."[16]

While it is certainly true that Jesus offers a salvation the Law could not offer, this sign miracle needs a better explanation. Two points are particularly important. In the first place, the signs in the Gospel of John were for the purpose of identifying Jesus as the Messiah. John 20:31 says that these signs were included "that you may believe that Jesus is the Messiah, the Son of God; and that believing you may have life in His name." Therefore, the signs were not given to describe the relationship between Judaism and Christianity or between the Mosaic Law and the

---

16. Beasley-Murray, *John*, 36.

New Covenant; instead, they are for establishing Jesus's identity as the promised Deliverer.

The second point is that the Mosaic Law was not fading away at that time. Was the Mosaic Covenant set aside before the inauguration of the New Covenant? If so, how did Jesus fulfill its demands? In Galatians 4:4–5, Paul tells us that Jesus had to be born under the Law and live under the Law so that he could fulfill the demands of the Law and provide redemption. The Mosaic Covenant would be replaced with the New Covenant at the crucifixion, but not before. Because these miraculous signs were to point to Jesus's identity, and because the Mosaic Covenant was still in effect, this interpretation, while ancient and still common, cannot be correct.

Instead, it is far better to see that here Jesus is introducing himself as the Prophet like Moses. Moses's first public miracle was turning the water of Egypt to blood, symbolizing judgment and death. In fact, in Exodus 7:19, it was not just the water in the Nile River or the water in streams and pools that were turned to blood, but also the water "both in vessels of wood and in *vessels of stone*."[17]

The first miracle of Jesus was a mirror-image of Moses's. The miracle of Moses was a plague and symbolized God's judgment, that of Jesus was a blessing and symbolized redemption and its accompanying joy.[18] With this, Jesus is presenting himself as the Prophet like Moses. In his first miracle, he shows himself to be the one of whom Moses spoke. This is seen as further signaling the time for the new exodus—a new exodus of salvation.[19] In turning the water to wine, Jesus is introducing himself by presenting his credentials—he is the Prophet like Moses. The Messiah has arrived!

---

17. Emphasis added.

18. In Matthew 9:17, Jesus likened his call to discipleship and salvation to new wine.

19. See Glasson, *Moses in the Fourth Gospel*. There is much more to the blood/wine comparison in Scripture. See also Gen 37:31; 49:11. Also at the Last Supper, wine symbolizes blood.

9

Jesus, the Prophet, in Samaria and in Galilee

ANY NUMBER OF ARTISTS have created works in which there is a hidden face. Perhaps the scene looks like a mountain or a lake with overhanging tree branches, but hidden in the details is a face that is not immediately noticeable. Regardless of how carefully the face may be hidden, once you see it, you can never "un-see" it. In Deuteronomy 18:15–19, God promised to send a Prophet like Moses, who would carry God's own message and bear his own authority. Many Christians are not familiar with the prophecy, and thus never consider that Jesus functioned as this Prophet in his earthly life. However, once you see this Moses-like Prophet in the Gospels, his words and actions take on a new depth of meaning.

Having surveyed Jesus's childhood, baptism, temptation, and first miracle, we will now continue with the rest of his earthly ministry.

HIS ENCOUNTER WITH THE WOMAN OF SAMARIA

After a trip to Jerusalem for Passover, Jesus and his disciples were returning to Galilee by way of Samaria. In John 4, Jesus asks an Israelite woman of Samaria for a drink from the well, and this provokes a conversation. To begin with, we need to know who the Samaritans were. They were

Israelites; they were not Gentiles.[1] An ancient hatred and hostility existed between the northern and southern tribes that goes back to the time of the Judges, though the decisive break between the two came with the foolishness of Rehoboam (1 Kgs 12). This hostility was religious and cultural in nature. Although idolatry was common in both the northern kingdom of Israel and in the southern kingdom of Judah, the northern kingdom was particularly given over to idolatry. Furthermore, they had rejected worship in Jerusalem at the temple and had established alternative places of worship. Finally, these Israelites, now called Samaritans, did not accept any of the God-given Scriptures except their own version of the Pentateuch.

The Samaritans were Israelites, but they were apostate, or deviant, in their faith. They were viewed as unclean by the Judean Jews. There were three barriers between this woman and Jesus: she was a Samaritan; she was a woman; and she carried a burden of shame and guilt. Jesus would reveal to this woman who he was, and in the process, he would reveal who she was.

The woman at the well identifies Jesus as the Prophet like Moses. How do we know? How does she connect the dots? Because of the way she answers him. She says, "Sir, I perceive that You are a prophet" (v. 19). Literally it reads, "Prophet You are." By answering in this way, it is likely that she is proclaiming Jesus to be *the* Prophet. Even though the definite article, "the," is not found in the Greek text, a principle of Greek grammar dictates that with this particular grammatical construction the definite article may be assumed.[2]

Even more significant is the fact that the Samaritans did not accept the books of the Prophets or the Writings. They were only looking for this Prophet who was prophesied in Deuteronomy 18. So how does she identify Jesus as the anticipated Prophet? There are two primary reasons she is able to make the connection: (1) their discussion regarding "water" (vv. 7–15) and (2) Jesus's supernatural knowledge of her private life (vv. 16–18).

---

1. See Jervell, "The Lost Sheep of the House of Israel," 113–32. See also, Schnabel, *Early Christian Mission*, 672.

2. This is referred to as Colwell's Rule. Colwell's Rule says that if a predicate nominative precedes the linking verb (copula), it drops the definite article most (87 percent) of the time; therefore, it should not be translated as an indefinite noun simply because of the absence of the article. See also R. Brown, *The Gospel According to John 1–12*, 171.

The discussion regarding water. Why would the discussion of water point to this Prophet like Moses? Moses miraculously provided water to the people of Israel in the wilderness on three occasions. In the first two incidents, water flowed from a rock (Exod 17:1–6 and Num 20:1–11), and in the third (Num 21:16–18), water sprung up from a well. Significantly, the area where the water was provided through a well is called Mattanah,[3] which means "gift."

In John 4:10, Jesus tells the woman, "If you knew the gift [Heb., *mattanah*] of God, and who it is who says to you, 'Give Me a drink,' you would have asked Him, and He would have given you living water." A few verses later he says, "Whoever drinks of the water that I will give him shall never thirst; but the water that I will give him will become in him *a well of water* springing up to eternal life" (v. 14).[4] With this, Jesus presents himself to this Samaritan woman as the Prophet like Moses, providing the living water of salvation.[5]

Supernatural knowledge. Her dawning recognition of Jesus's identity is confirmed when Jesus reveals his knowledge of her marital and moral failures. Certainly, it was possible for a prophet, such as Elijah, to possess knowledge supernaturally;[6] however, in Samaritan tradition, "if one shows supernatural knowledge, that one must be the *Taheb*."[7] The *Taheb*, or Restorer, in Samaritan thought was the Prophet like Moses.[8]

On that day long ago, a woman learned who she was—a very thirsty Samaritan. She discovered a thirst she didn't even know she had. A thirst that water could not quench. She also learned who Jesus was—the Prophet like Moses, who could provide living water in her personal wilderness.

---

3. Num 21:18.

4. Emphasis added.

5. Cho, *Jesus as Prophet in the Fourth Gospel*, 175. Chen says, "The Lord's provision of water at this well not only recalls both passages about water from the rock but also uses terminology and themes in common with other passages related to the Messianic vision of the Pentateuch" (Chen, *The Messianic Vision of the Pentateuch*, 208). See also Chen's discussion on pages 208 and 209.

6. For example, see 2 Kgs 5:25–27.

7. Cho, *Jesus as Prophet in the Fourth Gospel*, 179.

8. See, for example, Shomron, "The Taheb, the Restorer, A Prophet like Moses." Also, Tsedaka, *Understanding the Israelite-Samaritans*, 14.

THE SERMON IN NAZARETH

When they arrive in Galilee, Jesus goes to the synagogue in Nazareth, his hometown. All three synoptic Gospels refer to this sermon, but only Luke gives the substance of the message.[9] In Luke 4:18–19, Jesus reads from Isaiah 61: "THE SPIRIT OF THE LORD IS UPON ME, BECAUSE HE ANOINTED ME TO PREACH THE GOSPEL TO THE POOR. HE HAS SENT ME TO PROCLAIM RELEASE TO THE CAPTIVES, AND RECOVERY OF SIGHT TO THE BLIND, TO SET FREE THOSE WHO ARE OPPRESSED, TO PROCLAIM THE ACCEPTABLE YEAR OF THE LORD." Jesus is saying that he fulfills this prophecy in Isaiah.

Here, Jesus explicitly claims to be the Servant of Isaiah 61; he claims to have been anointed with the Spirit; and he claims to have been sent by the Lord, by Jehovah. What sort of leaders were anointed with the Spirit? Prophets. Who was the Servant of Isaiah 61? The Prophet like Moses. Who was to be sent by the Father? The Messianic Deliverer.

Jesus meets the resistance and unbelief of his townspeople by saying, "No prophet is welcome in his hometown" (Luke 4:24). He then identifies with the rejection faced by the prophets who had preceded him (vv. 25–27).

THE SERMON ON THE MOUNT

After moving his headquarters to Capernaum and calling his twelve disciples, Jesus delivers the Sermon on the Mount. In Deuteronomy 18:15–19, God had promised to send a Prophet like Moses, who would carry God's own message and bear his own authority. Regarding the Sermon on the Mount, Frederic Godet, writing in 1899, pronounced that "the mount where Jesus speaks is as the Sinai of the new covenant."[10] Jesus is acting and teaching as the Prophet like Moses. Prior to the Sermon on the Mount, Jesus fasted for forty days and nights. Before receiving the Law on Mount Sinai, Moses did as well.

This observation also leads us to consider the structure of the Sermon on the Mount. The opening words of The Sermon on the Mount, in Matthew 5, are similar to the biblical texts about Moses ascending Mount Sinai in Deuteronomy 9:9, where Moses says, "When I went up to the

---

9. Matt 13:54–58; Mark 6:1–6; Luke 4:16–30.
10. Godet, *Introduction to the New Testament*, 131.

mountain to receive the tablets of stone, the tablets of the covenant which the LORD had made with you, then I remained on the mountain forty days and nights."

The word translated "remained" can either mean "abode," "remained," or "stayed," and this is reflected in our translations.[11] But the primary meaning of the word is "sat." In other words, Moses "sat" on the mountain. Dale Allison examined Jewish literature of this time outside of the Bible and concluded: "The image of Moses sitting on Sinai . . . was firmly established in the imagination of pre-Christian Jews."[12] In the introduction to the Sermon on the Mount we read, "When Jesus saw the crowds, He went up on the mountain; and after He sat down, His disciples came to Him" (Matt 5:1).

There is also similarity between Moses's descent from Mount Sinai and Jesus's descent from the mountain in Matthew. Exodus 34:29 says, "It came about when Moses was coming down from Mount Sinai. . . ." Compare this with Matthew 8:1: "When Jesus came down from the mountain. . . ." These parallels seem to be intentional.[13] From first to last, in delivering this sermon, Jesus is modeling his teaching to reflect his identity as the Prophet like Moses delivering a new Torah.

> A. Poor in spirit blessed, for theirs is the kingdom of heaven
> B. Mourners blessed, for they will be comforted
>   C. Meek blessed, for they will inherit the earth
>   D. Hungry blessed, for they will be filled
>   D'. Merciful blessed, for they will be shown mercy
>   C'. Pure blessed, for they will see God
> B'. Peacemakers blessed, for they will be called sons of God
> A'. Persecuted blessed, for theirs is the kingdom of heaven

Sermon on the Mount

In fact, the Beatitudes at the beginning of the Sermon on the Mount are organized in such a manner that there is a parallelism between the first and last elements, the second and the next-to-last, and so forth. This is called a chiasm. Not only are the Beatitudes organized this way, but so is the entire Sermon on the Mount. What adds to this interest is that

---

11. Heb., ישב, *yashav*. The text says, ואשב, "then I remained."
12. Allison, *The New Moses*, 179.
13. Allison, *The New Moses*, 179–80.

Psalm 90, the Psalm of Moses, is also written as a chiasm. Even in the structure of his teaching, Jesus is alluding to his authority as the prophesied Prophet of Deuteronomy 18.

In Deuteronomy 18, the prophecy of the coming Prophet like Moses is given in the context of false and unreliable sources of revelation. Prior to the prophecy (Deut 18:9–14), Moses warns against foreign diviners, pagan mediums, and idolatrous sorcerers. In the passage that follows the prophecy (Deut 18:20–22), he warns against domestic, Israelite false prophets. In between these passages of warning against false sources of truth, we find the prophecy of the Prophet who only speaks and does what God tells him.

In the Sermon on the Mount, Jesus also warns against false prophets. He says, "Beware of the false prophets who come to you in sheep's clothing, but inwardly are ravenous wolves" (Matt 7:15). This highlights Jesus as the only true source of knowledge regarding the way to find deliverance from sin and entrance into the Messianic Kingdom. He speaks and does only what God tells him.

In his sermon, Jesus emphasizes the importance of "hearing these words of Mine" and acting upon them (Matt 7:24, 26). To truly understand what he is saying, we must remember the warnings in Deuteronomy 18 about failing to listen and obey him. God says in verse 15, "You shall listen to him," and in verse 19, he says, "It shall come about that whoever will not listen to My words which he shall speak in My name, I Myself will require it of him."

Jesus addresses the issue of authority even further when he examines the relationship between the Pharisaic legal traditions and his own teaching (Matt 5:17–19). In this sermon and in the Gospels generally, the primary question is whether the oral traditions of the Pharisees carry any authority for the way the disciples of Jesus are to live. The Pharisees claim these traditions were derived from Moses and that, in following them, they are simply being faithful to Moses. Jesus rebukes the Pharisees and denies that these traditions carry any authority.[14]

In this passage, Jesus focuses attention not on his view of the Law, but on the Law's view of him. He is the Prophet to whom the Law pointed. Faith in Jesus as the authoritative Prophet prophesied in Deuteronomy 18 was now seen as essential to Torah. Those who did not follow him were

---

14. See Prettel, "Messianic Judaism and Tradition," 136–86; see also, Sibley, "The Jewish Disciples in the Book of Acts," 211–12.

apostate in their relationship to Torah. They were building on a foundation of sand.

In the Sermon on the Mount, Jesus teaches his disciples about a way of life that is focused on internal attitudes of love for God and love for neighbor that go far beyond the focus of the Pharisees, and even that of the Mosaic Law, for one greater than Moses has come. Jesus is not intensifying the demands of the Law as much as he is internalizing the demands of the Law. The Sermon outlines the attitudes of life a disciple of Jesus should have. Once we understand the significance of Jesus as the Prophet like Moses, we can better understand the importance of becoming one of his disciples and living the *halakah* (the way of life) God wants us to live. The authoritative Prophet like Moses has made it clear.

THE RAISING OF THE WIDOW'S SON

Later, Jesus and his disciples leave Capernaum for the village of Nain. It was one of several villages around the base of a small mountain in Galilee, the Hill of Moreh. Two villages lay on opposite sides of the mountain: Nain and Shunem. The prophet Elisha raised a woman's only son from the dead in Shunem (2 Kgs 4:8–37), and Jesus would raise a woman's only son at Nain (Luke 7:11–17). Sometimes Jesus's miracles take place while he is on the way to a specific destination, but on this occasion, Scripture suggests that Jesus leads his disciples to Nain, a distance of thirty-two miles with an elevation gain of 1,440 feet (from—680 feet to 760 feet), and then returns.

The text suggests that Jesus intends to come here specifically. Since the dead were to be buried within twenty-four hours of their death, the implication is that Jesus supernaturally knows about this widow and her son before he and the disciples leave Capernaum. He comes specifically to raise this young man from the dead. Why? What is the point? If Jesus's actions are intended to send a message, what is it?

Because of the proximity of Nain to Shunem and the parallels with the miracle of Elisha, his miracle at Nain moves the crowds to identify him as the "great prophet" (Luke 7:16). Only the most prominent of the prophets, Elijah and Elisha, had raised the dead, so *the* Prophet who was to come was doubtless in their minds."[15] But neither of these Old Testament prophets had raised the dead with merely a spoken word.

15. Alford, *Alford's Greek Testament*, 506.

Elisha was known for the many miracles he performed—twice as many as Elijah. There are fourteen miracles attributed to Elijah in Scripture, but twenty-eight to Elisha. It is interesting that Elisha was anointed with a double portion of Elijah's spirit (2 Kgs 2:9–11). Elijah is also associated with one resurrection (2 Kgs 17:17–24), but Elisha with two (2 Kgs 4:18–37; 13:20–21).

It is also interesting that Elijah played a part in the ministries of both Elisha and Jesus, for both were "introduced," in one sense, by Elijah. Elijah preceded Elisha and was present as Elisha was anointed by the Spirit. John the Baptist, who came "in the spirit and power of Elijah" (Luke 1:17), preceded Jesus's ministry, introduced him to the nation, and was present as Jesus was anointed with the Spirit. In fact, attention quickly shifts from the young man who was raised from the dead to Jesus, the "great prophet" that God had raised up (Luke 7:16).

JESUS AND THE DISCIPLES OF JOHN

Immediately following the account of Jesus raising the widow's son at Nain, we find the disciples of John the Baptist coming to Jesus seeking reassurance that he is indeed the "the Expected One" (Luke 7:18–23). Jesus responds, "Go and report to John what you have seen and heard: the BLIND RECEIVE SIGHT, the lame walk, the lepers are cleansed, and the deaf hear, the dead are raised up, the POOR HAVE THE GOSPEL PREACHED TO THEM (v. 22)." His response is based on Isaiah 61, the text for his sermon in Nazareth. His reference to "the dead" being raised up refers to the widow's son.

Jesus would raise at least three: the widow's only son, Jairus's only daughter (Luke 8:40–42, 49–56), and Mary and Martha's only brother, Lazarus (John 11:1–44). Jairus's daughter had been dead for several minutes, the widow's son for several hours, and Lazarus for several days.

In Luke 7:24–29, Jesus speaks about John the Baptist in glowing terms. He says that John is indeed a prophet, "and more than a prophet" (v. 26). He goes on to say that John is the fulfillment of Malachi 3:1, the one who would prepare the way for the Messiah (Luke 7:27). Finally, he says, "Among those born of women, there is no one greater than John" (v. 28).

By elevating John the Baptist, he is also signifying that he himself is more than a prophet. He is the Messiah, the Son of God. In fact, only two chapters later, Jesus would be conversing with both Moses and Elijah (Luke 9:28–31)! Jesus is not merely a prophet, but the ultimate Prophet, the Messiah. Elisha's name means, "My God, save" (from *eli*, my God, and [*ya*]*sha*, save). Jesus's name, Yeshua, simply means "salvation."[16]

THE SIGN OF JONAH

During Jesus's second tour of Galilee, a year or so later, the scribes and Pharisees ask him to perform a "sign." He had been performing supernatural miracles since the wedding feast in Cana. He responds to them, "An evil and adulterous generation craves for a sign; and yet no sign shall be given to it but the sign of Jonah the prophet; for just as Jonah was three days and three nights in the belly of the sea monster, so will the Son of Man be three days and three nights in the heart of the earth" (Matt 12:39–40). This is commonly thought to prophesy his burial, but it is really a prophecy emphasizing his resurrection, for Jonah did not remain in the fish. The contrast Jesus is making is between the repentance and belief of the Ninevites and the failure of the scribes and Pharisees to respond in the same way.

In any case, Jesus says, "Behold, something greater than Jonah is here" (v. 41). He is a prophet, like Jonah in some respects, but greater. On this same tour of Galilee, he visits Nazareth once again (Matt 13:53–58). Again, the townspeople take offense at him, and Jesus replies, "A prophet is not without honor except in his hometown, and in his own household" (v. 57). A respected New Testament scholar, Dale Allison, says that this verse "stands as Jesus' indirect confession of himself as 'prophet.'"[17]

THE FEEDING OF THE FIVE THOUSAND

After sending out the Twelve with miraculous powers and a message about the Kingdom, even as Moses had sent out twelve to gather information

---

16. It has become popular to claim that Yeshua is simply a short form of Yehoshua (Joshua), and that therefore Jesus's name was originally Joshua. There is absolutely no biblical warrant for claiming his name was originally Joshua. Yehoshua means, "Yahveh saves" ("Jehovah saves"), but the only name given to Messiah in Scripture is Yeshúa (Matt 1:21), the masculine form of the feminine noun, *yeshuáh* (salvation). Peter said, "There is no other name under heaven that has been given among men, by which we must be saved" (Acts 4:12).

17. Allison, *The New Moses*, 314.

about the Land, Jesus takes the apostles into an uninhabited area. This is the setting for the feeding of the five thousand, the only miracle recorded by all four Gospels.[18] All the accounts contain elements that point to Jesus's identity as the Prophet like Moses,[19] but none as clearly as John. In fact, Christopher Maronde points out that John frequently emphasizes Jesus's connection with Moses. He says,

> The most significant Old Testament figure to be brought into the Gospel of John . . . is Moses. In John, a document steeped in the rich theology and history of the Old Testament, it is only natural that Moses would have a prominent place. He is the agent of God's deliverance used to bring Israel out of Egypt. He is prophet and king, bringing the law and covenant of Yahweh to his people. David, Jacob, and Abraham all deserve mention, but Moses towers over them all.[20]

In John 5, Jesus calls Moses to his defense in his disputation with the religious leaders when he says, "Do not think that I will accuse you before the Father; the one who accuses you is Moses, in whom you have set your hope. For if you believed Moses, you would believe Me, for he wrote about Me" (John 5:45–46). Here, Jesus is explicitly claiming to be the Prophet of whom Moses had written.[21] Moses is also prominent in John 6–9.

In John's account of the feeding of the five thousand, the clearest reference to Jesus as the Prophet like Moses comes from the crowd. Following the miraculous provision of food, the crowd says: "This is truly *the Prophet who is to come into the world*" (John 6:14, emphasis added). They saw the parallel between Jesus's miraculous provision of food in the uninhabited countryside[22] and Moses's miraculous provision of food in the wilderness.

One scholar points out that this recognition by the crowd "indicates that they already have knowledge about the Jewish eschatological tradition of the Prophet like Moses promised in Deut. 18.15–18."[23] He says

---

18. Matt 14:13–21; Mark 6:32–44; Luke 9:10–17; John 6:1–15.
19. See Allison, *The New Moses*, 238–42.
20. Maronde, "Moses in the Gospel of John," 23.
21. The reference to Moses in John 5:45 could conceivably refer to Genesis 49:10 or to other messianic prophecies in the Torah, but with the response of the crowd in 6:14, it should be seen as pointing to Deuteronomy 18:15–19.
22. Mark says it was "lonely" place (6:31, 32) and a "desolate" place (6:35).
23. Cho, *Jesus as Prophet in the Fourth Gospel*, 215.

that when the crowd gives voice to this identification, "Jesus seems not to deny the prophetic identity for himself. This implicitly indicates that Jesus accepts the title 'the prophet' for his identity."[24] Other miracles also serve as indications of both Jesus's identity and function as the Prophet.[25]

JESUS "PASSES BY"

After the feeding of the five thousand, Matthew, Mark, and John all record an episode where Jesus comes to the disciples's aid: on the Sea of Galilee, in the midst of a storm, in the dark of night.[26] Mark, however, includes a detail that is not mentioned by the others. Mark has increasingly been understood against its Jewish background,[27] and Dane Ortlund says Mark's purpose was to present Jesus as the Prophet like Moses "who inaugurates the new exodus."[28] In Mark's account, he says, "He came to them, walking on the sea; *and He intended to pass by them*" (v. 48).[29] This doesn't seem to make any sense, because the reason Jesus has come to them is because they are "straining at the oars" (v. 48). He has come to their aid! Why would he intend to pass them by?

In Exodus 33 and 34, God revealed himself to Moses, as he caused his glory to "pass by," while Moses had been put in a cleft of the rock (33:22). Four times in this passage the same verb is used (to pass by, עבר, *avar*), and it is only used of the Lord who passes by. In Exodus 33:19 God says, "I Myself will make all My goodness pass before you." Exodus 34:6-7 says: "Then the LORD passed by in front of him and proclaimed, 'The LORD, the LORD God, compassionate and gracious, slow to anger, and abounding in lovingkindness and truth; who keeps lovingkindness for thousands, who forgives iniquity, transgression and sin.'"[30] In these

---

24. Cho, *Jesus as Prophet in the Fourth Gospel*, 215. See also, A. Moore, *Signs of Salvation*, 25.

25. See Feiler, "Jesus the Prophet," 158–61; Maronde, "Moses in the Gospel of John," 23; and Allison, *The New Moses*, 207–13. See also, M. Saucy, *The Kingdom of God in the Teaching of Jesus*, 123, n. 94.

26. Matt 14:24–33; Mark 6:47–52; John 6:16–21.

27. Blackburn, *Theios Anēr and the Markan Miracle Traditions*.

28. D. Ortlund, "The Old Testament Background," 321. See also Bailey, "A Banquet of Death and a Banquet of Life," 78–82.

29. Emphasis added.

30. See Gurtner, "'Old Exodus' and 'New Exodus,'" 57–58.

passages, the Lord passes by to reveal himself as a gracious and compassionate Savior.[31]

The same terms used here are also used of the Lord in the closing verses of the prologue of John's Gospel. The way Richard Bauckham puts it, John says that "God, who has never been seen by human eyes, has been revealed in the human life of Christ Jesus, who reflects his Father's glory and is full of grace and truth."[32] He continues, "Moses could only hear God's word proclaiming *that* God is full of grace and truth. He could not see God's glory. But in the Word made flesh, God's glory was seen in human form, and grace and truth"[33] were made manifest.

When we turn to Mark 6 and to this episode on the Sea of Galilee, we need to understand that it is pointing to Jesus as the Prophet like Moses. Whereas God revealed himself to Moses as he passed by, on this occasion, Jesus reveals himself to his disciples as the divine Prophet, as the Lord God himself. God told Moses, "I AM WHO I AM" (Exod 3:14), and Jesus says to the disciples, "Take courage, I AM" (though it is translated, "it is I").[34]

THE TRANSFIGURATION

Several months later, Jesus takes Peter, James, and John and climbs "a high mountain" (Matt 17:1; Mark 9:2). All three synoptic Gospels record this episode of the transfiguration of Jesus.[35] The mountain is not named, perhaps because the drama and the details of these accounts of Jesus on the Mount of Transfiguration were to call to mind the account of Moses on Mount Sinai (Exod 24). After six days in which the glory of the Lord remained on Mount Sinai, Moses went up on the seventh day (Exod 24:16). Here, six days after the Father has revealed Jesus's identity to his disciples at Caesarea Philippi, they go up to the Mount of Transfiguration on the seventh day (Matt 17:1; Mark 9:2).

---

31. D. Ortlund also points out, "The first time Jesus calmed the sea in Mark, the account ends with the disciples asking, 'Who then is this?' (Mark 4:41). In Mark's second account of Jesus calming the sea, two chapters later, this question is answered." D. Ortlund, "The Old Testament Background," 334.

32. Bauckham, *Jesus and the God of Israel*, 55.

33. Bauckham, *Jesus and the God of Israel*, 55, emphasis in the original.

34. Matt 14:27; Mark 6:50; John 6:20.

35. Matt 17:1–8; Mark 9:2–8; Luke 9:28–36.

When Moses went up on Mount Sinai, he was accompanied by Aaron and two others who were brothers, Nadab and Abihu (Exod 24:1). On the Mount of Transfiguration, Jesus is accompanied by Peter and two brothers, James and John (Matt 17:1). There is also a cloud. In Exodus 19:9, God told Moses, "Behold, I shall come to you in a thick cloud."[36] We read in Mark 9:7 that a cloud envelops Jesus and his disciples. As Jim Congdon says, "As Moses had entered the cloud and divine light with the result that his face shone, so Jesus shone with heaven's light, and before Him appeared Moses and Elijah, the only Old Testament saints to receive a revelation on 'the mountain.'"[37] A. M. Ramsey writes, "Moses went up into the Mount . . . and when he came down to the people the skin of his face shone. Here, in contrast is the new and greater Moses, whose face shines not with a reflected glory but with the unborrowed glory as of the sun's own rays."[38]

Not only do these accounts include the facts that Jesus ascends a mountain and that his face and garments shine as they are overshadowed by the cloud, but Mark 9:7 says, "a voice came out of the cloud," even as the Lord had spoken to Moses (Exod 24:16). Years later, as Moses reflected on Israel's encounter with the Lord at Mount Sinai, he told the Israelites, "Then the LORD spoke to you from the midst of the fire [i.e., on the mountain]; you heard the sound of words, but you saw no form—only a voice" (Deut 4:12).

Luke's account gives the subject matter of the conversation Jesus has with Elijah and Moses, namely, "of His departure which He was about to accomplish at Jerusalem" (Luke 9:31). The word for "departure" is literally "exodus," so Jesus is speaking to them of his coming "exodus." Matthew not only records the general topic, but the very words of the voice from heaven that declare, "This is My beloved Son, with whom I am well-pleased" (17:5). In Isaiah 42:1, the Lord refers to his Servant as "My chosen one in whom My soul delights." As we have seen, the Servant of the Lord is identified as the Prophet like Moses; so here, Jesus is identified as this ultimate Prophet.[39] The voice from heaven continues with the admonition, "Listen to Him!" This points to Deuteronomy 18:15[40]—another,

---

36. See also Exod 24:15.

37. Congdon, "The Mosaic Law and Christian Ethics," 149. See also Evans, "Exodus in the New Testament," 454, and also Gurtner, "'Old Exodus' and 'New Exodus,'" 58.

38. Ramsey, *The Glory of God*, 120.

39. Allison, *The New Moses*, 244.

40. In Luke, this is a verbatim quotation from the LXX.

and an unmistakable, identification of Jesus as the Prophet like Moses. As Allison says, "It is natural to see in [Matthew] 17:1–9 the greater than Moses theme; for, at the last, Moses and Elijah disappear, and the reader is left with the command to 'hear him,' that is, the one Son of God, Jesus."[41]

Another observation is that when Moses was at the base of Mount Sinai, he erected an altar "with twelve pillars for the twelve tribes of Israel" (Exod 24:4). At the Mount of Transfiguration, Jesus descends and is with his twelve apostles (Matt 10:2–3), representing the twelve tribes of Israel.[42]

David Moessner makes a compelling case that from this point on, as Jesus journeys to Jerusalem, he is speaking with authority as the anticipated Prophet, foretold in Deuteronomy 18. He says, "In 9:1—19:44 Luke presents nothing less than the Prophet like Moses in a New Exodus unfolding with a dramatic tension all its own."[43] Here, he claims that Jesus both recapitulates and consummates the story of Moses. He goes on to say, "It has often been observed that in Luke 4:14—9:50 the *works* of Jesus are presented, whereas in 9:51—18:14 the *words* of Jesus in parables, instruction, table discourses, individual logia, and so forth, are given."[44] In fact, he claims that Luke "casts the entire public ministry of Jesus as the calling and fate of an eschatological prophet."[45]

Near the end of Jesus's journey toward Jerusalem, Jesus encounters the rich young ruler.[46] The rich young ruler is not able to attach himself to Jesus, because he is unable to detach himself from his possessions.[47] He is keeping the Law of Moses, but he refuses to follow the Prophet like Moses. This episode only underscores Moessner's point.

---

41. Allison, *The New Moses*, 247.

42. The apostles were not from each of the tribes, but they are seen as representing the tribes based on their number and the Lord's statement that they would judge the twelve tribes of Israel in the future (Matt 19:28).

43. Moessner, *Lord of the Banquet*, 46.

44. Moessner, *Lord of the Banquet*, 120.

45. Moessner, *Lord of the Banquet*, 47.

46. Mark 10:17–31; Matt 19:16—20:16; Luke 18:18–30.

47. Brown and Roberts, *The Gospel of Matthew*, 180.

10

Jesus, the Prophet, in Jerusalem

JESUS AND THE FEAST OF TABERNACLES

IN JOHN 7, JESUS has left Galilee to go up to Jerusalem for the Feast of Tabernacles (v. 10).[1] This was a fall pilgrimage festival, commemorating the booths, or tabernacles, that characterized the lives of the Israelites during their wilderness wanderings. Of course, these temporary shelters became symbolic of the need for dependence upon the Lord. This point was also reinforced by the timing of the festival, since it came when all crops had been gathered and processed (e.g., the wine and the olive oil). The harvest connection, however, also associated the festival with the end-times ingathering of the nations (see Zech 14:16–21).

On each day of the festival, the priest would lead a procession from the temple down to the Pool of Siloam, where he would fill a golden pitcher with a little more than half a gallon of water and return to the temple. This would be poured out at the base of the altar as a libation, symbolizing God's miraculous provision of water in the wilderness.[2]

---

1. See Lev 23:33–43.

2. According to *m. Sukkah*, 9, the volume of water was three *logs*, or about .56 gallons. See *Mishnayot: Seder Moed*, 339–40, n. 4. See also Edersheim, *The Temple, Its Ministry and Services*, 268–82.

When Jesus arrives, he teaches in the courts of the temple on two days of the feast. On the first occasion, he speaks of Moses and the Law (John 7:14–24), subjects which were especially on the minds of his hearers in the context of the feast.

The next occasion is the final and climactic day of the eight-day celebration.³ John reports: "Now on the last day, the great *day* of the feast, Jesus stood and cried out, saying, 'If any man is thirsty, let him come to Me and drink. He who believes in Me, as the Scripture said, "From his innermost being shall flow rivers of living water"'" (John 7:37–38).⁴ This is similar to what he had told the woman of Samaria in John 4 about "living water."⁵ The reaction of the crowd is similar to that of the woman: "Some of the people therefore, when they heard these words, were saying, 'This certainly is the Prophet'" (v. 40).

JESUS AND THE JEWISH LEADERS

Due to the failure of the religious leadership to recognize Jesus as the Prophet sent from God, everything about him is an affront to them.

Relationship. As the Son of God, Jesus is one with the Father. His relationship with God is infinitely closer than that of Moses. Following the healing of the lame man at the Pool of Bethesda, he says, "My Father is working until now, and I Myself am working," and in saying this he is "calling God His own Father, making Himself equal with God" (John 5:17–18). He claims the power to forgive sin when he heals the paralytic, lowered through the roof of Peter's house in Capernaum (Luke 5:20–21). Prior to the crucifixion, the high priest asks him, "Are You the Messiah, the Son of the Blessed One?" His answer is unequivocal: "I am; and you shall see THE SON OF MAN SITTING AT THE RIGHT HAND OF POWER, and COMING WITH THE CLOUDS OF HEAVEN" (Mark 14:61–62).

---

3. The festival lasted seven days (Deut 16:13, 15; Lev 23:33; Ezek 45:25), but it was followed by an octave, a concluding assembly on the eighth day (Lev 23:36, 39).

4. Regarding the reference to the Scripture, Sailhamer has a helpful comment: "John adds, 'By this he meant the Spirit, whom those who believe in him were later to receive. Up to that time the Spirit had not been given, since Jesus had not yet been glorified' (v. 39). With this explanation, we are enabled to link Jesus's words to the OT's promise of the Spirit (Ezek 36:26) as well as to understand the relationship between Jesus's work and the sending of the Spirit at Pentecost in Ac 2." Sailhamer, *NIV Compact Bible Commentary*, 490. However, it may well be that Joel 2:28–29 was the Scripture in mind.

5. See Zech 14:8.

Authority. In all the encounters Jesus has with the religious authorities, he is presented as an authoritative teacher of Torah. This was even true when he visited the temple as a boy (Luke 2:46–47). He knows the Book of Moses and the Law better than they do. As we have seen, authoritative proclamation was also to characterize the Prophet like Moses.

Jesus has a genuine concern for the temple, and it should come as no surprise that he exercises authority with respect to its holiness. Again, in these attitudes toward the temple, he is seen to be like Moses. It was Moses, after all, who instituted the tabernacle (which was the precursor of the temple) and oversaw the establishment of the priesthood.

In Mark 2:28, Jesus makes the audacious claim to be "Lord even of the Sabbath." Because most of the Pharisees do not recognize him as the one of whom Moses had spoken, this is considered blasphemous. But Jesus is only speaking as the Father directs him.

This kind of authority did not sit well with the Israelites in Moses's day, nor does it with the Sanhedrin in Jesus's day. The attitude of Israel's leadership toward Moses could be expressed with the words of Exodus 2:14: "Who made you a prince or a judge over us?" On two separate occasions, Moses faced the prospect of death by stoning at the hands of the people.[6] This is the sort of resistance both Moses and Jesus faced. In Matthew 21:23, the leaders ask Jesus, "By what authority are You doing these things, and who gave you this authority?"

Miracles. The response to Jesus on the part of the religious leadership is negative—beginning at his baptism and continuing throughout his earthly ministry. This is seen in John 9 with the healing of the man born blind, and it seems to grow stronger and harden as Jesus teaches and performs miracles. As mentioned previously, miracles were primarily associated with the role of the prophet, rather than the messianic offices of priest and king. The miracle-working ministry of Messiah is especially reminiscent of Moses and of the Deliver he foreshadowed.[7]

On one of the occasions when Moses faced opposition (Num 14:11), God asked him, "How long will this people spurn Me? And how long will they not believe in Me despite all the signs which I have performed

---

6. See Exod 17:4; Num 14:10.

7. Evans calls attention to the passage in Mark 8:11–12 where the Pharisees request of Jesus "a sign from heaven." He writes, "One thinks of Isaiah's appeal to Ahaz: 'Ask a sign of the Lord your God; let it be deep as Sheol or high as heaven.'" This may not be particularly relevant, but the comparison is of interest. Evans, "Prophet, Sage, Healer, Messiah, and Martyr," 1220.

in their midst?" The wording is very similar in John 12:37: "But though He [Jesus] had performed so many signs before them, *yet* they were not believing in Him."

Following the cleansing of the temple, we read that the chief priests and the scribes see the amazing things he has done (Matt 21:15). Allison relates this to "the very last words in the Pentateuch," which speak of the Prophet like Moses who will exceed the mighty power and wonders which Moses had performed.[8]

Prophecy. With this as background, it is significant that Jesus is aware of his coming violent death.[9] His death and the destruction of the temple are specific prophecies that came true, just as he had said.

Opposition. In the account of the healing of the man born blind in John 9, the irony of the position in which the religious leaders find themselves is beautifully highlighted. The formerly blind man testifies to the religious leaders that Jesus is "the Prophet" [i.e., like Moses (v. 17)].[10] Yet even as they are rejecting Jesus and His disciple, they are claiming to be the disciples of Moses![11] Each of the Gospels bears witness to this hostility.

In Matthew 21, Jesus's authority is challenged to the point that he relieves the chief priests and Levites of their spiritual authority and transfers it to the apostles as the leadership of the remnant of Israel (vv. 43, 45).[12] Today, their authority is exercised through the Scriptures of the New Covenant, all of which bear the stamp of apostolic authority[13] and are foundational for the church of Jesus (Eph 3:30).

Nevertheless, the resistance of the chief priests and Pharisees results in Jesus's seven-fold pronouncement of woe against the scribes and

---

8. Allison, *The New Moses*, 251.

9. Cho, *Jesus as Prophet in the Fourth Gospel*, 159–64.

10. Although the definite article is not present, the predicate nominative precedes the copulative verb, and the context requires invoking Colwell's Rule (see above, p. 106, n. 2). After the blind man's confession, the leaders threaten to expel anyone who confesses Jesus *as Messiah* from the synagogue (v. 22). For the same construction, see also v. 5. The lack of the article may, counterintuitively, draw more attention and emphasis than its presence.

11. See Sibley, "The Messianic Jewish Apologetic Purpose of John 9."

12. See D. Turner, *Israel's Last Prophet*, 236–51. "Kingdom of God," in this context is a reference to the authority to proclaim the way to citizenship in the Kingdom (see also Matt 23:13). For a helpful discussion of "nation," see Saldarini, *Matthew's Christian-Jewish Community*, 59–60.

13. Note that this authority is passed from one defined set of authorities, "the chief priests and the Pharisees" (e.g., the Sanhedrin) to another, the apostles. See also 1 Thess 2:3–4, 6.

Pharisees in Matthew 23.[14] This is in sharp contrast to the response of the crowds who are saying, "This is the prophet Jesus, from Nazareth in Galilee" (Matt 21:11).[15] The hostility of the priests and Levites is suggestive of the rebellion of Korah and the Levites in Numbers 16. These leaders extend the antagonism they have for Jesus toward his apostles and disciples as well.

God's prophets always experienced rejection, and this would be supremely evident in the death of the Servant of the Lord, the Prophet like Moses. Michael Brown says, "It is only when we see Jesus as a prophet that we can rightly understand the conflict and controversy that surrounded him."[16] Even as Moses had offered himself as an atoning redeemer (Exod 32:32), the Prophet of Deuteronomy 18:15 would willingly offer himself. Only in this manner could atonement be made, not only for Messiah's own people, but for "all the families of the earth" (Gen 12:3).

Looking at the larger picture, David Turner sees John the Baptist as the "penultimate [or, next to last] rejected prophet," Jesus as the "ultimate rejected prophet," and Jesus's disciples as "future rejected prophets."[17] This identity with Moses extends through the Old Testament prophets and the Suffering Servant to John the Baptist, Jesus, and to the believer today.

Reflecting on the death of Moses on Mount Nebo and the final journey of Jesus from Galilee to Jerusalem, Moessner comments,

> As the Prophet like Moses of Deuteronomy, Jesus must journey to die in Jerusalem, not simply because God so willed it but because God so willed that the Exodus redemption led by Moses be consummated in the Exodus of the Prophet who, like him, must die to effect new deliverance for the people.[18]

One thing is clear regarding the rejection of Jesus—it was prophesied centuries earlier in the Psalms and in Isaiah. Therefore, it could not postpone the Kingdom or change God's program, for it had been incorporated into his plan from the beginning.

---

14. D. Turner, *Israel's Last Prophet*, 269–397.

15. See D. Turner, *Israel's Last Prophet*, 236–51; Saldarini, *Matthew's Christian-Jewish Community*, 184; Kinzer, Postmissionary *Messianic Judaism*, 106–7, 124. Saldarini sees those to whom authority is passed to be the Matthean community, whereas Kinzer understands them to be the Pharisees. D. Turner, correctly in my view, understands the apostles to be the recipients of "the kingdom of God."

16. M. Brown, "Yeshua the Prophet," 5.

17. D. Turner, *Israel's Last Prophet*, 11.

18. Moessner, *Lord of the Banquet*, 323.

THE JUDGMENT

The plagues should be seen as God's judgment on Egypt, executed through Moses. In Exodus 18:13, we read of Moses serving as a judge for the people from morning until evening. "Judging" in this context means ruling or governing. In the verses that follow, we read of Jethro's suggestion that men be selected "who fear God, men of truth" (v. 21), who could assist Moses in judging the people. If Moses is presented as a judge, so is the Messianic Prophet of whom he spoke. In John 5:22, Jesus says, "Not even the Father judges anyone, but He has given all judgment to the Son." Jesus tells the parable of the pounds in Luke 19, in which the "nobleman" goes to "a distant country to receive a kingdom for himself" (v. 12). Upon his return, he would render judgment regarding their stewardship of his resources. As is clear from the context, the nobleman in the parable represents Jesus.

Not only do both Moses and Jesus serve as judges, but even as Moses had appointed leaders to judge the people (Exod 18:19–22), so Jesus assigns this responsibility to his apostles. Jesus addresses the apostles in Matthew 19:28: "Truly I say to you, that you who have followed Me, in the regeneration when the Son of Man will sit on His glorious throne, you also shall sit upon twelve thrones, judging the twelve tribes of Israel." Here, we have the Prophet like Moses as the Judge—like Moses, who also enlists others to participate with him, even as Moses had.[19]

Finally, there is another striking parallel with reference to God's judgment. Apart from a small remnant, the Exodus generation was not permitted to enjoy life in the Promised Land but died in the wilderness over a period of forty years following the Exodus. In a similar manner, apart from the remnant of the people (the disciples of Jesus), Jesus's generation would suffer the ineffectiveness of the temple sacrifices and the absence of God's presence for forty years. At the end of this forty years (the years following the crucifixion), the temple and the city of Jerusalem would be destroyed. Nevertheless, the "mighty minority,"[20] that is, the remnant of Jewish believers in Jesus, has been preserved and exists to this day as a guarantee that God will yet restore the nation to the Land and to himself.

---

19. First Corinthians 6:2–3 says that believers will judge angels. This probably has reference to a judgment of fallen angels in which believers will play a role.

20. Jervell, "The Mighty Minority," 26–51.

THE OLIVET DISCOURSE

At the end of the Exodus, and shortly before his death, Moses addressed the hundreds of thousands of Israelites who were being sent out to conquer the Promised Land. He was probably seated on a hill, overlooking the Land. This address we know as the book of Deuteronomy. In the same way, near the end of his earthly ministry, shortly before his death, Jesus addressed his disciples who were being sent out to preach the gospel to the whole world (Matt 24:14). He was seated on the Mount of Olives, overlooking the temple and Jerusalem. This address is commonly known as the Olivet Discourse. Moses prepared the people by reminding them of the past—the wilderness wanderings, the Law, and the conquests the Lord had enabled Israel to make of the nations to the east of the Land. Jesus prepared his disciples by prophesying the future.

Pagan practices, divination, witchcraft, and spiritists are condemned in Deuteronomy 18:9–14. These warnings set up the prophecy of the Prophet like Moses to come. He would be the only reliable source of truth. Just like Moses, Jesus also warned his disciples about false prophets and false messiahs in the future (Matt 24:4–5, 11, 23–26).

In Matthew 24:4 he says, "See to it that no one misleads you." Then in verse 11 he says, "Many false prophets will arise and will mislead many." Finally, in verse 24, Jesus warns that "false messiahs and false prophets will arise and will show great signs and wonders, so as to mislead, if possible, even the elect." Each of these warnings seems to relate directly to the identity of Jesus as the Messiah. In this last warning, these false prophets bear a resemblance to the magicians in Pharaoh's court who tried to undermine Moses's ministry and authority by their own signs and wonders.[21]

As we have seen, Moses and the line of prophets who followed him were opposed, persecuted, and sometimes even murdered. Likewise, Jesus warns his followers of murderous persecution in Matthew 24:9 and in verses 16–18. In verse 9, speaking of the Tribulation, he says, "Then they will deliver you to tribulation, and will kill you, and you will be hated by all nations because of My name." Later, with reference to the Great Tribulation (the last half of this seven-year period), when they would see the abomination of desolation in the temple, "then" the elect are to flee immediately (vv. 16–18).[22]

---

21. Exod 7:11–12, 22. See also 2 Tim 3:8.
22. For an interpretation of Matthew 24:34, see Appendix Two.

THE LAST SUPPER AND CRUCIFIXION

In light of the many parallels we have seen, it is not difficult to see Jesus as the Prophet like Moses in the Lord's Supper. The Last Supper is recounted in all four Gospels[23] and is presented as the fulfillment envisioned by the sacrifice at the original Passover. Even though Moses is most prominently associated with the covenant at Mount Sinai, in which the sacrificial system provided temporary atonement for sin through the sacrifice of a bull or a female goat,[24] he also instituted the Passover. The offering of a male lamb in the first Passover anticipated the sacrificial death of the Servant of the Lord (Isa 52:13—53:12), who would provide ultimate atonement for sin.

Isaiah says that the Messiah would "not open His mouth," but was "like a lamb that is led to slaughter" (Isa 53:7). Moses commanded the slaying of a lamb; the Prophet of whom he spoke would offer himself as the Lamb. Moses instituted the Passover; the Prophet like Moses fulfilled it. At the beginning of his earthly ministry, he had been introduced as "the Lamb of God who takes away the sin of the world" (John 1:29); he will end his life as the Passover Lamb, providing ultimate atonement for sin. In Revelation, Messiah is referred to twenty-six times as the Lamb.

During the Last Supper, Jesus says, "This is My blood of the covenant, which is poured out for many" (Mark 14:24). Evans relates "blood of the covenant" here to Exodus 24:8: "So Moses took the blood and sprinkled it on the people, and said, 'Behold the blood of the covenant, which the LORD has made with you in accordance with all these words.'" He says, "In announcing that the wine represented his 'blood of the covenant' and then sharing it with his disciples, Jesus has inaugurated the (new) covenant for the people of Israel, represented by his twelve disciples."[25]

The last clause, "which is poured out for many," is connected to Isaiah 53:12: "He poured out Himself to death, and was numbered with the transgressors; yet He Himself bore the sin of many, and interceded for the transgressors." Evans comments, "The allusion to the Suffering Servant enables Jesus to link the covenantal language of Exodus 24 and Jeremiah

---

23. Matt 26:17–30; Mark 14:12–25; Luke 22:7–23; John 13.

24. See Lev 4—7:10; 17:11.

25. Evans, "Exodus in the New Testament," 449. See J. Brown, "Exodus in Matthew's Gospel," 36; also Gurtner, "'Old Exodus' and 'New Exodus,'" 59.

31 with the figure with whom Jesus identifies."[26] The Lord's Supper does not replace Passover but fulfills it.

With his sinless life, his atoning death, and his resurrection, Jesus fulfilled three of the feasts of Israel: Unleavened Bread, Passover, and First Fruits. His sinless life rendered his sacrifice acceptable; his death inaugurated the New Covenant; and the resurrection made him "the first fruits of those who are asleep" (1 Cor 15:20). It is worth noting also that no prophet after Moses ever instituted a covenant until Jesus instituted a better covenant (Heb 7:22; 8:6).

Since Isaiah presents the Prophet like Moses as the Suffering Servant, it is also significant that he prophesies that he would be "numbered with the transgressors" (Isa 53:12) and that his grave would be "assigned with wicked men, yet He was with a rich man in His death" (Isa 53:9). In Matthew, we learn that Jesus is crucified between two thieves (27:38). Yet he is buried by two wealthy members of the Sanhedrin who had not agreed with the decision to offer Jesus up to the Romans—Joseph of Arimathea and Nicodemus.[27] This was a fulfillment of the prophecies of Isaiah. Isaiah also prophesies the resurrection when he says, "He will see His offspring, He will prolong His days, and the good pleasure of the LORD will prosper in His hand" (Isa 53:10b). In his suffering, death, burial, and resurrection, Jesus is proven again to be the great Prophet, the Lamb of God who takes away the sin of the world.

THE ENCOUNTER ON THE ROAD TO EMMAUS

Luke 24 records Jesus's encounter with two disciples on the road to Emmaus. These disciples apparently had identified Jesus as the Prophet like Moses, but they had not anticipated his death. When they mention the things that have happened in Jerusalem, Jesus asks them, "What things?" They answer, "The things about Jesus the Nazarene, who was a prophet mighty in deed and word in the sight of God and all the people" (Luke 24:19).

If the disciples on the Emmaus road are slow to fully recognize Jesus's identity (or to understand exactly how the events of his life, death,

---

26. Evans, "Exodus in the New Testament," 451.
27. See Mark 15:43; Luke 23:51; John 19:39–43.

and resurrection related to prophecy in the Scriptures), it is because "their eyes were prevented from recognizing Him" (Luke 24:16).[28]

As they go on the way, Jesus does not rebuke the disciples for their ignorance or their misunderstanding of the sacred Scriptures. Instead, he rebukes them because they do not *recognize* him from those very Scriptures! He says, "O foolish men and slow of heart to believe in all that the prophets have spoken!" (Luke 24:25). Then, he begins with Moses and explains these things to his disciples, likely using Deuteronomy 18 to help them understand his work. They stop at the home of Cleopas, probably one of the two disciples. It is here, in the breaking of bread, that "their eyes were opened and they recognized Him" (Luke 24:31). Jesus is not merely a prophet, even one "mighty in deed and word," but he is *the* Prophet, the Messiah, the Son of God.

Later, as the two disciples are reporting their experiences to the apostles and other disciples, Jesus appears in their midst. He gives them more instruction in the Scriptures, and in his conclusion, he says, "These are My words which I spoke to you while I was still with you, that *all things* which are written about Me in the Law of Moses and the Prophets and the Psalms must be fulfilled."[29]

THE SERMONS OF PETER AND STEPHEN

The only explicit New Testament citations of Deuteronomy 18:15 are in the book of Acts. In their sermons, Peter and Stephen draw attention to Jesus's identity as the Prophet like Moses during his earthly ministry. Regarding the encounter on the road to Emmaus, Paul Frede Feiler says: "Luke ... through Cleopas' summary of Jesus' earthly ministry, prepares the reader for the explicit identification of Jesus as the prophet like Moses in Acts 3:22–23."[30]

Preaching about Jesus in the courts of the temple, Peter proclaims, "Moses said, 'THE LORD GOD SHALL RAISE UP FOR YOU A PROPHET LIKE ME FROM YOUR BRETHREN; TO HIM YOU SHALL GIVE HEED in everything He says to you. And it will be that every soul that does not heed that prophet shall be utterly destroyed from among the people'" (Acts

---

28. For an excellent explanation of the disciples' "eye-opening" experience on this occasion, see D. Ortlund, "'And Their Eyes Were Opened, and They Knew,'" 717–28.

29. Luke 24:44, emphasis added.

30. Feiler, "Jesus the Prophet," 188.

3:22–23). Here, it is not that Jesus and Moses are adversaries, but Moses actually serves as a witness to the identity of Jesus—more than that, Moses is the prosecuting attorney, demanding obedience to him and warning that the only alternative is destruction.[31]

As Feiler says, "The quotation bases a soteriological imperative upon a Christological claim."[32] In other words, salvation is dependent on a recognition of who he was and is. It is because Jesus is the Prophet like Moses, and therefore the Messiah, that faith in him is necessary for salvation. The Jewish people must listen to Jesus or suffer the judgment of God, even as their forefathers in the wilderness.

Then, in Acts 7, which records Stephen's sermon immediately before his martyrdom, Stephen quotes the prophecy from Deuteronomy 18. He makes the point that Jesus was the Prophet like Moses, and the leaders had not heeded the warning to listen to him, but instead had offered him up for crucifixion. In Acts 7:37 he says, "This is the Moses who said to the sons of Israel, 'God will raise up for you a prophet like me from your brethren.'" Moses and Jesus were alike in that they both led God's people out of captivity. With miraculous signs and power, Moses led the Israelites out of physical bondage and slavery in Egypt. Jesus, having been raised from the dead (the ultimate miraculous sign) and possessing an even greater power, led his disciples out of spiritual bondage and slavery to sin and death.

In this context, it is important to understand that the Prophet like Moses does not *reject* Israel, but instead he has *divided* Israel. In the book of Acts, as Jacob Jervell says, "Israel has not rejected the gospel, but has become divided over the issue."[33] Though the majority has rejected the gospel, the remnant has not. The references in Acts indicate that although Jesus is no longer physically present, the authority that accompanies the gospel message is that of the Prophet like Moses. It comes with a warning not to be ignored.

The author of Hebrews seems to allude to Jesus's previous ministry as the Prophet like Moses when he writes, "For this reason, we must pay much closer attention to what we have heard. . . . God also testifying with them [i.e., the eyewitnesses], both by signs and wonders and by various

---

31. The warning here comes from Leviticus 23:29, but it is consistent with the warning in Deuteronomy 18:19.

32. Feiler, "Jesus the Prophet," 47.

33. Jervell, "The Divided People of God," 49. See also the excellent discussion of "this generation" in Saldarini, *Matthew's Jewish Community*, 40–43.

miracles and by gifts of the Holy Spirit according to His own will" (Heb 2:1, 4). In his authoritative preaching and teaching, in the miraculous signs which accompanied them, and in his claims to be the one of whom Moses spoke, Jesus demonstrates his singular role in the Gospels is that of the Prophet like Moses. The kinship of rejection and death connected the great prophets of the Bible; should these things not also characterize the ultimate Prophet? Why would we expect Jesus to be more acceptable than the prophets of Israel?[34]

Before we conclude this discussion, we must reflect for a moment on the events of Pentecost and their significance for us. When Jesus was baptized by John, the order was first baptism, then the anointing with the Spirit. With the events of Pentecost, the order is reversed: first comes the anointing with the Spirit as the Holy Spirit is "poured out" (Acts 2:17), then water baptism follows. This experience is repeated in this order with Gentiles (Acts 10:44–46) and with Jewish disciples of John the Baptist who believe in Jesus but know nothing of the Spirit (Acts 18:24–26; 19:1–6).

At conversion, we are also baptized with the Holy Spirit (1 Cor 12:13), but should this baptism with the Spirit be considered an anointment with the Spirit? Yes, for Paul says, "Now He who establishes us with you in Messiah and anointed us is God, who also sealed us and gave us the Spirit in our hearts as a pledge" (2 Cor 1:21–22). Following this anointment at our conversion, we are to be baptized. If we have been anointed with the Holy Spirit, we are to proclaim the authoritative message of salvation to others, and we are to be prepared for opposition and, if necessary, to suffer for his sake.

CONCLUSION

Having looked at our Lord's earthly ministry—on the dusty roads of Israel and in the courts of the temple—through the lens of the Hebrew Scriptures, our eyes have been fully opened. I feel something like the disciples felt on the road to Emmaus, after Jesus led them through a similar exercise. Luke 24:32 says, "They said to one another, 'Were not our hearts burning within us while He was speaking to us on the road, while He was

---

34. It is worth mentioning that in the future, when Satan's power is unrestrained, he uses a prophet—the false prophet—to deceive the nations (Rev 13:11–18).

explaining the Scriptures to us?'" I hope you will re-read the Gospels with new eyes and a burning heart.

Charles Wesley expressed the reason the remnant of Israel longed for his appearing and the reason we should long for him as well.

> Come, thou long expected Jesus
> Born to set Thy people free;
> From our fears and sins release us;
> Let us find our rest in Thee
> Israel's Strength and Consolation
> Hope of all the earth Thou art;
> Dear Desire of every nation
> Joy of every longing heart.[35]

---

35. Wesley, "Come, Thou Long Expected Jesus."

11

When Did Jesus Begin His Priestly Role?

A GODLY PASTOR'S WIFE, full of compassion for those in need, was also the principal of a Christian school. She learned that wearing more than one "hat" can be challenging. On one occasion, a teacher was going through severe hardships in her personal life that were making it impossible for her to do her job in the classroom. Problems were mounting. She needed to be dismissed. Unsure how best to handle the situation, this compassionate principal consulted the chairman of her board for advice. He reminded her, "You are not a pastor's wife here, but an administrator. You must do what is best for the students and for the school." Her difficulty was the tension between these two roles. As we have seen, Messiah is a prophet, priest, and king, yet without any conflict. He served as *the* Prophet, and he would yet serve as *the* Priest and King.

Some consider the death and resurrection of Jesus, on the one hand, and the return of Jesus, on the other, as the two great pillars of our faith. We look back to the work of the Lord in securing our salvation on the cross, and we look forward to his return, our blessed hope. What about the present? Is he still ministering to us in the present? What is his role now, and how does it relate to us?

Just as the Israelites could not enter their inheritance without the death of Moses, so the Prophet like Moses had to die to bring believers into their salvation. As we have seen, Isaiah presented Jesus as the

Suffering Servant, the one who would offer himself for us. Jesus is the sacrificial lamb.

When he returns in the future as King, he is depicted as the Lion of the Tribe of Judah (Rev 5:5). We turn attention now to Jesus as our High Priest. We are between the Lamb (i.e., the Servant) and the Lion (i.e., the King). In nature, this would not be a very good place to be. But Scripture emphasizes it is a blessing. Understanding the priestly ministry of Jesus is particularly relevant for believers today, for this is the current ministry of our Lord on our behalf.

Because of a great deal of confusion and conflicting claims, it is important to be clear about the timing of Jesus's ministry as our High Priest. When did he take up this office? Did Jesus begin his priestly ministry before his crucifixion? Did he begin his priestly ministry before his ascension? When Messiah began his priestly ministry, did he also begin his kingly reign? These questions need to be addressed before we can study what his ministry as priest involves.

DID JESUS BEGIN HIS PRIESTLY MINISTRY BEFORE HIS CRUCIFIXION?

To answer this question, we should examine the reasons for thinking he began serving as priest while he was with his disciples. Is there evidence in the Gospels for Jesus to have had a priestly ministry before his crucifixion?

A few scholars ignore the messianic role of the Prophet like Moses and claim that Jesus is to be understood in the Gospels as a priest.[1] Can this really be true? To be sure, there are aspects of Jesus's earthly ministry that do seem to be priestly at first glance. In the Gospels, we find that Jesus lived a holy and a pure life, he dealt with impurity in others, he washed feet, he interceded for others, and he offered himself as an atoning sacrifice. These are all characteristics some would point to as evidence that Jesus functioned as a priest in the Gospels. Let's examine these characteristics to see if they really do support a priestly ministry.

---

1. Here, I would call attention to Nicholas Perrin, *Jesus the Priest*. See also his article, "Jesus as Priest in the Gospels." Perrin seems to build on the work of John Baigent ("Jesus as Priest," 34–44). Some see the prophetic, kingly, and priestly offices operating simultaneously in Jesus's earthly ministry. Allen seems to hint at this. See Allen, *Lukan Authorship of Hebrews*, 198–214.

Personal purity. Beginning with his virgin birth, the purity of Jesus's nature surpassed that of all priests who had preceded him. With his victory over temptation and sin, his life surpassed all other human attempts to please God. His purity was necessary for his sacrificial death, but does it demonstrate a priestly role? Actually, it was his purity that qualified him as a suitable sacrifice, as the Lamb of God. Without the purity of his nature and of his life, his sacrificial death would not have been sufficient as an atonement for our sin. The Passover lamb was to be without defect. The purity of the lamb, however, did not make the lamb a priest! The purity of Jesus testified to his identity as the Son of God, but not to his role as priest. If personal purity is not sufficient grounds, what about ceremonial purity?

Ceremonial purity. Some claim that Jesus's encounters with ritual impurity suggest a priestly role. For example, the woman with an issue of blood (Luke 8:43–48) was considered to be ritually unclean according to the Mosaic Law.[2] Anything she touched was considered unclean (e.g., her bed or her chair), and anyone who touched those things was considered unclean. Yet when the woman touched the fringe of Jesus's garment, rather than impurity flowing to Jesus, healing and cleansing power flowed from him and gave her the possibility of being ritually pure for the first time in twelve years.[3] Yet, this should not necessarily be seen as a priestly act, for even the high priest would be defiled by contact with impurity. Instead, her cleansing should be associated with Messiah's identity as the Son of God.[4]

The Gospels also record several incidents in which Jesus dealt with lepers. In his Galilean ministry, he healed an unnamed leper. The incident immediately followed the Sermon on the Mount, in which Jesus showed himself to be the Prophet like Moses. In this passage, the leper associates healing with cleansing. He says, "Lord, if You are willing, You can make me clean."[5] Jesus stretches out his hand, touches him, and says, "I am willing; be cleansed," and the leper is healed. In touching this leper, rather than the impurity rendering Jesus impure, the process is reversed—that which was impure becomes cleansed. Even so, Jesus sends the cleansed lepers to the priest to present an offering as Moses had commanded. (It

---

2. See Mark 5:24–34; Luke 8:42–48; Lev 15:25–30.
3. Mark 5:25–34; Luke 8:43–48.
4. Ps 2:7; Matt 3:17; Heb 1:2, 5, 8; 2:6; 3:5–6; 5:8. Moses was the Lord's servant (Josh 1:1).
5. Matt 8:2. See also Matt 8:1–4; Mark 1:40–45; Luke 5:12–16.

is also interesting to note that the first person in the Bible to be healed of leprosy was Moses in Exodus 4:6–7.)

Later, we read of an incident in which Jesus and his disciples are at the home of Simon the Leper.[6] Nothing is said of him, except that his home provides the setting for the story that follows. The episode virtually requires the understanding that Simon was formerly a leper, but he has been healed, most likely by Jesus. It may even be possible, though this is speculative, that he is the unnamed leper Jesus had healed earlier. Finally, in Luke 17:11–19, Jesus meets ten lepers, who call out to him for mercy. Jesus heals them from a distance, but not before instructing them to go and show themselves to the priests. Would this have been necessary if Jesus had been serving as a priest at that time?

The authority of Jesus. Jesus also had many conflicts with the religious authorities over Sabbath activities, the washing of hands, plucking grain, etc. As we have seen, his authority over these matters should be seen as a connection to the Prophet like Moses, who has authority concerning the Law, rather than as a connection to the priesthood. Furthermore, his authority is greater than that of the religious leadership, for he speaks with God's authority. In fact, in Matthew 12, Jesus claims to be "greater than the Temple" (v. 6), "greater than Jonah" (v. 41), and "greater than Solomon" (v. 42).

Foot washing. Because foot washing was associated with priestly ritual in Exodus 40, when Jesus washed his disciples's feet, as recorded in John 13:5, some assume this to have been a priestly action. We also find in Exodus 30:17–21 that priests were to wash their hands and feet before their service in the tabernacle. But foot washing was certainly not exclusively, or even primarily, a priestly function.[7]

Foot washing was part of personal hygiene and comfort. In a culture and climate where sandals were worn by everyone and roads were dusty, the washing of feet was customary and expected. In fact, the first four mentions of the word "feet" in the Bible involve washing dirty feet.[8] In each case, water was provided by the host so that visitors could wash their own feet.

By Jesus's day, foot washing was generally the responsibility of servants. A host or hostess could offer this service as an expression of hospitality, but

---

6. Matt 26:6; Mark 14:3.
7. Coloe, "Welcome into the Household of God," 408.
8. Gen 18:4; 19:2; 24:32; 43:24.

it was ordinarily carried out by servants.[9] Edward Klink, commenting on Jesus washing the disciples's feet, says, "This majestic scene depicts almost beyond the capacity of words the humble service and sacrifice of our Lord and the kind of Lord he is—the Servant. . . . When Jesus washed the feet of his disciples, he enacted his role as the Servant, a role which he most fully performed by his death on the cross."[10] Moses was the servant of the Lord; how much more was Jesus the Servant of the Lord.

Intercession. Without question, prayer was expected of priests. They were to pronounce the benediction daily at the tabernacle—later at the temple—and on other occasions. This benediction is the well-known blessing found in Numbers 6:24–26. Nevertheless, although it may come as a surprise for some, apart from this benediction, intercession was not expressly a part of priestly duties on the Day of Atonement. The only prayer required of the high priest was one of confessing the sins of the people (Lev 16:21). Furthermore, intercessory prayer was certainly not seen as exclusively, or even primarily, a priestly function. Intercessory prayer was more characteristic of the prophets than the priests.

Jesus was a man of prayer. In the Synoptics, there are several passages that speak of Jesus praying for his disciples[11] and advocating for them in the heavenly court.[12] Jesus spent time in prayer.[13] He taught his disciples to pray.[14] Jesus was compassionate, even though the majority rejected him. In Matthew 23:37–39, he expresses his longing to harbor Jerusalem's inhabitants under his saving embrace:

> Jerusalem, Jerusalem, who kills the prophets and stones those who are sent to her! How often I wanted to gather your children together, the way a hen gathers her chicks under her wings, and you were unwilling. Behold, your house is being left to you desolate! For I say to you, from now on you shall not see Me until you say, "BLESSED IS HE WHO COMES IN THE NAME OF THE LORD!"

Jesus also prayed for those who were responsible for his death. Prayer and intercession were characteristic of Jesus's earthly ministry.

---

9. J. Thomas, *Footwashing in John 13*, 42.
10. Klink, *John*, 587–88.
11. E.g., Luke 22:32.
12. E.g., Matt 10:32; Luke 12:8.
13. E.g., Luke 6:12; 11:1; 22:45.
14. E.g., Matt 6:5–15; 7:7–11.

In his Gospel, John records what is often called Jesus's "Farewell Discourse" (John 14–17). Jesus delivers these words to his disciples as they are observing the Passover Seder (the lengthy and orderly meal in which the events of the Exodus are recounted and celebrated). The Farewell Discourse of Jesus is similar to the farewell speeches of Jacob, Joshua, and David. The entire book of Deuteronomy can be seen as Moses's "farewell speeches to Israel."[15]

In comparing Deuteronomy to the Farewell Discourse of Jesus, it seems they are both expressions of the covenants they are inaugurating—the Mosaic Covenant and the New Covenant.[16] Andreas Köstenberger comments, "The parallels between the Johannine farewell discourse and covenant language in Moses' parting Deuteronomic instructions are underscored by the preponderance of the five major verb themes of Exodus 33–34 and Deuteronomy ('love,' 'obey,' 'live,' 'know,' and 'see') in the Johannine discourse, particularly in 14:15–24."[17] In the farewell discourse of Moses in Deuteronomy 32 and 33, there are also two sections of poetry. Raymond Brown comments:

> One in [Deut 32] where Moses turns from the people to address the heavens, the other in [Deut 33] where Moses blesses the tribes for the future. So also in John 17, Jesus turns to heaven and addresses the Father, but much of what he says concerns the future of his disciples.[18]

The Farewell Discourse of Jesus concludes with what has been called his "High Priestly Prayer" (John 17).[19] With this terminology, it is obvious that many see in this intercessory prayer the action of a high priest praying for his people.

There are two reasons some believe this prayer points to Jesus serving as a priest. (1) The structure of his prayer is similar to the order of sacrifices on the Day of Atonement. First, he prays for himself, then for his disciples (both current and future). (2) Jesus uses the verb "sanctify." In his prayer, Jesus uses this word (sometimes translated "consecrate") three

---

15. Klink, *John*, 571.
16. Klink, *John*, 571.
17. Köstenberger, "Exodus in John," 104.
18. R. Brown, *The Gospel According to John XIII–XXI*, 744.
19. It was first called the "high priestly prayer" by David Chytraeus (1531–1600).

times (vv. 17–19).[20] Do these features provide sufficient justification for the claim that Jesus is functioning as a priest during his earthly ministry?

While there are similarities to the Day of Atonement sacrifices, there are also major differences. On the Day of Atonement, a bull was sacrificed to provide atonement for the high priest and his household (Lev 16:6). Then two goats were presented, one of which was sacrificed while the other was to serve as the scapegoat, bearing the sin of the people into the wilderness (Lev 16:22). With the atonement of Jesus, there was no second sacrifice. Furthermore, while the ceremony of the Day of Atonement provided temporary atonement for the nation, the crucifixion provides ultimate atonement, but only for those who become disciples of Jesus.

Regarding the use of the verb "to sanctify" in John 17:17–19, priests were not the only ones to "sanctify" people or places. In Exodus 19, Moses was to consecrate the people (v. 10, 14), the priests were to consecrate themselves (v. 22), and Moses consecrated Mount Sinai (vv. 23). In 2 Samuel 8:11, David consecrated gifts and spoils of war. In Exodus 13:1–2, Moses sanctified all the first-born sons of Israel.[21]

The question remains: Does Jesus's prayer life (or specifically his "High Priestly Prayer") represent priestly action that demonstrates he had assumed his office as our High Priest?

Following an examination of the evidence that the high priestly ministry of Jesus might be found in the Gospels, John Baigent, a New Testament scholar in London, concludes that although there are similarities between the ministry of Jesus as it is presented in John with what we find in Hebrews, there is no reason to think that John's view of Jesus was that of a high priest during his earthly ministry.[22] Nowhere in the Gospels is he ever referred to as a priest. Instead, he is functioning as the Greater Moses, offering his farewell address and a prayer of intercession.

Nevertheless, Jesus's intercessory prayer in John 17 should be seen as an example of the kind of intercession he is making now as our great High Priest. Intercession is currently a major aspect of his heavenly ministry (Heb 7:25), and in John 17, he seems to be demonstrating the type of intercessory ministry he would have in the future.

---

20. ἁγιάζω, *agiazo*.

21. Additional examples could also be provided, but in every case, the same verb is used (קדש, *qadash*).

22. Baigent, "Jesus as Priest," 38. See also Attridge, "How Priestly Is the 'High Priestly Prayer' of John 17?" 1–14.

EVIDENCE OF A CHANGE IN JESUS'S ROLE

To support the view that Jesus transitioned sequentially from his prophetic role to his priestly role, we should consider carefully three features found in the Gospels. First, we will look at Jesus's repeated announcements of his coming departure. Then we will consider two sets of "bookends" recorded by Luke that mark the beginning and end of Jesus's ministry as the Prophet like Moses. The first "bookend" consists of two 40-day periods, and the second of two benedictions.

The absence of Jesus. Almost twenty times in the Gospels, Jesus speaks of his departure.[23] John records approximately twelve of these sayings. For example, in John 13:33, Jesus says, "Little children, I am with you a little while longer. You will seek Me; and as I said to the Jews, now I also say to you, 'Where I am going, you cannot come.'" In each of these verses, though not with these exact words, Jesus is saying, "I am leaving!"

Repeatedly in Matthew, Mark, and Luke, Jesus speaks of his coming death. The first time is following Peter's confession at Caesarea Philippi.[24] The second time is after his transfiguration.[25] Eventually, on his final trip to Jerusalem, Jesus again details not only his death, but the torture and abuse that would precede it.[26] There are also references to his death in John. More generally, in John 16:5 Jesus says, "But now I am going to Him who sent Me." With Jesus's coming departure, his disciples would be "troubled" and filled with grief[27] and would need a Comforter.[28] It is also for this reason, among others, that believers then and now are to long for his return. In repeatedly announcing his departure, he is preparing his disciples for a change in their relationship to him.

They had known him as the Prophet—the Messiah, the Son of God—but soon, they would know him as their High Priest.[29] The absence of Jesus is a powerful indication of just such a change in role. While physically present, he had ministered as the Prophet like Moses. Soon

---

23. See also, Mark 14:7, 21; Luke 22:22; John 8:14, 21; 13:3, 36; 14:2–4, 12, 18; 16:16–19, 28.
24. Matt 16:21–23; Mark 8:31–32; Luke 9:21–22.
25. Matt 17:22–23; Mark 9:30–32; Luke 9:43–45.
26. Matt 20:17–19; Mark 10:32–34; Luke 18:31–34.
27. John 14:1–3; 20:20, 22.
28. John 14:16, 25–26.
29. Heb 2:17; 3:1; 4:14–15; 5:10, etc.

he would exercise his role as their great High Priest from heaven. In his absence, he would send the Spirit.

The forty-day periods. Luke records two different periods of forty days in the earthly life of Jesus. Following his baptism, the Spirit led him into the wilderness to be tempted by Satan (Luke 4:1–13). At this time, he fasted for forty days and forty nights, as Moses had (Exod 43:28). This forty-day period at the beginning of his earthly ministry was a time of testing. At the end of his ministry, between the resurrection and ascension, Luke bears witness to another forty-day period, a time of teaching (Acts 1:3). These frame his earthly ministry. It seems to have been more than a coincidence.

With his victory over the temptations of Satan, Jesus proved himself to be the promised Prophet. He lived the life of faith that Moses could not live. He entered the Land from the Jordan—something Moses was not allowed to do. If the first forty-day period, with its parallels to the life of Moses, demonstrated his qualifications to be the Prophet, his last forty-day period demonstrated the conclusion of this role, as he taught his disciples and prepared them for his ascension. One scholar suggests that the disciples "learned more in those forty days than in the three years they had daily associated with him."[30] In any case, these two periods serve to bracket Jesus's ministry as the Prophet like Moses.

The benedictions. David Allen points out another frame, or *inclusio*, found in the Gospel of Luke—two benedictions. This frame also clarifies the transition from Jesus's role as the Prophet like Moses to the assumption of his priestly role.[31]

In the first chapter of Luke, Zacharias is stricken dumb, so that when he exits the temple, he is unable to speak. Luke records the scene: "The people were waiting for Zacharias, and were wondering at his delay in the temple. But when he came out, he was unable to speak to them" (Luke 1:21–22a). A crowd is waiting for him to exit the temple, raise his hands, and bless them with the priestly benediction.[32] But on this occasion, the blessing goes unspoken, for he is mute. At the conclusion of the Gospel

---

30. Bavinck, *Sin and Salvation in Christ*, 444; as cited by G. Ortlund, "Resurrected as Messiah," 754.

31. Allen, *Lukan Authorship of Hebrews*, 207–10. Allen argues that Jesus is presented as priest in the Gospel of Luke but does note that comparatively little is said of this in the Gospel, compared with the evidence in Hebrews (which he suggests was written by Luke as well). This may indicate that Jesus's identity as priest is signaled in the Gospel, but his current ministry as the Priest like Melchizedek is highlighted in Hebrews.

32. Num 6:24–26. See *m. Tamid* 7:2.

of Luke, Jesus and his disciples go to the Mount of Olives. Again, Luke describes the scene: "And He led them out as far as Bethany, and *He lifted up His hands and blessed them*. While He was blessing them, He parted from them" (Luke 24:50–51, emphasis added). Could it be that here Jesus delivers the blessing Zacharias was unable to pronounce?[33] What was that blessing? Most likely Jesus's last words before his ascension were: "The LORD bless you, and keep you; the LORD make His face shine on you, and be gracious to you; the LORD lift up His countenance on you, and give you peace" (Num 6:24–26).[34] With this blessing, he now assumes his role as the Priest like Melchizedek. Allen says, "Luke presents Jesus as the High Priest, as one who is qualified for His position . . . because of His radical holiness . . . as well as His sacrifice for sins."[35]

As the Servant of the Lord and Prophet like Moses, he suffered rejection and death. This was a biblical prerequisite for his priestly ministry. Everything in the earthly ministry of Jesus until the ascension was preparatory for his ministry as the Priest like Melchizedek. This included his sinless life, his rejection (culminating with his death on the cross), and his resurrection. Each of these aspects not only fulfilled prophecy, but they provided the basis for his high priestly ministry.[36]

It is interesting to note that there do not seem to be any explicit references in Scripture to his role as the Prophet like Moses being eternal, everlasting, or enduring (as is true of the roles of Priest and King). The New Covenant he established through his blood is eternal, and his death as the Lamb of God has eternal effects and is the basis for his roles as priest and king. The work he did as the Prophet is celebrated, for he was the Lamb of God and is identified as such thirty-one times throughout Revelation alone. Furthermore, his prophetic activity of intercession

---

33. This is the suggestion of P. A. Stempvoort, as cited by Allen. See Allen, *Lukan Authorship of Hebrews*, 209.

34. Compare also the blessing of Melchizedek in Genesis 14:19–20.

35. Allen, *Lukan Authorship of Hebrews*, 213.

36. See G. Ortlund, "Resurrected as Messiah," 756. David M. Moffitt writes regarding the testimony of Hebrews:

> The author's use of Exodus to emphasize the liberating/Passover and covenant inaugurating effect of Jesus's death, together with his equally important emphasis on the subsequent high-priestly work of Jesus in the Father's presence in the heavenly holy of holies, allows the conclusion that the author of Hebrews both distinguished between the roles and importance of Passover (associated with Jesus's death) and Yom Kippur (associated with Jesus's ascension), while also holding these two salvific elements together in the very narrative and person of the incarnate Son of God. (Moffitt, "Exodus in Hebrews," 163.)

characterizes his present activity as our Priest, and Scripture preserves his teaching. From this, we can conclude that though the inauguration of these roles is sequential, the characteristics and offices are cumulative.

The announcements of his coming departure, his forty days of teaching, and the blessing of his disciples at his ascension point to his new role as our great High Priest.

Evidence from Hebrews. David Schrock writes, "From the introduction (1:1–4) to the benediction (13:20–21), Hebrews is dedicated to Christ's high priesthood."[37] Indeed, Hebrews provides the strongest evidence for believing that Jesus's priestly ministry followed his service as the Prophet. Some have argued that in offering himself as a sacrifice for sin, Jesus was functioning as a priest. However, in speaking of Jesus's taking on flesh and suffering temptation and death, Hebrews 2:17 says, "He had to be made like His brethren in all things, *so that He might become* a merciful and faithful high priest in things pertaining to God, to make propitiation for the sins of the people."[38] He had not yet become a priest.

Instead of seeing Jesus's offering of his life as a priestly action, it should be seen as a prerequisite for his priestly ministry. Here in Hebrews, just as in the Gospel of Luke, the suffering and death of Jesus are described as qualifications for his ministry as a priest. His priesthood had to follow his earthly suffering.[39] His suffering equipped him for his priestly ministry, "for only by suffering would he be able to deal gently with the weak, as every priest must."[40] His suffering and death were experienced as the Servant of the Lord, as the Prophet like Moses, even as was prophesied in Isaiah 53.

The death of Jesus was also necessary for the inauguration of the New Covenant. Hebrews 7:12 says, "For when the priesthood is changed, of necessity there takes place a change of law also." For Jesus, who was from the Tribe of Judah, to serve as a priest while the Mosaic Covenant was in effect would have been inconceivable to the author of Hebrews. The requirements of the Mosaic Covenant did not end until the establishment of the New Covenant with the crucifixion of Jesus.[41] For Jesus to be a priest, the Mosaic Covenant had to have been made "obsolete"

---

37. Schrock, *The Royal Priesthood and the Glory of God*, 157.
38. Emphasis is mine.
39. See also Heb 1:3; 5:8–9; 10:12; 12:2.
40. G. Ortlund, "Resurrected as Messiah," 753.
41. See also Heb 9:15; 1 Cor 11:25.

(Heb 8:13), for it required Levitical priests. Both Melchizedek and Jethro functioned prior to the institution of the Mosaic Covenant.

Hebrews 7:16 says that the priesthood of Jesus would be "according to the power of an indestructible life." Once again, this indicates that his ministry as the Priest could only begin following the resurrection.[42] To be a priest, Jesus had to have an indestructible life.

The evidence from Hebrews is conclusive. For Jesus to serve as a priest: (1) he had to have completed his earthly ministry, (2) the Mosaic Covenant had to have been rendered obsolete, and (3) he had to have an indestructible life. Hebrews makes it clear that Jesus could not have begun to function as a priest before His crucifixion.

DID JESUS BEGIN HIS PRIESTLY MINISTRY BEFORE HIS ASCENSION?

Many people assume that Messiah's saving work was essentially finished on the cross, paving the way for his ascension into heaven, where, as one author characterized it, "His only work is to pray."[43] What we sometimes fail to recognize is that atonement was a process. First, the sacrificial animal had to be the prescribed animal, and it had to meet certain requirements. It had to be "without defect."[44] Without meeting those requirements, the death would have been meaningless. Yet even with the death of the sacrificial animal, the process was not complete, for the sacrifice had to be offered, or presented, before the Lord.

It is important to understand the symbolism of Passover. Then we will look at evidence from Luke, Acts, and Hebrews.

The symbolism of Passover. The Passover lamb pointed forward to the ultimate atonement. The lamb was a substitute for the firstborn male of the family. But the imagery was expanded with the Suffering Servant of Isaiah 53. The ultimate sacrifice would correspond more closely to the Passover lamb than to the Levitical offerings. In the New Testament, Jesus fulfills this role.

The Passover lamb had to be "without defect" (Exod 12:5). First, we should remember that John makes a point of noting that though the

---

42. G. Ortlund, "Resurrected as Messiah," 755.

43. N. Moore, "Sacrifice, Session and Intercession," 521. He is here expressing a view he does not hold.

44. Cf., Exod 29:1; Lev 1:3, 10; 3:1, etc.

Roman soldiers broke the legs of the two thieves, they did not break Jesus's legs (John 19:31–33). He was physically without blemish. Secondly, of course, Jesus had to live a perfect life. Scripture says, "For we do not have a high priest who cannot sympathize with our weaknesses, but One who has been tempted in all things as we are, yet without sin" (Heb 4:15). The unleavened bread used in both the Passover ceremony and in the Lord's Supper symbolizes his spotless life, free of leaven.

The payment was made, but in the original Passover, the blood still had to be placed on the doorposts and the lintels of the doors. Each step of the Passover was significant, but the climax would come when the Lord would pass through. Exodus 12:23 says, "The LORD will pass through to smite the Egyptians; and when He sees the blood on the lintel and on the two doorposts, the LORD will pass over the door and will not allow the destroyer to come into your houses to smite you." The application of the blood to the doorposts and lintel was as important as the sacrifice itself.

In what way did Jesus present his death to the Father? We don't know, but it may have been with the nail prints in his hands and feet and the scar in his side. These were the marks presented to Thomas as proof of his death (John 20:25). The need for this presentation of his death before the Father helps us to understand the significance of the ascension in completing the process.

Evidence from Luke and Acts. The evidence from Luke and Acts seems to indicate that his function as the Priest like Melchizedek began with the ascension. In this two-part work, Luke is silent regarding the sacrificial significance of the crucifixion. Nowhere does Luke connect Jesus's death to salvation. Instead, in Acts he links salvation to Jesus's exaltation rather than to his death. David Moffitt reaches the same conclusion when he says, "Luke plainly does connect the salvific benefits of repentance, the forgiveness of sins, and purification with Jesus' heavenly ascension and elevation to God's right hand more clearly and consistently than he ever does with the crucifixion."[45]

Moffitt also calls attention to Acts 5:30–31: "The God of our fathers raised up Jesus, whom you had put to death by hanging Him on a cross. He is the one whom God exalted to His right hand as a Prince and a Savior, to grant repentance to Israel, and forgiveness of sins." The exaltation of Jesus to heaven "as a Prince and a Savior, [was] to grant repentance to Israel, and forgiveness of sins." Moffitt says, "Here . . . the cross is not

---

45. Moffitt, "Atonement at the Right Hand," 554.

identified as the element in the larger narrative of the Christ event that produces these atoning results. Rather, the exaltation of Jesus to God's right hand provides these benefits."[46]

Evidence from Paul. As a prisoner of Rome, Paul had time to write what are called his "Prison Epistles," one of which is his letter to the Ephesians. J. Armitage Robinson considered Ephesians to be "the crown of St. Paul's writings."[47] Paul's burden was for believers, in Ephesus and everywhere, to deepen their appreciation for, and understanding of, the work of Messiah—in the past, as the ultimate Prophet and Servant of the Lord, and in the present, as our great High Priest. He wanted them to be confirmed and built up in their faith. This concern was for the individual readers, but also for the Church—the body of Christ—as a whole.

Paul prays for his readers:

> *I pray that* the eyes of your heart may be enlightened, so that you may know what is the hope of His calling, what are the riches of the glory of His inheritance in the saints, and what is the surpassing greatness of His power toward us who believe. *These are* in accordance with the working of the strength of His might which He brought about in Messiah, when He raised Him from the dead, and seated Him at His right hand in the heavenly *places*. (Eph 1:18–20)

From Paul's inspired perspective, it is of utmost importance that we really understand not merely the facts of what Jesus has done and is doing, but that we meditate on the implications for our own lives. He wants "the eyes of our heart to be enlightened."

Paul's assignment for us is to truly know and understand three realities. First is "the hope of His calling." This "hope" is the certainty of our salvation, our resurrection, and of eternal life, which is ours through God's grace in salvation. Second is "the riches of the glory of His inheritance in the saints." This refers not to our inheritance (which has just been described),[48] but to the Father's inheritance—his own people. We need to comprehend the great value he places on us and his desire for our complete transformation—that we "should be to the praise of His glory" (Eph 1:12). The third reality is "the surpassing greatness of His power toward us" (v. 19). In other words, we need to know that this transformation is

---

46. Moffitt, "Atonement at the Right Hand," 570.
47. Robinson, *St. Paul's Epistle to the Ephesians*, vii.
48. See Eph 1:11.

not dependent on our own ability or willpower, but it is related to his power. He is able to make us suitable for his Kingdom. This power is at work in all believers, "beyond all that we ask or think," for it is "the power that works within us" (Eph 3:20).

How is all this possible? It is possible because of what Messiah has done and is doing. "In Him, we have redemption through His blood, the forgiveness of our trespasses" (Eph 1:7). Yes, it was "brought about in Messiah, when [God] raised Him from the dead" (Eph 1:20a). This speaks of his atoning death and resurrection as the Servant of the Lord spoken of by Isaiah, based on the prophecy of the Prophet like Moses. But his resurrection led to his ascension, in which God "seated Him at His right hand in the heavenly places" (Eph 1:20b). By saying this, Paul indicates that with the ascension, Jesus has become the Priest after the order of Melchizedek (as in Ps 110:1, 4).

There is a correspondence here: As his death and resurrection as the Prophet is directly related to our salvation from the *penalty* of sin, so his ascension is directly related to the work he is continuing to do in our lives, releasing us from the *power* of sin. This is summed up perfectly in Ephesians 2:4–6: "But God, being rich in mercy, because of His great love with which He loved us, even when we were dead in our transgressions, made us alive together with Messiah (by grace you have been saved), and raised us up with Him, and seated us with Him in the heavenly *places* in [Messiah] Jesus."

Evidence from Hebrews. The evidence from Hebrews seems to corroborate that his function as the Priest like Melchizedek had to follow not only his crucifixion, but his resurrection. Gavin Ortlund says, "Several factors indicate that Christ's appointment to this [priestly] office should be seen as coinciding with the event of his exaltation/ascension/enthronement."[49]

Hebrews 1:1–2 speaks of Messiah's role as the Servant: "God, after He spoke long ago to the fathers in the prophets in many portions and in many ways, in these last days has spoken to us in His Son." The next verse says, "When He had made purification of sins, He sat down at the right hand of the Majesty on high."[50] This indicates that his transition from Prophet/Servant to Priest was with his ascension.

---

49. G. Ortlund, "Resurrected as Messiah," 752.
50. See also Heb 12:2.

Hebrews 8:1 says, "Now the main point in what has been said is this: we have such a high priest, who has taken His seat at the right hand of the throne of the Majesty in the heavens." Notice the tenses. When it says, "We have such a high priest," this speaks of his present ministry. When it says, "who has taken His seat," it is speaking of his finished work in the past. Hebrews 1:3 has already said that he would not take his seat as Priest until he had made purification of sins. First, the payment has been made for our sin—atonement has been secured. Secondly, Jesus has taken his seat. Now, in the present, we are being sanctified. "We have such a high priest," and his ongoing work is in the lives of believers.

Hebrews 6:19-20 says, "This hope we have as an anchor of the soul, a hope both sure and steadfast and one which enters within the veil, where Jesus has entered as a forerunner for us, having become a high priest forever according to the order of Melchizedek." His priestly ministry began at the ascension, and he ministers now "behind the veil" (Heb 9:24) in heaven.

Scripture stresses the importance of the ascension. Gavin Ortlund says, "In Heb 5:9-10, the saving significance of Christ's priestly appointment is emphasized and more clearly identified with the priestly order of Melchizedek."[51] This presentation of his sacrificial death was the initial ministry of the High Priest, and its importance is underscored by the symbolism of Passover in Luke, Acts, and Hebrews.

DID HIS PRIESTLY MINISTRY ALSO INAUGURATE HIS REIGN AS KING?

Melchizedek was both priest and king. Is Jesus presently serving concurrently as both priest and king? Notice the fact that Psalm 110:1 points to Messiah's exaltation to Yahweh's right hand, "until" he (i.e., Yahweh) subdues Jesus's enemies. He does not assume his role as our King "until" God has subdued his enemies. The use of "until" seems to indicate that his function as Priest begins prior to his reign as King. So, the inaugurations of his two roles of priest and king are initiated sequentially, not simultaneously. First, he serves as our High Priest, then he will also serve as our King.[52]

51. G. Ortlund, "Resurrected as Messiah," 752.

52. G. Ortlund believes that Jesus's role as King began with the resurrection, on the basis of Acts 2:30-32 and 13:30-35. However, these passages only indicate that the resurrection made his reign as King possible, because it preserved him from corruption.

Even so, he will always be our Priest. Psalm 110:4 says, "The LORD has sworn and will not change His mind, You are a priest forever according to the order of Melchizedek." Nine times in Hebrews words such as "eternal," "forever," and "permanently" are used to describe his priesthood.[53] So, his ministry as the Priest begins with his ascension and exaltation and continues, even as he begins his reign as King at the Second Coming. His reign is to begin after the Lord has put his enemies under his feet.

CONCLUSION

To this point, we have seen that Jesus could not have functioned as our High Priest during his earthly ministry. We have also seen that Jesus could not have served as our High Priest before the ascension. Jesus currently exercises his session as our High Priest, and when he returns, he will also reign as King.

He also mentions Romans 1:3–4 ("Resurrected as Messiah," 760–61), but these verses do not mention Jesus's reign as king.

53. Heb 5:6; 6:20; 7:3, 17, 21, 24 (2x), 25, 28.

12

What Does His Priestly Order Tell Us About His Ministry?

HAVING ATTEMPTED TO ANSWER these questions about the timing of Jesus's ministry as our great High Priest, we will now turn attention to the ministry itself. The author of Hebrews wrote, "Therefore, holy brethren, partakers of a heavenly calling, consider Jesus, the Apostle and High Priest of our confession" (Heb 3:1). In this chapter, we will consider two questions: what does his priestly order tell us about his ministry, and where does he exercise his priestly ministry?

THE ORDER OF MELCHIZEDEK

To understand the present ministry of Jesus, we should give more thought to the "alternative" order of priests—the order of Melchizedek. Melchizedek is the first priest mentioned in the Bible, and he was a priest of God Most High (Gen 14:18). The next priest mentioned[1] is Jethro, priest of Midian and Moses's father-in-law (Exod 3:1). The first mention of the Aaronic priesthood of Israel does not occur until Exodus 40:15, and the implication is that Aaron served as the first high priest.[2] We can gain

---

1. That is, apart from Potiphera, an Egyptian priest (Gen 41:45).

2. For more on the order of Melchizedek in the Old Testament, see Mathews, *Melchizedek's Alternative Priestly Order*.

insight as we look at Melchizedek, Jethro, and Jesus. We have already seen some similarities between Melchizedek and Jethro, but are there other parallels?

In Genesis we read that (1) Melchizedek, the priest of Salem, blessed Abram in the name of the Most High God (Gen 14:18). (2) This had followed Abram's success in battle over the four kings who had captured Lot and his family. (3) Melchizedek praised God for his rescue of Abram from the four kings saying, "Blessed be Abram of God Most High . . . who has delivered your enemies into your hand" (Gen 14:19f). (4) Melchizedek brought out bread (i.e., food) and wine for a meal (Gen 14:18).

Likewise, in Exodus we read that (1) Jethro, the priest of Midian, came out with Moses's wife and sons to bless Moses (2) following Moses's success in battle over the Amalekites (Exod 17:8–16). Moses also brought news of the deliverance from the Egyptians (Exod 18:8–11), and (3) Jethro praised God, saying, "Blessed be the LORD, who delivered you from the hand of the Egyptians . . . The LORD is greater than all the gods" (Exod 18:10–11). (4) Then Jethro brought out a burnt offering and sacrifices for a meal, which he ate with Moses and Aaron.[3]

In Genesis 15:2, immediately after Abram's encounter with Melchizedek, Abram's servant is referred to as his heir. His name was Eliezer. In Exodus 18:4, Jethro brings Moses's family to meet him, and reference is made to his son, Eliezer.[4] These and other parallels between Melchizedek and Jethro serve to link these two so that Jethro is to be seen as another priest like Melchizedek.

Since Jesus is a priest after the order of Melchizedek, we should also expect parallels between these Old Testament priests and Jesus. Jesus has blessed his disciples with the greatest of all blessings, the blessing of salvation. This blessing came after he had won a great victory over the greatest enemies of all—sin and death. We anticipate sharing with him the marriage feast of the Lamb (Rev 19:7–9). Whatever else may be on the menu at that celestial celebration, we know we will have bread and wine, for Jesus said, "But I say to you, I will not drink of this fruit of the vine from now on until that day when I drink it new with you in My Father's kingdom" (Matt 26:29).

---

3. See Sailhamer, *NIV Compact Bible Commentary*, 85–86.

4. Sailhamer, *The Pentateuch as Narrative*, 280. Sailhamer also brings out additional parallels in the following page.

THE ORDERS OF AARON AND OF MELCHIZEDEK

Because many New Testament scholars try to understand the priesthood of Jesus in light of the Aaronic priesthood found in the Pentateuch, it is important to draw a sharp distinction between this priesthood and that of Melchizedek. This is not to deny the similarities between temple ritual and the ministry of Jesus as High Priest,[5] but the differences must also be taken into account.

First, unlike the high priest, Jesus did not need to make a sin offering for himself. When you look at the passages that describe the ministries of Melchizedek and Jethro, there is no record of either of them ever offering a sin offering or any atoning sacrifice. In Genesis 14, there is no reference to sacrifice at all, and in Exodus 18:12, we read only that Jethro "took a burnt offering and sacrifices for God." Here, there is no mention of atonement, but instead, the context suggests that this was an offering of thanks for God's deliverance of Moses and the Israelites from Egypt.

Second, in contrast to the Levitical high priest, who only entered the Holy of Holies once annually, Jesus remains there. When Isaiah saw the Lord seated on a throne in the temple, he was presented as a priest, but not a priest of the Aaronic order. In the New Testament, we are told that Jesus "has taken His seat at the right hand of the throne of the Majesty in the heavens" (Heb 8:1).

Third, the Day of Atonement primarily looked to the past; it dealt with the forgiveness of past sin. The priestly ministry of Jesus is primarily looking to the present and future; it has in view the preparation of a holy people.[6] In the Old Testament, the Passover lamb was not viewed as an atoning sacrifice. Instead, it pointed to the future, and ultimate, atonement of Messiah. In general, as our High Priest, Jesus is concerned with both sanctification and blessing.

Fourth, unlike the priests of old, Jesus was made our High Priest with a divine oath. The author of Hebrews points this out in Hebrews 7:20–22 and 28. Here, the author of Hebrews points to God's oath in Psalm 110:4: "The LORD has sworn and will not change His mind, 'You are a priest forever according to the order of Melchizedek.'" Unlike the Aaronic priests, who were ordained according to their ancestry in the

---

5. There are clear allusions to both the Day of Atonement and the sin offerings (e.g., cf. Heb 13:10–12; Lev 4:21; 16:17; 23:26–32).

6. See N. Moore, "Sacrifice, Session and Intercession," 535–36.

Tribe of Levi, Jesus was made our High Priest by an oath of God himself. His result is that Jesus is "the guarantee of a better covenant" (Heb 7:22).

The Greek word translated "guarantee" never appears anywhere else in the New Testament.[7] A corresponding Hebrew word is used, for example, in Genesis 43:9, when Judah offered to be "surety" for his brother Benjamin.[8] Both of these Hebrew and Greek words carry the same basic meaning, one who stands in place of another. As our advocate and substitute, Jesus guarantees the fulfillment of the New Covenant.

WHERE DOES JESUS EXERCISE HIS PRIESTLY MINISTRY?

Most people automatically assume that if Jesus is seated on a throne, he is reigning as a king. However, following the ascension, Scripture makes a distinction between his initial priestly ministry and his subsequent ministry as our eternal Priest/King.

Paying attention to the throne upon which he is seated is crucially important. Mark 16:19 says, "So then, when the Lord Jesus had spoken to them, He was received up into heaven and sat down *at the right hand of God*." This is also what we find in Hebrews 1:3: "When He had made purification of sins, He sat down *at the right hand of the Majesty on high*." Again, in Hebrews 8:1 we read: "We have such a high priest, who has taken His seat *at the right hand of the throne of the Majesty in the heavens*."[9] Notice that he is seated at the right hand of the Father as our High Priest.

We read in Psalm 110: "The LORD says to my LORD: 'Sit at My right hand until I make Your enemies a footstool for Your feet.'... The LORD has sworn and will not change His mind 'You are a priest forever according to the order of Melchizedek'" (vv. 1, 4). Psalm 110, the Gospel of Mark, and Hebrews (not to mention Luke, Paul, and Peter) give unanimous testimony that Jesus is currently functioning as our High Priest, and he is seated at the right hand of the Father.

Are we to imagine two thrones at present—one of which belongs to the Father and another throne to the right which is occupied by Jesus? Apparently not, for Scripture seems to indicate that the Father's throne

---

7. ἔγγυος, *engyos*.

8. עָרַב, *arav*. See also Gen 44:32.

9. Emphasis in each passage is mine. See also Luke 22:69; Acts 5:31; Rom 8:34; Eph 1:20; Heb 1:13; 10:12; 12:2; 1 Pet 3:22.

includes a seat for Jesus at his right hand, on the same throne. It is one throne with at least two seats.

Notice carefully what Jesus promised in his message to the Laodicean church: "He who overcomes, I will grant to him to sit down with Me *on My throne*, as I also overcame and sat down with My Father *on His throne*" (Rev 3:21).[10] Jesus "overcame" when he died, was raised from the dead, and ascended. With the ascension, Jesus sat on the Father's throne—a single throne on which both the Father and Son are currently seated.

But here we see that there are two thrones: the Father's throne, on which both Jesus and the Father are seated, and another ("My throne"). When Jesus returns in the Second Coming, he will be seated on his own throne, but, like the Father's throne, it will also have at least one additional seat, for he promises the one who overcomes a seat on his throne. Revelation 3:21 is perfectly consistent with the testimony of the Scriptures we have just reviewed. It is clear that Jesus is now seated at the right hand of the Father and is serving as the Priest like Melchizedek.

The next question is: What does Jesus do as our High Priest? The short answer is that he saves us and transforms us. The next two chapters are devoted to fleshing out these two aspects of his present ministry.

---

10. Emphasis is my own.

13

What Does He Do? He Saves Us!

In his classic book *Mere Christianity*, C. S. Lewis described our present life in this world:

> This universe is at war.... It is a civil war, a rebellion, and ... we are living in a part of the universe occupied by the rebel. Enemy-occupied territory—that is what this world is. Christianity is the story of how the rightful king has landed, you might say landed in disguise, and is calling us to take part in a great campaign of sabotage.[1]

Later, he raises a question many have and then proceeds to answer it: "Why is God landing in this enemy-occupied world in disguise and starting a sort of secret society to undermine the devil? Why is He not landing in force, invading it? ... He wants to give us the chance of joining His side freely."[2] The "undercover Messiah" has come to gather his disciples, citizens of his Kingdom, and prepare them for service. Before he assumes his role as King, he is currently directing this spiritual battle as our great High Priest.

---

1. Lewis, *Mere Christianity*, 86.
2. Lewis, *Mere Christianity*, 114.

THE PRIESTLY MINISTRY OF JESUS AND THE PRIESTHOOD OF THE BELIEVER

Christians often speak of the doctrine of the priesthood of the believer. This refers to the truth that individual Christians may read and understand the Scriptures without depending upon an earthly priest or pope and that we may pray to the Lord directly without going through a human intermediary. It means that there is no essential difference between clergy and laity, but that all believers are ministers (Eph 4:11–13). Yet, when we examine the Scriptures, we find an overwhelming emphasis on the priesthood of Jesus. Although we should believe in what the doctrine of the "priesthood of the believer" stands for, the terminology itself is problematic.

When a search is made of the words "priest" or "priesthood" in the New Testament, following the book of Acts, we find they occur a total of forty times.[3] Seventeen times the words refer directly to Jesus as our High Priest, sixteen times the words are used in a context where the Levitical priesthood is contrasted with that of Jesus, and one reference is to Melchizedek himself. In other words, the terms are used thirty-four times in contexts about Jesus as our Priest like Melchizedek. The remaining six refer to believers. That is a ratio of almost six to one. We will address those that refer to believers later.

When the Bible speaks of Jesus as our High Priest, the emphasis is not merely on his identity, but on that which his ministry as our Priest entails. As the author of Hebrews says, "Therefore, holy brethren, partakers of a heavenly calling, consider Jesus, the Apostle and High Priest of our confession" (3:1). Jesus is currently serving as our High Priest.

THE INSTRUMENTS OR AGENTS HE USES

Since Jesus is actively serving as High Priest, does he have agents or instruments that assist him? He said that when he would depart physically, he would send the Holy Spirit (see John 14:15).[4] I want to suggest that the

---

3. Rom 15:16; Heb 2:17; 3:1; 4:14, 15; 5:1, 5, 6, 10; 6:20; 7:1, 3, 5, 11 (2x), 12, 14, 15, 17, 21, 23, 24, 26, 27, 28; 8:1, 3, 4; 9:6, 7, 11, 25; 10:11, 21; 13:11; 1 Pet 2:5, 9; Rev 1:6; 5:10; 20:6.

4. More could be said about the ministry of the Holy Spirit, but the point here and in what follows is to understand the ministry of the Spirit as derivative and supportive of Jesus's role as High Priest. Many of the New Testament passages make this connection, as will be seen.

Holy Spirit is the primary agent of our great High Priest. At Pentecost, the Spirit descended, because Jesus had ascended. There is a direct relationship. In his sermon on that momentous day of the birth of the church, Peter said, "Therefore [Jesus] having been exalted to the right hand of God, and having received from the Father the promise of the Holy Spirit, He has poured forth this which you both see and hear" (Acts 2:33).

When we read of the explosive growth of the early church in the book of Acts, we correctly point to the Holy Spirit as the key to this growth. But we often fail to recognize that behind the Spirit's work is the high priestly ministry of Jesus. It is Jesus who has sent the Spirit and who directs the Spirit. Jesus said, "When the Helper comes, whom I will send to you from the Father, that is the Spirit of truth who proceeds from the Father, He will testify about Me" (John 15:26).

In John 16:13–15 Jesus said:

> But when He, the Spirit of truth, comes, He will guide you into all the truth; for He will not speak on His own initiative, but whatever He hears, He will speak; and He will disclose to you what is to come. He shall glorify Me, for He will take of Mine and will disclose *it* to you. All things that the Father has are Mine; therefore I said that He takes of Mine and will disclose *it* to you.

The Holy Spirit is the agent of Jesus on earth.[5]

If the ministry of the Lord as our Priest is to build up his body, the church, on earth, he began by laying the foundation with his apostles and prophets (Eph 2:20). Directly and through the Holy Spirit, the Lord revealed truth to "His holy apostles and prophets" (Eph 3:5). They were the human instruments used in writing the New Testament Scriptures.

Many times, as Paul wrote his epistles, he referred to himself as a servant or slave of Messiah.[6] In this, Paul was not alone, for James, Peter, Jude, and John all claimed to write under the direction, and in the service, of Jesus through the Holy Spirit.[7] Therefore, the Scriptures themselves serve as the written Word of God and are thus an instrument of the Spirit and of our High Priest. As the Lord exercises his priestly ministry, the Holy Spirit is his agent on earth, and the Scripture is his sword (Heb 4:12).

---

5. John 14:16, 26; 15:26–27; 16:7–15.

6. See Rom 1:1; Gal 1:10; etc.

7. See Jas 1:1; 2 Pet 1:1; Jude 1:1; Rev 1:1. Of course, all Scripture in inspired by the Holy Spirit.

HIS MINISTRY IN SALVATION

The question for us now is, "What is he doing as our High Priest?" In short, he is making new citizens of the Kingdom,[8] and he is preparing them for that Kingdom. In the process, he is directing believers and transforming their lives.

Under the direction of our high and exalted Priest, the Holy Spirit convicts of sin and of righteousness (John 16:8), and he illumines our minds to understand and receive the gospel message. He also mediates the presence of Jesus to his disciples. As Jesus himself told his disciples, "Lo, I am with you always, even to the end of the age" (Matt 28:20). Even when he is not here, through his Holy Spirit, our Helper, Jesus is with us.

He grants citizenship in the Kingdom. Jesus secured our citizenship in the Kingdom at great cost. Therefore, we are able to receive it as a gift. People are convicted of their sin, receive the message of salvation, repent of their sin, and place their trust in Jesus for salvation. This is what is involved in becoming a disciple of Jesus and a citizen of his Kingdom.

In the sixty-three years between 1892 and 1954, over fifteen million immigrants passed through Ellis Island in New York Bay to become U.S. citizens. The process for citizenship was carefully and thoughtfully prepared, and immigrants went through the system efficiently. Immigrants were carefully documented and registered. They were given health evaluations, and if there were medical problems, they were treated at the hospital. Those with incurable or disabling ailments were excluded and returned to their country of origin. Only 2 percent were barred entry.

Next were the interviews and the legal inspections to determine their identities, places of origin, occupations, and whether the immigrants had criminal records. Criminals were not given citizenship. Those who completed this lengthy process were granted citizenship, passports were presented, and the new citizens were then able to enter the country and begin their new lives as Americans.

Citizenship in the coming Messianic Kingdom involves a process as well, but it is almost the opposite of the merit-based system at Ellis Island—it is a grace-based system. Citizenship is granted on the basis of God's grace, received through faith. It is a gift. As new citizens, we are registered, sealed by and baptized in the Holy Spirit, and given spiritual

---

8. "Kingdom of heaven" and "Kingdom of God" are synonymous and can be used interchangeably. They refer to the Messianic Kingdom initially. See Compton, "The 'Kingdom of Heaven/God' and the Church," 176–202.

gifts or abilities. Then, as we await the arrival of the future Kingdom in which we now have citizenship, we undergo a process to better prepare us for our lives in that Kingdom. As citizens of a heavenly kingdom, we are not human beings having a spiritual experience, but spiritual beings having a human experience. This world is not our home.

As we learn how to live in this future Kingdom, we have temporary assignments in enemy territory. Here, we are tested, strengthened, and made ready for our new lives. What one author wrote concerning the purpose of 1 Peter could just as well describe much of the New Testament. Of 1 Peter he said, "This epistle could be understood as a handbook written for ambassadors to a hostile foreign land. The author, knowing persecution would arise, carefully prescribed conduct designed to bring honor to the One they represented."[9] Paul wrote, "We are ambassadors for Messiah" (2 Cor 5:20). Let's look at this grace-filled process more carefully.

He intercedes for the lost. The epistle to the Hebrews has much to say about Jesus as a priest and, specifically, as the Priest like Melchizedek.[10] The emphasis in Hebrews is not merely his identity as High Priest, but his current ministry as a priest: "He is able to save forever those who draw near to God through Him, since He always lives to make intercession for them" (Heb 7:25; see Rom 8:34). Formerly, as we have seen, intercession characterized the role of prophets more than that of priests. However, intercession continues to characterize his ministry as our great High Priest.

Here, in Hebrews 7:25, the intercession of Jesus is connected to his ability to save. He wants people to be saved, and he draws the lost to himself.

He calls, he saves, and he seals. Ephesians 1:13 is more specific about the exact moment we receive the Holy Spirit: "In him you also, after listening to the message of truth, the gospel of your salvation—having also believed, you were sealed in Him with the promised Holy Spirit." Romans 8:9 explains simply that "if anyone does not have the Spirit of Messiah, he does not belong to him." Today, believers receive the Holy Spirit the moment they accept Jesus as Lord and Savior. In John 3:5 Jesus says, "Unless one is born of water and the Spirit, he cannot enter into the kingdom of God." When we trust in Jesus, God immediately seals us with his Spirit (2 Cor 1:22). Hebrews 12:23 says that we are "enrolled in heaven."

---

9. Raymer, "1 Peter," 838.
10. E.g., see 3:1; 4:14, 15; 5:5–6, 10; 6:20; 7:1—8:14; etc.

He baptizes with the Holy Spirit. Jesus's ministry as the Prophet began with his anointment and baptism with the Spirit. As our High Priest, he baptizes his disciples with the Spirit. John the Baptist spoke of this connection between Jesus and the Spirit. John 1:32–33 says:

> And John testified saying, "I have seen the Spirit descending as a dove out of heaven, and He remained upon Him. I did not recognize Him, but He who sent me to baptize in water said to me, 'He upon whom you see the Spirit descending and remaining upon Him, this is the One who baptizes in the Holy Spirit.'"[11]

Just before the ascension, Jesus told his disciples, "You will be baptized with the Holy Spirit not many days from now" (Acts 1:5). Less than two weeks later, at the Jewish festival of Pentecost (the Feast of Weeks, or *Shavu'ot*), Jesus not only baptized his disciples with the Holy Spirit but drew many others into salvation and baptism as well (Acts 2). We next read of the baptism with the Spirit in connection with the salvation of Cornelius and his household (Acts 11:15–16). Peter recognized this as the fulfillment of what Jesus had promised.

Paul talks about this baptism in the Spirit in 1 Corinthians 12:13. Speaking of the experience of all believers, he says, "For by one Spirit we were *all* baptized into one body, whether Jews or Greeks, whether slaves or free, and we were *all* made to drink of one Spirit." Paul also makes mention of our baptism in the Spirit in Ephesians 4:4–6 when he speaks of the unity we have as believers. He says, "There is one body and one Spirit, just as also you were called in one hope of your calling; one Lord, one faith, *one baptism*, one God and Father of all who is over all and through all and in all."[12] He who was baptized as the Prophet like Moses will yet baptize his disciples with the Spirit as our great High Priest.

Some believe baptism in the Spirit is separate from conversion and subsequent to salvation.[13] Often, they say it should be accompanied by an ecstatic utterance of "tongues." On the contrary, these passages plainly speak of this baptism with the Spirit in connection with a salvation experience. When a person repents of sin, places his trust in Jesus's atoning death for the forgiveness of sin, and commits himself to the Lord, the Holy Spirit takes up residence in his spirit. The Apostle John speaks of

---

11. See also Matt 3:11; Mark 1:8; Luke 3:16.
12. Emphasis is mine in both passages.
13. E.G., cf. Fee, "Baptism in the Holy Spirit," 87–99.

this same spiritual baptism as an anointing. He says that Jesus has anointed us and that this anointing abides with us and teaches us (1 John 2:27).

Through his intercession, he calls people to salvation, he saves and seals them with the Holy Spirit, and he baptizes them with the Holy Spirit. This is all part of our transformation from citizens of "the old country" to citizens of the coming Kingdom.

He seats us in the heavenlies. In Ephesians 2, Paul writes that we were dead in transgressions and sins (v. 1), because we followed the ways of this world. We were all objects of God's wrath and in need of God's grace (vv. 2–3). But Paul uses three very unusual verbs to describe the condition of believers. First, he says that we have been made alive together with the Messiah spiritually (v. 5). Second, we have been raised up with him spiritually. And third, we have been seated with him in the heavenly places (v. 6).[14] That is to say, believers are no longer mere earthlings—we now have an exalted status and resources. We are sons and daughters of God through no merit of our own.

In these verses, Paul draws a parallel between the actual physical experience of Jesus and our own actual, though spiritual, experience. Jesus died, was raised, and was physically seated in the heavenly realms, and these are the spiritual experiences of the new believer.[15] Paul continues in verse 7 to speak of our future in "the ages to come." In each of his roles, Jesus provides for us in the past, the present, and the future.

Paul then writes of the present results of the past ministry of the Messiah (Eph 2:11–22). Here, his emphasis is on the unity Jesus accomplished by breaking down the barriers between Jews and Gentiles.

He gives us spiritual gifts. Although we have been seated with Messiah in the heavenlies in a spiritual sense, we remain on the earth to live a new, resurrected life in connection with him. For this reason, he has given gifted individuals to equip us—apostles, prophets, evangelists, and pastors and teachers (Eph 4:11). Through the apostles and prophets, we have been given the Scriptures of the New Testament. Evangelists, pastors and teachers are given to evangelize, pastor, and teach, but they are also given, Paul says, "for the equipping of the saints for the work of service, to the building up of the body of Messiah; until we all attain to the unity of the faith, and of the knowledge of the Son of God, to a mature man,

---

14. See also Col 3:1–2.
15. See Hoehner, *Ephesians*, 329–35.

to the measure of the stature which belongs to the fullness of Messiah" (Eph 4:12–13).

In addition to the gift of these individuals, at salvation we are each given spiritual gifts. These are discussed in Romans 12 and 1 Corinthians 12:4–11, though these may not be comprehensive lists. As we use these gifts in serving the Lord, they also produce unity as we work together through the Holy Spirit to encourage and build up one another.

Our High Priest intercedes for the lost. He saves, seals, and baptizes us with the Spirit. At the same time, he seats us in the heavenly places and gives us spiritual gifts for service and unity with other believers. All of these things are associated with the new citizenship we receive at our conversion.

14

What Does He Do? He Transforms Us!

Unlike the process at Ellis Island, Jesus takes in criminals, prostitutes, drug addicts, self-centered prima donnas, greedy materialists, foul-mouthed grouches, self-righteous Pharisees, and passive-aggressive rebels. He accepts those who are broken, sick, and blind. No one comes to him with riches, for everyone who comes is completely bankrupt. Paul claims,

> For consider your calling, brethren, that there were not many wise according to the flesh, not many mighty, not many noble; but God has chosen the foolish things of the world to shame the wise, and God has chosen the weak things of the world to shame the things which are strong, and the base things of the world and the despised God has chosen, the things that are not, so that He may nullify the things that are, so that no man may boast before God. (1 Cor 1:26–29)

Imagine with me how we must appear to the angels. Like most new immigrants, when we gain our citizenship in the everlasting Kingdom, we don't know how to speak the language. As we begin to learn, our accent is thick; we stumble over the words, and we have much to learn. Even as we are learning the language, our thoughts are still in our mother tongue. We also have too much of the "old country" about us. Our clothing is foreign, and our customs are strange. Our reactions to things are inappropriate. But we will change over time. The truth is that we may have been saved from the penalty of sin, but the power of sin is still very strong in our lives.

HIS MINISTRY IN SANCTIFICATION

As our High Priest, Jesus prepares us for life as citizens of the Kingdom serving as ambassadors in hostile territory. Having saved us and granted us citizenship in that Kingdom, he is now preparing us. He renews our minds, unifies his disciples, and makes us holy in thought and life. Ultimately, he welcomes us to our new country and Kingdom. As he brings Israel to salvation and makes it a priestly nation, he also extends his blessings to gentile believers from the nations.

He renews our minds. The way we look at life must change. We usually view life with a self-serving, if not self-centered, perspective. Many approach life with either pessimism or fear, and others with pride and hubris. We need to learn to be oriented toward others, rather than ourselves, and to be full of gratitude, hope, and joy. The way we react to circumstances should change when we come to saving faith

Our priorities should shift. Some people know much more about movies, actors, and actresses; for others, it could be pop music and musical groups; and for yet others, it might be sports teams, player statistics, and team standings. None of these things are evil or wrong, but our emphasis should shift from these things of the "old world" to the things that are eternal. Paul writes, "Therefore, if you have been raised up with Messiah, keep seeking the things above, where Messiah is, seated at the right hand of God. Set your mind on the things above, not on the things that are on earth" (Col 3:1–2). How well do we know the Bible? What role does prayer have in our lives? Do we know how to share the gospel with someone else? Are we kind and thoughtful of others?

Not only are our affections and priorities misplaced, but our ideas and ways of thinking are wrong. For many generations, the American worldview was largely shaped by biblical values, even if not consistently. Today, Americans have been profoundly influenced by naturalism and the theory of evolution, Eastern religious worldviews, and a subjective perspective on truth and identity. Modern culture has so changed its views of human sexuality that for many people, God's design has been confused or completely rejected. The biblical view of the sanctity of life is also scorned. Abortion and euthanasia are accepted and celebrated. Superstitious and mystical belief systems are popular. The good news is that Jesus renews our minds. Paul exhorts us, "Have this attitude in yourselves which was also in Messiah Jesus" (Phil 2:5; see also Eph 4:23).

This teaching is not limited to Paul. James says, "You adulteresses, do you not know that friendship with the world is hostility toward God? Therefore, whoever wishes to be a friend of the world makes himself an enemy of God. Or do you think that the Scripture speaks to no purpose: 'He jealously desires the Spirit which He has made to dwell in us'?" (Jas 4:4–5). Our interests are to be focused on him rather than on the things of this world.

He produces unity. When we are baptized in the Spirit, we become temples, or dwellings, of the Holy Spirit. Paul says: "Do you not know that you are a temple of God, and that the Spirit of God dwells in you?"[1] Changing the imagery, Paul also says we have become the body of Messiah.[2] In Romans 12:5 Paul says, "So we, who are many, are one body in Messiah, and individually members one of another."[3] This imagery is designed to communicate our interdependence and the need for a servant mentality as we become more others-focused.

Not only are we joined to one another, but we are also joined, collectively, to him. When he appeared to Saul on the road to Damascus, he said, "Saul, Saul, why are you persecuting Me?" (Acts 9:4). This was the cry of the Head on behalf of his body. When we are persecuted for his sake, he is affected. He is our great High Priest. He is able to sympathize with us, and he is able to give us whatever we need.

He makes us holy. The greatest ministry of our Priest is the preparation of a holy people. Paul says that "God causes all things to work together for good to those who love God, to those who are called according to His purpose" (Rom 8:28). That good purpose to which we are progressing is "to become conformed to the image of His Son" (Rom 8:29). This is the blessing he bestows, and it is the outgrowth of his redemptive work. He paid the price for our sin when he died on the cross, and his ascension secured our salvation. Now, having been saved from the penalty of sin, we are being saved from the power of sin. In this, we are being prepared for the Kingdom. As Peter would say, you have been born again. You have "[obtained] an inheritance which is imperishable and undefiled and will not fade away, reserved in heaven for you . . . [namely] a salvation ready to be revealed in the last time" (1 Pet 1:4–5).

He works in us, through the Holy Spirit, to produce lives that please him. In reading the New Testament, it is striking how many times

---

1. 1 Cor 3:16. See also Eph 2:11–22; 3:17.
2. Eph 4:12. See also 1 Cor 10:17; 12:27; Rom 12:5.
3. See also 1 Cor 10:17; 12:27; Eph 4:12; Heb 13:3.

gratitude and love are stressed—love for God and love for our neighbors. All the while, Jesus is interceding for us—for his own. Paul writes, "Jesus is He who died, yes, rather who was raised, who is at the right hand of God, who also intercedes for us" (Rom 8:34). He is preparing a people for his Kingdom.

He gives assurance. There are times in the lives of believers when the enemy attacks us with doubts about our salvation. At times like this, Jesus, our High Priest, through his Spirit and through the Word, brings the assurance we need. Hebrews 6:19–20 says, "This hope we have as an anchor of the soul, a *hope* both sure and steadfast and one which enters within the veil, where Jesus has entered as a forerunner for us, having become a high priest forever according to the order of Melchizedek." David Allen says, "The enthroned Christ in the heavenly sanctuary as our forerunner is the guarantee that we shall one day enter heaven as well. As our anchor of hope, he secures our entrance."[4] Jesus gives us the assurance we need.

He advocates. An advocate is a lawyer. If you're not in trouble, you probably don't need a lawyer. A lawyer is usually someone who can stand up for you and help you when you are in need. You only need *the* Advocate if you're a sinner. The Apostle John wrote, "My little children, I am writing these things to you so that you may not sin. And if anyone sins, we have an Advocate with the Father, Jesus Messiah the righteous" (1 John 2:1). John did not say, "If anyone sins, he has forfeited his Advocate."

Only when we understand the enormity of our sin problem can we truly appreciate our need for Jesus as our advocate. The Bible says that sin is every act we commit that is contrary to the will of God (1 John 3:4). Sin is also every word we speak that is contrary to the will of God (Matt 12:36–37). Not only that, but sin is every thought we think that is contrary to the will of God (Rom 12:2). As if that were not enough, sin is also every good deed that we should be doing that we fail to do (Jas 4:17). Since sin is every action, word, and thought contrary to God's will and every failure to do what is right, how many times a day would you think we sin? Certainly, the number would be in the hundreds, if not thousands. How many sins in a year? How many in a lifetime?

Of course, Jesus died for our sin. If we have trusted in him, it has been forgiven. But Satan will bring up our sin to accuse us and to discourage us. One of his most effective tools is guilt. We need an advocate!

---

4. Allen, *Hebrews*, 403.

The priesthood of Jesus is crucially important, for not only is he working in our lives to shape and transform us, but he is constantly advocating for us.

In Zechariah's vision, he saw "Joshua, the high priest, standing before the angel of the LORD, and Satan standing at his right hand to accuse him" (Zech 3:1). Even though Joshua's garments were filthy, before Satan could speak one word of accusation, we read (v. 2), "the LORD said to Satan, 'The LORD rebuke you, Satan!'"

This is actually speaking of the removal of sin from Israel and its spiritual restoration. But we who are Gentiles also share in this. Joshua, this priest, is presented as one who points to the coming Messiah, who is our advocate. So Jesus is our High Priest and advocate as well. And what an advocate we have! Jesus, our great High Priest, seated at the right hand of the Father in the heavenlies, and endowed with all authority, is praying for you and for me. This is true not only with regard to our sin, but to whatever need we may have. There is nothing we will face in this life that is beyond his ability as our advocate.

He motivates and enables us to do his will. Situational awareness is very important. Think of driving. Some people drive with a very short horizon. They only are aware of cars, road conditions, and road signs as they encounter them. Situational awareness expands the horizon so that problems are anticipated by looking far ahead. When it comes to our lives as citizens of the Kingdom, situational awareness involves being aware of what is happening around us, taking everything into account, and adjusting our behavior and attitudes in light of God's purposes to prepare us for his Kingdom. In addition to looking for an immediate application of a Scripture passage to a crisis or challenge we may be facing, we should consider how a passage or life lesson will contribute to our future life as citizens of the Kingdom. He gives us situational awareness.

He gives us both the desire and the ability to live for him. Philippians 2:13 says, "For it is God who is at work in you, both to will and to work for His good pleasure." Having this desire to serve the Lord prepares us for our life in the Kingdom. Paul writes, "For we are His workmanship, created in Messiah Jesus for good works, which God prepared beforehand so that we would walk in them" (Eph 2:10).

He welcomes us home. Several years ago, I was asked to present a conference paper on the life of Lilli Wolff, a Jewish believer in Jesus. She had been a Holocaust survivor, had moved to Dallas, had become a believer, and was also a member of our church when I was young. I needed her obituary as a part of my research.

I went to our church library, and in the back, where church archives were kept, I was directed to large three-ring binders full of mylar pockets. Whenever a church member would die, his or her newspaper obituary was cut out and collected in these binders. As I turned the pages, I recognized the names of people I had known years ago. Most were contemporaries of my parents; some had been my Sunday School teachers. It was as though I could see an entire congregation who had formerly comprised the membership of our church. They are all now in heaven.

Shortly afterward, at the conclusion of a Sunday morning worship service, I watched as dozens of people came forward to publicly profess their faith in Jesus. Putting these images together, it seemed the church was a large spiritual vortex—bringing in the newly redeemed, nurturing them to maturity and service as they swirled around, and then sending them on into heaven. Jesus is currently preparing the citizenry of his coming Kingdom. This is the Father's purpose for now, even as he said so many centuries ago in 1 Samuel 2:35: "But I will raise up for Myself a permanently faithful priest who will do according to what is in My heart and in My soul; and I will build Him a permanently faithful house, and My Anointed One [Messiah] will walk before Me always."[5]

Not only is this true of us as individuals, but the day will come when he will meet us all and welcome his body, the church, home. In 1 Thessalonians 4:16–17 we read, "For the Lord Himself will descend from heaven with a shout, with the voice of the archangel, and with the trumpet of God and . . . we . . . will be caught up . . . in the clouds to meet the Lord in the air, and so we shall always be with the Lord."

"A HOLY NATION" AND "A KINGDOM OF PRIESTS"

He restores Israel as a holy nation. Many of my fellow gentile Christian brothers and sisters tend to see the endgame, the final act of history, as the salvation of the nations and the Rapture of the church. The Old Testament was mostly about the Jewish people, finally the gospel went to the Gentiles, and one day, the Lord will take us to be with him. End of story.

If this is the way you see the storyline of Scripture, you are in for a surprise ending, for the Bible presents it differently. During all but the

---

5. Author's translation.

earliest period the Old Testament, God made covenants with Israel alone. Salvation was limited to Israel. For a Gentile to be saved, he or she had to become a part of the people of Israel (see John 4:22; Eph 2:11–12). Gentiles, as Gentiles, could not be saved, and only a small number were saved—by becoming attached to the people of Israel.[6]

In the New Testament, we read of the initial Jewishness of the early church, but for most of the history of the church, only a remnant of Jewish people has been saved. Paul specifically addresses this in Romans 11. He speaks of the remnant and its importance in verses 1–6. In verses 7–10, he speaks of the divinely-ordained blindness of the majority of the people, and in verses 11–24, he explains how God has used the spiritual blindness that afflicts the majority of Israel to open the door for Gentiles to be saved.

But Paul goes on to say that when "the fullness of the Gentiles has come in" (v. 25), then "all Israel will be saved" (v. 26). In fact, the remnant of Jewish believers today is something like a down payment or a guarantee that one day, the entire Jewish population of that time will be restored to the Land of Israel and will be brought to repentance and salvation through faith in Jesus, their Messiah.

This was prophesied many times in the Old Testament. Ezekiel 36 and 37 are very clear about the physical restoration of the Jewish people to the Land being followed by the national spiritual restoration of the people to the Lord. Before that day arrives, however, Jesus is presently also calling disciples from the nations, even as was promised to Abram: "In you all the families of the earth will be blessed" (Gen 12:3).[7]

Paul tells us in Romans 11 (vv. 11–12, 25–26) that God will first gather the fullness of the Gentiles, and then "all Israel will be saved." He writes in verses 30–32:

> For just as you [i.e., Gentiles] once were disobedient to God, but now have been shown mercy because of their [i.e., the majority of the Jewish people's] disobedience, so these [i.e., Jewish people] also now have been disobedient, that because of the mercy shown to you they also may now be shown mercy. For God has shut up all in disobedience so that He may show mercy to all.

---

6. It is sometimes suggested that the people of Nineveh were redeemed under the preaching of Jonah. However, there is no indication of more than an acknowledgment of God's identity and a repentance that forestalled God's certain judgment on the Ninevites (Assyrians). Judgment would come less than one and a half centuries later (cf. Nahum). See Jer 18:7–10.

7. See Gen 12:1–3; 21:12d; 26:3–5; 28:12–16.

The New Covenant was made with the people of Israel, and those of us who are Gentiles have been grafted in so that we partake of the spiritual blessings that were originally promised to Abraham and the patriarchs of Israel. In any case, eventually the people of Israel will be restored both to their Land and to their Messiah. This is the work of our High Priest.

He makes of the redeemed a kingdom of priests. Israel was to be the channel through which God would bring the blessings of salvation to the nations. As we have seen in Exodus 19:5–6, God had promised Israel, "Now then, if you will indeed obey My voice and keep My covenant, then you shall be My own possession among all the peoples, for all the earth is Mine; and you shall be to Me a kingdom of priests and a holy nation."[8]

When would Israel be "a holy nation"? Through Isaiah, God points in the future to a time when "all your people will be righteous" (Isa 60:21a). Consider Jeremiah 50:20: "In those days and at that time, declares the LORD, search will be made for the iniquity of Israel, but there will be none; and for the sins of Judah, but they will not be found; for I shall pardon those whom I leave as a remnant." We know very well of the sin of Israel, so this verse is nothing short of astounding!

How would this be possible? In Genesis 15:6, it is said of Abraham that "he believed in the LORD; and He reckoned it to him as righteousness." His faith in the Lord was accounted to him as righteousness. In Genesis 26:5, God told Isaac that "because Abraham obeyed Me and kept *My charge, My commandments, My statutes and My laws,*" if Isaac would remain in the Land, God would be with him and bless him. It is significant that what is said of Abraham is also said of obedience to the Mosaic Law: "You shall therefore love the LORD your God, and always keep *His charge, His statutes, His ordinances, and His commandments*" (Deut 11:1. Compare the terms that are used). Sailhamer notes that "the writer has never assumed that Abraham actually had a knowledge of the Law itself.... Thus Abraham is an example of one who shows the Law written on his heart."

Therefore, we are to anticipate a time when the people of Israel would have this same type of relationship with the Lord. With the promise of the New Covenant, the Lord said, "I will put My law within them, and on their heart I will write it; and I will be their God, and they shall be My people" (Jer 31:33). Ezekiel 37:24 says: "My servant David [i.e., the Messiah] will be king over them, and they [i.e., both Israel and Judah]

---

8. This is the author's translation. See the discussion above on pages 23–24.

will all have one shepherd; and they will walk in My ordinances, and keep My statutes, and observe them."

Within approximately thirty years of the inauguration of that New Covenant, the Apostle Peter wrote a letter to Jewish disciples of Jesus: "You . . . are being built up as a spiritual house for a holy priesthood" (1 Pet 2:5). He reiterated, "But you are a chosen race, a royal priesthood, a holy nation, a people for God's own possession" (1 Pet 2:9). So, Peter is referring to these Jewish believers, the remnant of Israel, as a fulfillment of this ancient promise. This remnant of Jewish believers through the centuries has been a guarantee of what is anticipated for the future.

Certainly, it would apply to the restored nation at the Second Coming. Through Zechariah, the Lord said, "I will pour out on the house of David and on the inhabitants of Jerusalem, the Spirit of grace and of supplication, so that they will look on Me whom they have pierced; and they will mourn for Him, as one mourns for an only son, and they will weep bitterly over Him like the bitter weeping over a first-born" (Zech 12:10).

A weeping such as that which filled Pharaoh's palace when Joseph revealed his identity to his brothers (Gen 45:2) will fill the Land of Israel when Jesus reveals his identity to his brothers. But their sorrow will quickly turn to everlasting joy. This passage indicates, as Paul puts it in Romans 11:26, that "all Israel will be saved."

When we looked at the forty references to "priest" or "priesthood" in Romans through Revelation, thirty-four applied to the priesthood of Jesus and six to believers. Three of these six references refer to Jewish believers (Rom 15:16; 1 Pet 2:5, 9). But when we turn to Revelation and examine the final three, there is a change.

John, writing to "the seven churches that are in Asia" (Rev 1:4), says, "He has made us to be a kingdom, priests to His God and Father—to Him be the glory and the dominion forever and ever. Amen" (Rev 1:6). Some claim that only Jewish believers could really understand all the allusions to the Old Testament that are found in the book, but that is not certain. These churches were likely composed of both Jewish and gentile believers. That leads us to the next reference in 5:10. Beginning with verse 8 we read:

> . . . the four living creatures and the twenty-four elders fell down before the Lamb . . . and they sang a new song, saying, "Worthy are You to take the book, and to break its seals; for You were slain, and purchased for God with Your blood men from every tribe and tongue and people and nation. And You have made

them to be a kingdom and priests to our God; and they will reign upon the earth." (Rev 5:8–10)

This clearly indicates that people from all nations have now been incorporated into this kingdom of priests. This is further supported in Revelation 20:6, which refers to all the redeemed who will be resurrected prior to the Messianic Kingdom.

It is important to note that the incorporation of gentile believers into this priesthood does not suggest that the church has replaced Israel, but rather that gentile believers are able to partake of the spiritual blessings that originally pertained to Israel, through the New Covenant.

The priests of old were concerned to remove impurity that would separate men from God in his holiness. Trespass and sin offerings were made to remove the barrier that sin created. With this in mind, when we look at these references to believers as priests in the New Testament, we find that Paul and Barnabas were "a light for the Gentiles, that [they] may bring salvation to the end of the earth" (Acts 13:47). Paul saw his evangelistic ministry among the Gentiles as a priestly work. It was to minister "as a priest the gospel of God, so that my offering of the Gentiles may become acceptable, sanctified by the Holy Spirit" (Rom 15:16).

This remnant of Jewish believers through the centuries has been a "deposit" or a foretaste of what is anticipated for the future. The essence of what it means to be a nation of priests is to be a nation helping others to be reconciled to God and presenting them as an offering. This is precisely what the early Jewish disciples of Yeshua (Jesus) did as they began to spread the gospel first, and especially, to their own people, and later to the gentile nations—many times at the cost of their lives. As a priesthood, we who have been sanctified by the blood of Jesus should share in the priestly task of evangelism. In this task, our great High Priest enables and intercedes for us. Even so, come, Lord Jesus!

15

Jesus as the King in the New Testament

IN THE 1500S, SCOTLAND was preparing against a possible invasion by the Spanish Armada. At the same time, King James VI of Scotland was to go to Norway to bring back his bride. The nation was anxious. It was a time of danger—the king would be absent. Robert Bruce was a minister of the Church of Scotland. He was a powerful preacher and Moderator of the General Assembly of the Church of Scotland. The king was very aware of how valuable the services of the church would be in maintaining public confidence and peace while he was away in Norway. In October 1589 he appointed Bruce as Privy Councilor and delegated his authority to him in his absence.

Sometime after that period of crisis, Robert Bruce was preaching before the king at Edinburgh, and the king was sitting in his own seat, with several of the nobility waiting on him. The king had a habit of talking with those around him during the sermon, and that's what he did on this particular occasion. Bruce soon noticed it, stopped in the middle of his sermon, and the king grew silent. Bruce continued. For a second time, the king began to talk to those around him, and again, Bruce stopped. When the king stopped talking, Bruce continued his sermon once more. When the king began talking a third time, Bruce addressed the king: "When the lion roareth, all the beasts of the field are at ease. The Lion of the Tribe of Judah is now roaring in the voice of his Gospel, and it becomes all the petty kings of the earth to be silent."[1]

Jesus is not one of the "petty kings of the earth." He is the Lion of the Tribe of Judah, the King of kings, and Lord of lords. His arrival as king has been anticipated since it was announced in Genesis 49:10, almost four thousand years ago. He is the ultimate King. His power is unlimited; his knowledge is unrestricted; his justice is uncompromising; his wisdom is unmatched; and his grace is unrestrained. He is holy, yet the depth of his love is bottomless. Having examined the ministry of Jesus as the Prophet like Moses and the Priest like Melchizedek, our focus will now be on Jesus as the King like David.

THE RIDDLE OF MESSIAH'S REJECTION AND REIGN

The messianic prophecies of the Hebrew Bible were sometimes thought to be perplexing. Part of the confusion comes from the seemingly contradictory images used. On the one hand, Messiah was to be a humble messiah, riding a donkey, suffering abuse and even death (Zech 9:9; Ps 22:1–18; Isa 52:13—53:12). On the other hand, he was to be a warrior-king, who would defeat Israel's enemies and establish a kingdom of righteousness and peace (Num 24:16–19; Isa 63:1–6; Zech 14:2–9; Ps 72).

These images are often blended. Like parallel mountain ranges seen from a distance, these portraits do not often reveal the span between them. As we now know, Messiah came first as the Prophet and Servant. Today he is our Priest. Someday, he will come again as our King. But this sequence is not often found in the Old Testament. Instead, these images are presented as overlapping.

Just consider two examples. The first messianic prophecy is found in Genesis 3:15, and in this one verse we find prophecies of both the first and second comings of Messiah. The first coming is as "the Seed of a woman," speaking of his virgin birth. As the Seed of a woman, he is stricken by the serpent. This speaks of the first coming of Messiah. But the verse also says that Messiah would crush the head of the serpent. This speaks of his future coming. There are many other prophecies that do the same thing. Another is Isaiah 9:6–7b:

> For a child will be born to us, a son will be given to us; and the government will rest on His shoulders; and His name will be

---

1. Original Source: Wodrow, *Sermons by the Rev. Robert Bruce*, 154.

called Wonderful Counselor, Mighty God, Eternal Father, Prince of Peace. There will be no end to the increase of *His* government or of peace, on the throne of David and over his kingdom.

The first two phrases speak of his first coming, and the rest speak of his second coming.

Here, again, the angel spoke of his birth, but then immediately pointed to the future—to the Second Coming, when the virgin's Son (Isa 7:14) would reign as King on the throne of David.

The rabbinic sages of the past could not reconcile how Messiah could be "a man of sorrows and acquainted with grief" (Isa 53:3) and yet be a king "on the throne of David and over his kingdom" (Isa 9:7). So, they developed the idea that there must be two messiahs, one who would come humbly, and another who would come in victory and majesty.[2]

This consensus was only disturbed when a Hassidic rebbe in New York was thought to be the messiah. Following the rebbe's stroke and confinement to a wheelchair until his death, his followers became convinced that instead of two messiahs, there would be only one, but with two appearances. Following his death, they expected him to rise from the dead and come back as "king messiah." To this day, in New York and in Israel, you can see posters and billboards with his picture and the epithet "King Messiah." He died in June 1994. To this day, his body remains in his tomb![3]

JESUS AS THE SON OF DAVID IN THE NEW TESTAMENT

What does the New Testament say about Jesus as the Son of David, and why does it matter? Jesus's birth in Bethlehem, the city of David, was in direct fulfillment not only of the promises made to David in 2 Samuel 7, but also of the prophecy in Micah 5:2: "From you [Bethlehem] One will go forth for Me to be ruler in Israel." The star that guided the wise men was the fulfillment of the ancient prophecy in Numbers 24:17: "A star shall come forth from Jacob, and a scepter shall rise from Israel." From the wise men and their gifts to the angelic host, everything about Jesus's

---

2. Based on the vision of the Four Craftsmen, found in Zech 1:18–21 (MT, Zech 2:1–4), *b. Sukkah* 52b identifies these four as Elijah, who would herald the arrival of Messiah, Messiah ben Yoseph, who would die in battle, the Righteous Priest, and Messiah ben David, who would be the Davidic King.

3. Rabbi Menachem Mendel Schneerson, 1902–1994.

birth points to his royal identity. The use of the title "the Son of David" indicates an heir apparent.

There are no fewer than five references to David in the genealogy of Jesus in Matthew 1:1–17. Then, in Matthew 1:20, Joseph is told not to be afraid of taking Mary to be his wife, and he is addressed as "Joseph, son of David"! For Matthew, the Davidic lineage of Jesus is tremendously important.

Jesus is referred to as the "Son of David" or as a descendant of David more than twenty times in the New Testament. He is called the Son of David by blind men (in seven references),[4] by the woman with an issue, by a Canaanite woman, by children, by an angel, and by Paul.[5] In Matthew 12:23 the Galilean crowds exclaimed, "This man cannot be the Son of David, can he?" But by the triumphal entry, recorded in Matthew 21:9, the Jerusalem crowd answered, "Hosanna to the Son of David"! The question had been put to rest.

The Pharisees were somewhat perplexed. They agreed that the Messiah was to be the Son of David (Matt 22:42), but they could not understand why his father, David, called him "Lord" in Psalm 110:1 (Matt 22:5; Acts 2:29–32). As Jesus framed the question in Matthew 22:45, "If David then calls Him 'Lord,' how is He his son?" In his teaching in the temple, Jesus clearly taught that he was not merely a son of David, but *the* Son of David. In Revelation 22:16, Jesus refers to himself as "the root and the offspring of David." In other words, Jesus says of himself that he is both the ancestor of David and David's descendant, both the root and the offspring!

This emphasis on Jesus as the Son of David in the Gospels encourages us to connect the life and earthly ministry of Jesus and the Davidic Covenant. References to Jesus as the Son of David speak of his royal identity as well as to his purpose of gathering a body of disciples who will be citizens of his Kingdom. As we have seen, this purpose could only have been accomplished through his service as the great Prophet, the Suffering Servant—the Lamb of God.

The Gospels and Acts are not alone in bearing witness to Jesus as the Son of David, Paul also speaks about Jesus as the Son of David. In 2 Timothy 2:8, Paul makes an interesting statement. He says, "Remember Jesus the Messiah, risen from the dead, descendant of David, according to

---

4. See Matt 9:27; 20:30–31; Mark 10:47–48; Luke 18:38–39.
5. See Matt 9:20; 15:22; 21:15; Luke 1:32; Rom 1:3.

my gospel." Here, in referring to Jesus, Paul makes two important points: (1) Jesus has risen from the dead, and (2) Jesus is a descendant of David. That Jesus was born as the Son of David was much more important to the apostles and early Jewish believers than it has been to many gentile believers, for it speaks of the importance of the Jewishness of Jesus, of his identity as King, and of the faithfulness of God.

The earthly life of Jesus as recorded in the Gospels had to have taken place when it did to fulfill prophecy about his arrival. In Daniel 9:26, we are told that Messiah would be "cut off," or killed, before the destruction of Jerusalem and the temple. This happened in AD 70. Furthermore, Genesis 49:10 says that the coming Messianic King had to have been from the Tribe of Judah as well as from the lineage of David. These records were destroyed and lost to history with the destruction of AD 70. No one since then could document such a lineage.

If Jesus was the Son of David, why did he not take the throne, exercise his royal prerogatives, and set up his kingdom? Some say he wanted to, but he couldn't because Israel rejected him. I am convinced there is a much better answer.

The experience of David pointed to the pattern his greater Son would follow. Samuel anointed David as king when he was a young man, perhaps when prepubescent (1 Sam 16:12–13). The prophet Samuel was sent to Bethlehem, to the house of Jesse, and anointed him there. Yet he did not begin his reign immediately. For the next period in David's life, perhaps fifteen years or more, David led a group of about four hundred men. Scripture describes them as "everyone who was in distress, and everyone who was in debt, and everyone who was discontented" (1 Sam 22:2). They followed freely, not under compulsion. Finally, when David was thirty years old, he was crowned king and began his reign on the throne (2 Sam 5:3–4).

Likewise, Jesus was born to be king. But, as we have seen, he has not yet taken his throne. He is now serving as our advocate and High Priest.[6] A template was set with David. There was an interval between his consecration (i.e., his anointment) as king and his coronation as king. In the meantime, his followers were those who were in distress and in debt, yet who followed him gladly and faithfully.[7] This is also true of Jesus (and of his disciples), and the day will yet come when he will take his throne and

---

6. Incidentally, it is interesting to note that in the Old Testament the ministries of the prophets and priests preceded the reign of Israel's kings.

7. See 2 Sam 2:4; 5:1–4.

begin to rule. David's kingdom was the greatest Israel had ever known. The Kingdom of David's Son will far exceed this and will encompass all the nations of the earth.

Let's examine this more closely. Before David was ruling as king (when he was on the run from King Saul), he and his men, with permission of the priest Ahimelech, ate consecrated bread that was only to be eaten by priests (Lev 24:5–9). This consecrated bread had been set aside, for it was holy (1 Sam 21:6), but this was seen as a permissible exception to the rule.

Jesus uses this acceptable exception to the law of the showbread to show that the Law was not absolute, but it is his authority, as the Son of David, which is absolute. Jesus and his hungry disciples picked heads of wheat and ate them on the Sabbath (Matt 12:1–8). This activity would normally have been legal (Deut 23:25), and it was to be seen as a legitimate exception to the normal practice of the Sabbath. But it was also legitimate for two other reasons: (1) the purpose of the Sabbath and (2) the authority of Jesus. Jesus first said, "The Sabbath was made for man, and not man for the Sabbath" (Mark 2:27). Then he claimed to be "Lord of the Sabbath" (Matt 12:8).

For our purposes here, it is worth noting that when David ate the consecrated bread, he had not yet been crowned king, though this was his God-ordained destiny (1 Sam 16:11–13). Likewise, when Jesus ate the grain on the Sabbath, he had not yet been crowned King, though He had been born to be the King (Matt 2:2).

This period of time before his coronation can also be seen in the language used. In Ezekiel 34:23–24 the Lord says, "Then I will set over them one shepherd, My servant David . . . and My servant David will be prince among them; I the LORD have spoken." Note that the shepherd would be God's servant, "David." Since this was written long after David had died (about four hundred years), Ezekiel is not actually referring to David, but instead to David's promised heir, the Son of David. Also, this coming Son of David, the Messiah, is to "be prince among them." Throughout the Bible, Messiah is referred to as a prince.

Here in Ezekiel 34, he is called a prince (*nasi*). In Isaiah 9:6, he is the "Prince of Peace" (*sar*). In Daniel 9:25, he is "Messiah the Prince" (*nagid*). In the New Testament, in Acts 3:15, Peter boldly proclaimed Jesus as "the Prince of life (*archegon*), the one whom God raised from the dead." And in Acts 5:31, Peter calls him "the one whom God exalted to His right hand as a Prince (*archegon*) and a Savior." These different words translated "prince" refer to a chief, a leader, or one who has a preeminent position, not necessarily a royal prince as we think of the word. Nevertheless, when considered in the light of his lineage as the Son of David, it is clear that he is no mere "leader," but the heir apparent, the Prince who is destined to reign as the King in the future.

JESUS AS THE KING LIKE DAVID IN THE NEW TESTAMENT

What excitement must have filled the hearts of those in Israel who were trusting in God's promises when this long-prophesied King, this Son of David, arrived and began his ministry. Yet there was much confusion. They could not understand why he did not begin to reign as King or establish a kingdom. After the resurrection, the disciples began to understand that though the King had arrived, the Kingdom would come later. So, while Jesus first functioned as the Prophet, and serves now as our princely Priest, all creation longs for the return of the King and the establishment of his Kingdom.

We must always keep in mind the distinction between Jesus's identity and the role in which he is functioning. On the one hand, the kingship of Jesus was proclaimed, and there are many references to his identity as a king throughout his earthly life. Yet, when we search the pages of the New Testament for evidence of kingly activities, there is remarkably little evidence. Some might point in general to the authority with which he taught, performed miracles, and interacted with the religious authorities. They may argue that only a king could claim such authority. However, the authority of God himself was also to characterize the Prophet like Moses. Not only that, but as the Priest like Melchizedek, Jesus is seated at the right hand of the Father. Jesus is never without the full authority of God. There is no messianic office that lacks ultimate authority. In each of his roles, he is always the Son of God and God the Son.

The New Testament evidence argues against his exercise of kingly authority or rule in either the first century or at the present time. Let's examine some of the evidence.

EVIDENCE PRIOR TO THE TRIUMPHAL ENTRY

Some argue Jesus was functioning as King over an invisible kingdom. They point to specific texts in the New Testament. But when we turn to them, we find that they are not persuasive in demonstrating that Jesus functioned as a king in his earthly ministry. Let's begin with passages prior to the triumphal entry.

Direct references. Although Jesus is often referred to as "the Son of David," which suggests his royal identity, he is only explicitly referred to as a king four times prior to the triumphal entry: (1) at the annunciation of his birth, by the angel Gabriel (Luke 1:32–33); (2) while still an infant, by the wise men (Matt 2:2); (3) early in his ministry, by Nathaniel (John 1:49); and (4) on an occasion when the crowd wanted to make him king (John 6:15). The first three of these references, though, are to his identity, rather than to his role. The fourth would have involved kingly activities, but this is a prospect Jesus rejected and from which he withdrew. These are the only direct references to Jesus as a king.

The use of Isaiah 61 in Nazareth. Did Jesus's sermon in Nazareth indicate he was functioning as King?[8] Following his baptism, Luke 4:14 says that "Jesus returned to Galilee in the power of the Spirit." He was preaching in the synagogues and arrived in Nazareth. Here, he took the scroll of Isaiah and began to read from chapter 61: "The Spirit of the LORD is upon Me, because He anointed Me to preach the gospel to the poor. He has sent Me to proclaim release to the captives, and recovery of sight to the blind, to set free those who are oppressed, to proclaim the favorable year of the LORD" (Isa 61:1–2a in Luke 4:18–19). Then he rolled up the scroll, gave it to the attendant, and said, "Today this Scripture has been fulfilled in your hearing" (Luke 4:21).

Jesus is reading from Isaiah 61, which says that the Servant of the Lord was anointed with the Spirit, who was "upon" him. Earlier in Isaiah (42:1), we read that the Servant of the Lord would be anointed with God's Spirit to carry out the same ministry as that outlined in chapter 61. If so, the anointing prophesied in Isaiah 61 must be the anointing, not of a king, but of the Servant of the Lord, the Prophet like Moses.

---

8. Among others, Darrell Bock sees a kingly role of Messiah in Isaiah 61. He says, "The key Christological point in this passage is the reference to Jesus as the promised Messiah (Christ) of the Old Testament, clearly a regal function, something that is his through his connection to David as David's seed." Bock, "The Reign of the Lord Christ," 44.

Not long before he returned to Nazareth, Jesus had been anointed with God's Spirit at his baptism to carry out his ministry. On that occasion, the voice from heaven said, "This is My beloved Son, in whom I am well-pleased" (Matt 3:17). It is virtually identical to the message that would come later from the bright cloud on the Mount of Transfiguration: "This is My beloved Son, with whom I am well-pleased" (Matt 17:5). These declarations seem to reflect Isaiah 42:1–9, and they identify Jesus as the Servant of the Lord (who also is equated with the Prophet like Moses), but not yet the King.

This was not the anointing of a king, but the anointing of the great Prophet. David Ravens comments, "At the anointing of David, the spirit of the Lord came upon him mightily (1 Sam 16:13) yet, perhaps surprisingly, Luke has chosen the anointing of a prophet as the model for the work of Jesus."[9] E. Earle Ellis says, "The Lord's appropriation of this Scripture [i.e., Isa 61] to himself apprised the audience, at least, that he was a prophet."[10] This was not merely his identity here, but he was actually serving in this capacity. In fact, Jesus confirmed this a few verses later when he said of himself, "No prophet is welcome in his hometown" (Luke 4:24).

This understanding is consistent with the selected text that Jesus read. As the passage in Isaiah 61 continues, we find verses that speak of judgment. As Edward E. Hindson says, "Both a 'year of favor' and a 'day of vengeance' are forthcoming. Many claim that Jesus stopped reading after the words 'favorable year' and did not go on to read 'day of vengeance' to indicate a clear distinction between His first and second comings."[11] This is the way Alec Motyer understands it: "What Isaiah sees as a double-faceted ministry the Lord Jesus apportions respectively to His first and second comings, the work of the Servant and of the Anointed Conqueror."[12]

Even if this were the case, we must consider whether kings alone "proclaim . . . the day of vengeance of our God." Was this not also the content of prophetic proclamation? Perhaps too much is made of the break in the passage, for Jesus also proclaimed God's coming judgment.[13]

---

9. Ravens, *Luke and the Restoration of Israel*, 115.
10. Ellis, *The Gospel of Luke*, 97.
11. Hindson, "Isaiah 61:1–6," 991.
12. Motyer, *The Prophecy of Isaiah*, 500.
13. Rather than to see the break in the middle of verse 2, it is far better to understand verses 1–3 as "the Servant/Messiah's announcement of his role" (Oswalt, *The Book of Isaiah*, 562).

Relatively early in his ministry, he proclaimed the danger of failing to heed his message because of riches or the idle pursuits of life (Luke 6:24–25). He pronounced judgment on Chorazin, Bethsaida, and Capernaum in Luke 10:13–15 because of the lack of faith he saw among the people. He pronounced judgment on those who refused to repent in Luke 13:2–5. He proclaimed the vengeance of God upon Jerusalem in Luke 19:43–44. In John 12:47–48, Jesus pronounced the Father's judgment on all who reject him and his message. It is more likely that when Jesus concluded his reading with "to proclaim the favorable year of the LORD"—and did not include "and the day of vengeance of our God"—it was because that next phrase did not suit his purpose for his particular message in Nazareth. He was expressing his compassion for his townspeople.

In Luke 19:11–27, as Jesus and his disciples were ascending the road from Jericho, approaching Jerusalem, the disciples were getting excited, because "they supposed that the kingdom of God was going to appear immediately" (v. 11). In order to correct their understanding, Jesus told a parable about "a certain nobleman [who] went to a distant country to receive a kingdom for himself, and then return" (v. 12). The parable deals with what his servants should have been doing in his absence. But the parable also unmistakably says that the nobleman, although assured of a kingdom, would have to go to a distant country to receive the kingdom, and only then would he return. Of course, the nobleman who would later become a king is none other than Jesus. In some ways, Jesus is a mysterious king. He is a king whose kingdom is yet future. He is a king who is not clamoring for the throne, but one who is patiently awaiting the Father's timing.

THE TRIUMPHAL ENTRY

At the triumphal entry, Psalm 118:26 is quoted by the crowds: "Blessed is He who comes in the name of the LORD," to which they added, "even the King of Israel" (John 12:13; Matt 21:9). Luke records the crowds saying, "Blessed is the King who comes in the name of the LORD" (Luke 19:38). This psalm (Ps 118) does not mention Messiah as a king. But with Jesus riding on the colt of a donkey, the crowd recognized the connection to another Old Testament passage, Zechariah 9:9: "Rejoice greatly, O daughter of Zion! Shout in triumph, O daughter of Jerusalem! Behold, your king is coming to you . . . mounted on a donkey, even on a colt, the foal of a donkey" (Matt 21:5; John 12:14–15). So instead of shouting "Blessed is the One who comes in the name of the LORD," as in Psalm 118, they imported the word "king" from Zechariah 9 and began to shout, "Blessed is the King who comes in the name of the LORD."

There is no question the crowds wanted a messianic king, for they had previously tried to make him a king (John 6:15). The curious feature is that by putting these two passages together, the message is not what they think. They wanted his rule immediately, but Psalm 118 speaks about the Messiah being rejected by the leadership of the nation. His rejection is like the rejection of Moses and the prophets, but it is preeminently the rejection of the Suffering Servant of Isaiah. Isaiah 53:3 had foretold this very response on the part of the nation's leadership.

Psalm 118 seems to take the joy associated with Israel's deliverance from Egypt as a metaphor for the spiritual deliverance Messiah will bring *despite* his rejection, or even *because* of his rejection. It speaks of Messiah as "the stone which the builders rejected" (v. 22). Nevertheless, the day of his rejection is referred to as "the day which the LORD has made," and we are admonished to "rejoice and be glad in it" (v. 24).

Why should we rejoice on the occasion of Messiah's rejection? Because it would be the day of salvation (Zech 9:9), and it will portend his becoming "the chief corner stone" and the reigning king. It is this which makes Good Friday truly good! Jesus is a mysterious king—a king, to be sure, but "disguised" in his role as the Suffering Servant, humble and mounted on a donkey.

The ancient rabbis recognized messianic significance in the person and activities of Moses, believing he foreshadowed a humble redeemer. In rabbinic literature we read:

> Rabbi Berekiah said in the name of Rabbi Isaac, "As the first redeemer was, so will be the last redeemer. What was said of the first redeemer? (Exodus 4). 'And Moses took his wife and his sons and placed them upon the donkey' (Ex 4:20). Thus it shall be with the last redeemer, as it is said, 'Humble and riding upon a donkey'" (Zch 9:9).[14]

The passage in Zechariah 9 continues in the next verse (v. 10) to speak of the Messianic King's military power, His establishment of peace among the nations, and the worldwide scope of his dominion. But this

---

14. *Eccl. Rab.* 1.28, cited and translated by Postell, "Typology in the Old Testament," 161.

verse, verse 10, is not quoted by the crowds or by the Gospels. Knut Heim says that for those familiar with the passage in Zechariah, the conclusion would be "that the evangelists [i.e., those who wrote the Gospels] may have intended to suggest that Christ had not yet come to rule the whole earth."[15] This is remarkably similar to Jesus's use of Isaiah 61:1–2a in the synagogue in Nazareth. Therefore, the reference to Jesus as a king during the triumphal entry reflects his true identity, to be sure, and also the desires of the people to make him a king on that occasion. But it does not indicate the actual reign of Jesus as a king at that time.

The triumphal entry should have raised the question, "What kind of a king is this?" He was not a king to reign in power and majesty, but a Servant to be rejected and to suffer. The power, majesty, and glorious kingdom would come, but not before the rejection, suffering, and death. The "builders" had to reject the stone before it could become "the chief corner stone" (Ps 118:22). Many today have a similar attitude to the crowds of Jesus's time: They want him to reign as king at present. Instead, he exercises all authority as our great High Priest and soon-coming King. The Kingdom itself, however, is not yet here.

FOLLOWING THE TRIUMPHAL ENTRY

What evidence do we find of Jesus's role as a king following the triumphal entry? The religious leaders brought the charge against Jesus that he claimed to be the Messiah, a king (Luke 23:2). When asked by Pilate directly if he was King of the Jews, Jesus answered that he was.[16] Jesus was then mocked for this claim by the religious leaders.[17]

Near the end of Matthew's Gospel, we read that the Romans placed a sign on the cross saying, "This is Jesus the King of the Jews" (Matt 27:37). This seems to be parallel with a passage near the beginning of Matthew. In Matthew 2:2, in the story of the birth and infancy of Jesus, the wise men came to Jerusalem and asked, "Where is He who is born King of the Jews?" Both at his birth and at his death, Jesus was proclaimed "King of the Jews." Both declarations were made in Jerusalem. Both declarations were made by Gentiles. At his birth, it was made by wise men from the East, and at his death, by Roman soldiers from the West. He was no more

---

15. Heim, "The Perfect King of Psalm 72," 247.
16. Matt 27:11; Mark 15:2, 9, 12; Luke 23:3; John 18:13.
17. Matt 27:29; Mark 15:18; Luke 23:37; John 19:3.

functioning as the King of the Jews when he was on the cross than when he was in the manger. His victory was that of the Son of God, the Servant of Isaiah 53. All these references are to his identity as King, not to his reign as King.

ACTS AND THE EPISTLES

In Acts and the Epistles there are only three references to Jesus as King, yet no indication of a current kingly role. The first is in Acts 17 when Paul was in Thessalonica, and "evil men" brought a charge before the city authorities that Jason extended hospitality to Paul and Silas. On this occasion, they reported that Jason, Paul, and Silas were saying "that there is another king, Jesus" (Acts 17:7). This is the only reference to Jesus as a king in Acts, and it was for the purpose of bringing slanderous charges of treason against the believers.

The second reference is in 1 Timothy 6. Paul writes:

> I charge you in the presence of God, who gives life to all things, and of Jesus the Messiah, who testified the good confession before Pontius Pilate, that you keep the commandment without stain or reproach until the appearing of our Lord Jesus the Messiah, which He will bring about at the proper time—He who is the blessed and only Sovereign, the King of kings and Lord of lords. (1 Tim 6:13–15)

Once again, his identity as King is proclaimed, yet he is not to reign as King "until . . . the proper time." This indicates that Messiah is not currently exercising his power as monarch, but one day, "which He will bring about at the proper time," he will return as "King of kings and Lord of lords." In Hebrews 1:8, we read of the Son's throne and "the righteous scepter [which] is the scepter of His kingdom." It is striking that there are only these few references to Jesus as King in Acts and all the Epistles, and they each point to his future reign.[18]

Some argue that the present activity of God in salvation and in the lives of believers is evidence of the kingdom. God's work in salvation is certainly evidence of the sovereignty of God and of his universal rule over the earth, but does it speak of the Messianic Kingdom? Some encourage

---

18. An examination of Colossians 1:13, which speaks of "the kingdom of His beloved Son," must wait for our study of the Messianic Kingdom in the New Testament in chapter 17. See discussion of Colossians 1:13 on page 219.

believers to "make Jesus king of your life." What is intended is not literally to "make Jesus king," but instead, this idea emphasizes our need to submit our lives to his authority. What do we find in Acts and in the Epistles?

Jesus taught his disciples about the Kingdom of God for forty days following the resurrection, yet when the Spirit was poured out on believers at Pentecost, there was no mention of the Kingdom. Peter concludes his sermon on that occasion with the declaration that God has made Jesus "both Lord and Messiah," but there is no mention of him as King (Acts 2:36). In Acts 2:47, we are told that the Lord was daily adding to the disciples's number, but nothing is said about the growth of the Kingdom. In the next chapter, following the healing of the lame man at the gate of the temple, Peter preached his second sermon. In his sermon, he never connected this miraculous healing to "kingdom authority" or to "kingdom power." Instead, Peter's appeal to his audience is based upon the authority Jesus exercised as the Prophet like Moses (Acts 3:22–23).

In Acts, Jesus would ascend from Jerusalem, and Jerusalem would be the city in which the promise of the Father would be fulfilled with the coming of the Spirit. It was not only in Jerusalem, but in the very courts of the temple that the church was birthed, and it was from this center that the Word would go forth into all the world. In fact, "the Word" is almost personified in Acts, as it seems to advance under its own power. In actuality, the Word of God was advancing by the power and direction of the Spirit. Of course, people (such as Peter and Paul) played their very important parts, but the Spirit was constantly advancing "the Word." David Peterson says:

> Word and Spirit are presented as the primary agents of the reigning Lord in forming and growing his church. Human characters have an important role to play in the story, as those who have encountered the heavenly Christ and who act as Spirit-empowered proclaimers of his word. Acts implies that the Lord Jesus will continue to fulfill his purpose in the world, even in the absence of apostles and prophetic figures such as Stephen, Philip and Paul (cf. Acts 20:28–32). The same word on the lips of Spirit-directed believers is able to reach new people groups and break through cultural and religious barriers to grow the church in ever-widening circles (e.g., Acts 8:4; 11:19–21).[19]

Even though he speaks of the "reigning Lord," in context, he is speaking of Jesus as the authority, the Head of the church, rather than as the

---

19. Peterson, *The Acts of the Apostles*, 48–49.

King of his Kingdom. Supporting evidence for Peterson's claim is found throughout the book of Acts, but he highlights four texts in particular:

- Acts 6:7—"The word of God kept on spreading, and the number of the disciples continued to increase greatly in Jerusalem, and a great many of the priests were becoming obedient to the faith."
- Acts 12:24—"But the word of God continued to grow and to be multiplied."
- Acts 13:49—"And the word of the Lord was being spread through the whole region."
- Acts 19:20—"So the word of the Lord was growing mightily and prevailing."[20]

The emphasis in all four of these texts is that the Word of God increased, multiplied, spread, and prevailed over opposition. May we not see the Word as an agent of the High Priest, Jesus?

The progress of the Word is also expressed as a part of the inexorable progress of the sovereign plan and activity of God.[21] One scholar points out that Acts does not have a single human protagonist. He says, "In Luke-Acts no single character remains on the human stage, but there is an overarching purpose, the purpose of God."[22] Another claims, "The plan of God is a distinctively Lukan theme which undergirds the whole of Luke-Acts, becoming especially prominent in the speeches of Acts."[23]

Interestingly, with this emphasis on the progress of the Word, the work of the Spirit, and the accomplishment of the plan of God, we do not read of the progress of the Kingdom. Nowhere in Acts do we find the language or the theology of the presence of a current form of the Kingdom. With references in the Epistles to Jesus as a king occurring only in 1 Timothy 6:15 and Hebrews 1:8 (and then only with regard to the future), neither do we find this emphasis in the Epistles, either.

---

20. See also, Acts 4:29, 31; 6:2, 4; 8:4, 14, 25; 11:1, 14; 13:5, 7; 44, 46, 48, etc.

21. See Peterson, "Luke's Theological Enterprise," 521–44.

22. Tannehill, "The Story of Israel within the Lukan Narrative," 325. See also Squires, "The Plan of God," 19–39.

23. Squires, *The Plan of God in Luke-Acts*, 1.

REVELATION

In the salutation of the book of Revelation, Jesus is referred to as "the faithful witness, the firstborn of the dead, and the ruler of the kings of the earth" (1:5). In the first case, John is using three descriptive phrases to state the identity of Jesus. Some see in them a chronological arrangement. (1) "The faithful witness" can just as easily be translated "the faithful martyr" and may be a reference to his death. (2) "The first-born of the dead" most likely refers to his post-resurrection life. (3) "The ruler of the kings of the earth" may well refer to the exercise of his sovereign power in the future. Whether or not this chronological scheme is adopted, this verse does not appear to state that he is currently exercising his authority as king.

In the next verse, John addresses his readers as those whom "He has made . . . to be a kingdom of priests to His God and Father" (v. 6). In this case, the "kingdom of priests" language is taken from Exodus 19:5, which is also used in 1 Peter 2:9-10, as we have seen. There it was addressed to Jewish believers in Jesus, and this is also conceivably the case with John's Revelation. It is clear that the book was addressed to seven churches in Asia (1:4). The use of the word "churches" does not provide an indication of the ethnicity of the members. The heavy use of the Hebrew Scriptures in the book has persuaded some that the recipients were Jewish believers in Jesus (as is true with Hebrews, James, 1 and 2 Peter, and possibly the Epistles of John). Richard Longenecker says, "That the Apocalypse of John stems from a Jewish Christian milieu and was addressed to Jewish Christians seems beyond all reasonable doubt."[24] The quotation from Exodus 19:5 in Revelation 1:6 and in 1 Peter only strengthens this understanding.

Even so, the Jewishness of the recipients is not decisive for the argument. The point is that in Revelation 1:5-7, Jesus is presented as having "released us from our sins by His blood," and "He has made us to be a kingdom, priests to His God and Father," even as in 1 Peter 2.

By the time we reach Revelation 5:9-10, he has prepared a people for his Kingdom from "every tribe and tongue and people and nation."

---

24. Longenecker, *Biblical Exegesis in the Apostolic Period*, 194. It has been noted that of its 404 verses, 278 contain references to the Hebrew Scriptures. There are more than five hundred Old Testament passages used in one way or another in the book. It is also worth noting that these allusions reflect Hebrew texts rather than Greek texts. John's understanding of the Old Testament is not to read New Testament theology into the Old, but to recognize the messianic nature of Old Testament revelation. See Johnson, "Revelation," 411.

More precisely, he has prepared a people for his kingdom, beginning with Israel, as in 1 Peter 2 (and perhaps Rev 1), but extending to all the families of the earth, as in Revelation 5.

The Lord gives John (and us) the outline for the book in Revelation 1:19: "Therefore write the things which you have seen, and the things which are, and the things which will take place after these things." To some extent, the book is laid out chronologically. In chapter 1, following the superscription (vv. 1–3) and the salutation (vv. 4–8), we find "the things which [John] has seen" (i.e., in the past). In the messages to the churches (chs. 2–3), we find "the things which are" (present tense). In chapters 4–22, we find "the things which will take place after these things" (future tense).[25]

Everything in chapters 4–22 is future; it is prophetic. The vast majority of it refers to the judgments of God on the earth during the Tribulation. References to Jesus as King may be found in 11:15; 17:14; and 19:16. In Revelation 11:15 we read: "Then the seventh angel sounded; and there were loud voices in heaven, saying, 'The kingdom of the world has become the kingdom of our Lord and of His Messiah; and He will reign forever and ever.'" The Kingdom will be discussed later, but here, it is important to see that his reign is yet future.[26] As Robert Thomas says, "The perspective of the verb tense is a point after the action of the seventh trumpet will have run its course, . . . but the verb views it as an already accomplished fact, . . . convey[ing] the absolute certainty of these future transactions by speaking of them as already past."[27]

In Revelation 15, we find a prelude to the bowl judgments in chapter 16. Here, we find a large assemblage of those who have remained faithful during the Tribulation, most likely through their martyrdom. We are told that they sing "the song of Moses, the bond-servant of God, and the song of the Lamb" (v. 3). The lyrics are given in verses 3 and 4. When we compare them with the Song of Moses in Exodus 15 (particularly v. 11), we find that the two songs are singing the same message with somewhat different lyrics. All of this is pointing to Jesus as the new, and ultimate, Moses.

In Revelation 16, the bowl judgments consist of a series of plagues on the earth. Michelle Fletcher observes: "The death of the firstborn is

---

25. For a defense of this verse as a three-stage outline of the book, see R. Thomas, *Revelation 8–22*, 113–16.

26. R. Thomas argues that attempts to interpret "the kingdom of our Lord" as the church fail on grammatical grounds. See R. Thomas, *Revelation 8–22*, 105–6.

27. R. Thomas, *Revelation 8–22*, 106.

strikingly absent from Revelation's plague cycle." She also notes: "Jesus is designated firstborn from the dead in the opening section (Rev. 1:5)."[28]

In Revelation 17:14 we read: "These will wage war against the Lamb, and the Lamb will overcome them, because He is Lord of lords and King of kings, and those who are with Him are the called and chosen and faithful." Thomas writes:

> Paul applies the title [Lord of lords and King of kings] to God the Father in 1 Tim. 6:15, but in Revelation the Son frequently has the same titles as the Father. The title "Lord of lords" occurs earliest in Deut. 10:17 as a title for God. Daniel 2:47 quotes Nebuchadnezzar as calling Daniel's God 'a Lord of kings'. These two titles marking the Lamb as supreme over all earthly power recur in 19:16 where at His return to earth in triumph the name appears on the part of His cloak that covers His thigh.[29]

The point is that in Revelation, Jesus defeats the forces of Antichrist (the ten-nation confederacy), pours out judgments on the earth, and takes the throne of David in Jerusalem where his reign is everlasting. He ends the rebellion not just of the nations (Ps 110), but also of Satan. This is when he takes the throne of David and reigns as King of kings and Lord of lords.

WHAT KIND OF KING WILL HE BE?

In C. S. Lewis's classic tale, *The Chronicles of Narnia*, he has Mr. Beaver telling the children, who have stumbled into this new world of Narnia, about Aslan. Aslan is the king, who is on the move, coming back to Narnia to rescue and redeem. Mr. Beaver says:

> "Don't you know who is the King of Beasts? Aslan is a lion—the Lion, the great Lion." "Ooh! Said Susan, "I'd thought he was a man. Is he—quite safe? I shall feel rather nervous about meeting a lion." "That you will, dearie, and no mistake," said Mrs. Beaver; "if there's anyone who can appear before Aslan without their knees knocking, they're either braver than most or else just silly." "Then he isn't safe?" said Lucy. "Safe?" said Mr. Beaver; "don't you hear what Mrs. Beaver tells you? Who said anything about safe? 'Course he isn't safe. But he's good. He's the King I tell you."[30]

28. Fletcher, "Reading Exodus in Revelation," 196–98.
29. R. Thomas, *Revelation 8–22*, 302.
30. Lewis, *The Lion, the Witch and the Wardrobe*, 85–86.

When Jesus comes as the King like David, he will come as the Lion of the Tribe of Judah, awesome in his power and majesty, yet righteous and full of grace and mercy to his own.

He will be a King like David, but he will also be a King like Melchizedek. Hebrews 7:1–2 says that Melchizedek, whose name means "king of righteousness," and who was also "king of Salem" (Gen 14:18), points to Jesus. As King like Melchizedek, Jesus will be a king of righteousness and also a king of peace.

In the words of Jeremiah:

> "Behold, the days are coming," declares the Lord, "when I will raise up for David a righteous Branch; and He will reign as king and act wisely and do justice and righteousness in the land. In His days Judah will be saved, and Israel will dwell securely; and this is His name by which He will be called, 'The Lord our Righteousness.'" (Jer 23:5–6)

Here we have the Son of David, and he is the Messiah, for he is called "righteous Branch," a messianic title. Like David, he will reign as a king, but like Melchizedek (Heb., "King of Righteousness"), he will do justice and righteousness (Heb., *tsedek*). He will be "The Lord our Righteousness."

As the King like David, he will be the Lion of the Tribe of Judah; as the King and Priest like Melchizedek, he will be as the Lamb of God, who has taken away the sin of the world and is interceding for his own. In his very person, the lion and the lamb will lie down together. In the words of Psalm 85:10, "lovingkindness and truth have met together; righteousness and peace have kissed each other."

Jesus is King, and those of us who follow him today follow freely, not under compulsion. We owe literally everything to him! The Spirit comforts us in his absence, and we are to pray for the coming of his Kingdom, when his perfect will is to be done on earth as in heaven. That day will come, when Jesus returns, takes his throne in Jerusalem, and establishes righteousness and peace. As we await his return, may he find us faithful with the resources he has entrusted to us!

THE ANOINTING OF JESUS

Before we conclude, we should consider the anointing of Jesus. Jesus was anointed with the Spirit at his baptism, and this is the anointing appropriate for prophets. Priests and kings were anointed with oil. Jesus, however, was never anointed with oil. Oil is often a symbol of the Holy Spirit in Scripture. This would seem to suggest that the anointing with the Spirit is of a higher order than an anointing with oil. Anointment with the Spirit would apparently render the anointing with oil superfluous for the offices of priest and king.

Jesus's role as the Prophet like Moses, the Servant of the Lord, is foundational. The roles or offices of Priest and King are derived from that of the Prophet. Had he not come as the Prophet to offer deliverance through his suffering and death, he would not have qualified to serve as our Priest. Had he not come as the Prophet, he would not have had the right to reign. The many thousands that gather around the throne will sing, "Worthy is the Lamb that was slain to receive power and riches and wisdom and might and honor and glory and blessing" (Rev 5:12). He was the Lamb when he was slain. In this, he was the Prophet like Moses, the Servant of the Lord.

CONCLUSION

Understanding the identities of the Messiah and the way he fulfills these three roles is significant for truly understanding his person and work. Rather than learning of Jesus in the Gospels and glancing back to the Old Testament to see a few isolated prophecies that support what we find in the Gospels, we have followed the development of these messianic roles through the Old Testament, so that when Jesus bursts upon the scene, we see him, not differently, but from a new perspective.

His earthly ministry can hardly be understood apart from an appreciation for his ministry as the Prophet like Moses. Moses was a towering figure in the story of Israel. As Moses was sent by God to deliver Israel from bondage, so Jesus was sent from the Father to deliver men and women from bondage to sin. All the prophets after Moses served the Covenant established at Mount Sinai. Moses delivered the Law, and the prophets called Israel back to covenant faithfulness. God had revealed the Law to Moses through a very close and personal relationship.

How much greater was the relationship Jesus had with his Father? Jesus fulfilled the Law perfectly. He taught with authority. He demonstrated his authority over nature, sickness, death, and demons in his miracles. The New Covenant was established through his atoning death.

He is the Prophet *par excellence*. We must listen to him, for through the New Testament, he still speaks the very words of God.

His present ministry at the right hand of the Father must be understood in light of his ministry as the Priest like Melchizedek. If Melchizedek was the first of a superior and alternative priesthood to that of Aaron, how much more superior is the priesthood of Jesus! His present high priestly ministry of preparing a people for his Kingdom, interceding for them, advocating for them, and providing them with spiritual blessings is essential for their lives as citizens of his Kingdom. In the parable of the talents, the nobleman told his servants to "occupy til I come" (Luke 19:13, KJV). But believers are more than a colony of occupation. They are an insurgency. Jesus gave his instructions in Acts 1:8: ". . . you shall be My witnesses."

The blessings he bestows are the gift of salvation, the indwelling presence of the Holy Spirit, and the blessing of spiritual gifts, which have been given to build up the body of believers among "all the families of the earth" (Gen 12:3). "For we do not have a high priest who cannot sympathize with our weaknesses, but one who has been tempted in all things as *we are, yet* without sin" (Heb 4:15). Under the authority of our great High Priest, we serve as priests as well.

This chapter has attempted to demonstrate that his reign is yet future. This future ministry in power and glory as the King of kings is to begin with his Second Coming. With his coming, every knee will bow, and every tongue confess that he is Lord (Phil 2:9–10). After defeating and judging his enemies, he will set up his throne in the temple of Jerusalem and rule Israel and the nations with righteousness and justice. His rule will restore all creation, eradicate the effects of sin, and usher in a new order of righteousness and peace. This is the blessed hope. This should be the primary object of our prayer (Matt 6:9–10).

The certainty of his soon coming gives confidence in the face of suffering and opposition to the gospel and comfort in times of loss. The citizenship we have held, perhaps for many years, will allow us finally to come home. In the meantime, we are to be constantly watching, always ready for the return of our King—Shiloh, him to whom it belongs!

As the Prophet, his death on the cross paid the price for our salvation, and we have been freed from the penalty of sin. As the Priest, not only has he saved us from the penalty of sin, but he continues our salvation, for we are being saved from the power of sin. Finally, one glorious day, when he comes as King, our salvation will be complete, for we will be saved from the presence of sin. As Hebrews 9:28 (HCSB) says, "Messiah also, having been offered once to bear the sins of many, will appear a second time for salvation without reference to sin, to those who eagerly await Him." It is not coincidental that the angel told Joseph that Mary's child would be called Jesus [Yeshúa], "for He will save [salvation, *yeshuáh*] His people from their sins" (Matt 1:21).

God promised he would raise up a Prophet (Deut 18:15, 18), he promised to raise up a Priest (1 Sam 2:35), and he promised to raise up a King (2 Sam 7:12; Jer 23:5; 30:9). These would be the roles of the one, long-anticipated Son of David, whom God would raise up (2 Sam 23:1; Amos 9:11).

Philip Bliss composed many gospel songs that are still sung today. He was associated with Dwight L. Moody, the great evangelist in Chicago in the last half of the 1800s. Bliss wrote a hymn in 1876, shortly before his death. It was introduced when he was providing the music for an evangelist conducting a service at the state prison in Jackson, Michigan. The sermon, which was based on Isaiah 53, dealt with the crucifixion of Jesus. The title of the sermon was "Man of Sorrows." In thinking about what music would be appropriate, Bliss was struck by the paradox of Jesus's suffering and death being the occasion for our rejoicing, for it provided salvation! He also thought of the paradox of this Suffering Servant—so mistreated, so humiliated, so horribly abused, even to death—returning as our reigning King. The song begins:

> Man of Sorrows! What a name
> For the Son of God, who came
> Ruined sinners to reclaim.
> Hallelujah! What a Savior!

This was the Prophet like Moses. The last verse speaks of the King:

> When he comes, our glorious King,
> all his ransomed home to bring,
> then anew this song we'll sing:
> Hallelujah! What a Savior![31]

---

31. Bliss, "Hallelujah! What a Savior!" Also as, "'Man of Sorrows,' What a Name."

# Part 4

The Messianic Kingdom

SOME HOUSES ARE BUILT with "mud rooms" or vestibules, where you can take off your muddy boots, hang up your coat, or shed your soaked shirt. You are shielded from outside conditions, but you aren't yet really in the house. C. S. Lewis once criticized other novelists who wrote from an entirely secular perspective. He said their problem was that they did not "see this world as the vestibule of eternity."[32]

Our journey through the Scriptures in these pages should give us this very perspective. Our lives at present, as citizens of the future Messianic Kingdom, are like these mud rooms or vestibules. Here, we remove our dirty boots and the clothes that are stained and soiled, and we prepare to enter the house, the Kingdom for which we have been saved. Paul wrote to the Philippians: "For our citizenship is in heaven, from which also we eagerly wait for a Savior, the Lord Jesus the Messiah" (3:20).

The Messianic Kingdom is a massively important topic with many interpretations and competing opinions. Many biblical passages deal with the subject, and they give rise to what can seem to be a tangled jungle of interpretations and conclusions. Books on the topic of the Kingdom usually exceed four hundred pages, and one particular project is a three-volume work of 2,175 pages.[33] Obviously, we will not be able to answer every question or deal with every verse of Scripture. Instead, we will cover enough to map out a strategy for thinking about the Kingdom,

---

32. Lewis, *God in the Dock*, 221. Appreciation is expressed to Randy Newman for calling this to my attention. See Newman, *Mere Evangelism*, 79.

33. See Peters, *The Theocratic Kingdom of Our Lord Jesus*; McClain, *The Greatness of the Kingdom*; Vlach, *He Will Reign Forever*; Woods, *The Coming Kingdom*.

consider what I believe to be the most compelling position, and stimulate interest for further reading and study.

Our objective is to deal with the Scriptures in a clear and consistent way so that we can arrive at biblically sound conclusions about the Messianic Kingdom. I believe the most helpful approach is to study the Kingdom from the perspective of Messiah's roles, as we have examined them to this point. To begin with, a brief review of the Messianic King and his Kingdom in the Old Testament may be helpful.

16

The Messianic Kingdom in the Hebrew Scriptures

THE MESSIANIC KINGDOM SHOULD be understood against the background of Israel as a theocracy. Following the Exodus from Egypt, Israel was established as a theocratic nation in which God reigned as King. This was the only time in history in which God directly ruled a nation. Doug Bookman makes an important distinction: "That theocratic relationship, formed by Yahweh with Israel, was unique to human history. Thus, the term [i.e., theocracy] should not be taken as descriptive of God's perpetual rule over all creation."[1]

Israel's theocracy began with the Mosaic Covenant, ratified in Exodus 24:1–8 at Mount Sinai. Later, his enthronement as a cloud displaying his glory in the Holy of Holies of the tabernacle is dramatically portrayed in Exodus 40:34–38. As King, he appointed human leaders to implement his directions and to mediate his authority. Initially, he personally appointed leaders such as Moses, Aaron, and Joshua, and later, the judges, kings, and prophets of the nation. However, as Bookman notes that "throughout the years when the Glory-cloud was resident in the tabernacle/temple, every individual in that succession of human leaders was

---

1. Bookman, "The Nature of the Old Testament Theocracy," 352.

obligated to acknowledge that he was in fact ruling only as the proxy of King Yahweh."[2]

The leaders God appointed for the nation were not simply to govern the people or to ensure obedience, but God also desired a personal relationship with the people of Israel based on faith. Isaiah used the imagery of a vineyard to express God's passion for Israel to produce a harvest of faith in him and in his salvation. The goal was spiritual fruitfulness, but the vineyard was unproductive.

Nevertheless, this theocratic relationship continued until God departed from his throne in the temple and his cloud of glory left through the East Gate, as depicted in the vision of Ezekiel (Ezek 9–11). The theocracy lasted almost a thousand years, from the time when Israel was gathered at Mount Sinai (1446 BC) until the final days before the Babylonian conquest and subsequent exile (570 BC).

Following Judah's return from the Babylonian Captivity, the Second Temple was constructed to serve the spiritual needs of the people. Priests served once again in the temple, and the required sacrifices were offered, but these priests were false shepherds. God also sent prophets to proclaim his Word to the people, but too often their words fell on deaf ears.

In time, Messiah would come, but just as many of Israel's previous leaders had rejected the prophets, so they would reject God's Son. Not surprisingly, in Matthew 21:33–41, Jesus took up Isaiah's imagery of the vineyard and spoke of the wicked tenants who were responsible for it. In Matthew 21:43, Jesus took the spiritual authority of the nation from the Sanhedrin and chief priests and transferred it to the apostles.[3]

God's presence visited the temple again in the person of his Son. New Testament Scripture indicates that, even as the Shekinah had been a visible representation of God's presence, Jesus was that visible representation as well. Speaking of Jesus, the author of Hebrews wrote, "He is the radiance of His glory and the exact representation of His nature" (Heb 1:3). The word translated "radiance" is the Greek word[4] that means "radiance" or "effulgence, in the sense of brightness from a source."[5]

At Jesus's baptism and the transfiguration, God said, "This is My beloved Son in whom [or, with whom] I am well-pleased" (Matt 3:17; 17:5).

---

2. Bookman, "The Nature of the Old Testament Theocracy," 353.

3. See D. Turner, "Matthew 21:43 and the Future of Israel," 46–61; and D. Turner, *Matthew*, 515–20.

4. ἀπαύγασμα, *apaugasma*.

5. *BDAG*, 99.

In John 1:14 we read, "And the Word became flesh, and dwelt[6] among us, and we saw His glory, glory as of the only begotten from the Father, full of grace and truth." Second Peter 1:16–18 indicates that Jesus received this glory from the Father at his baptism, even as at his transfiguration, when "the Majestic Glory" said, "This is My beloved Son with whom I am well-pleased." Simon Kistemaker concludes that Peter and the apostles "personally saw Jesus' glory and honor from the time of his baptism to the day of his ascension."[7] Certainly, we can say that Jesus fulfilled a similar function as the Shekinah.

After Jesus condemned the scribes and Pharisees in Matthew 23, as he left the temple, he declared the temple devoid of God's presence (v. 38): "Behold, your house is being left to you desolate!" With his departure from the temple, God's presence left the temple, following the course of the departure of the Shekinah in Ezekiel 9–11. Jesus then taught from the Mount of Olives.

Along this line, the rending of the veil in the temple following the crucifixion was not to reveal that access to God was now open to all, although this is true, but to reveal that the temple was desolate, devoid of God's indwelling presence. "House" is used here in Matthew 23:28 the same way it is used in Acts 2:2, namely, of the temple. This verse in Matthew seems to be clearly referring to the temple itself, and not to the nation as a whole, as devoid of God's presence.

Through the New Testament Scriptures, which were written under the authority of the apostles and with the inspiration of the Holy Spirit, we see that God has preserved a remnant of Israel who are, to this day, placing their faith in Messiah Jesus. There is also the promise that the time will come when Israel, as the vineyard of the Lord, will be much more fruitful. Read the rest of the story of Isaiah's vineyard in Isaiah 27:2–6.

Yet this was not the end of the story. As we have seen, Ezekiel also foresaw the time when God would once again rule the nation, and the cloud of glory would return from the east (Ezek 43:1–9). This time, God's rule would be exercised by the Messiah. The Kingdom of Messiah was envisioned throughout the Scriptures. Let's look at some specific examples.

---

6. ἐσκήνωσεν, *eskenosen*, may allude to God's dwelling in the tabernacle.
7. Kistemaker, *Exposition of the Epistles of Peter and of the Epistle of Jude*, 266.

GENESIS 49:10

In Genesis 49:10 Jacob prophesied, "The scepter [i.e., the right to rule] shall not depart from Judah, nor the ruler's staff from between his feet, until Shiloh [or, Him to whom it belongs] comes, and to him shall be the obedience of the peoples." So, a king is to come from Judah—one to whom a special authority will be given.

NUMBERS 24:17

In Numbers 24:17 Balaam prophesied, "A star shall come forth from Jacob, a scepter shall rise from Israel, and shall crush through the forehead of Moab, and tear down all the sons of Sheth." Again, we have reference to a scepter or "a ruler's staff" and to crushing a head, as in Genesis 3:15, where it is Satan's head that is crushed.

DEUTERONOMY 33:7

In Genesis 49:10, Jacob had said this king would come from Judah, and this promise reappears in Deuteronomy 33:7: "Hear, O LORD, the voice of Judah, and bring him [i.e., this king, the One to whom it belongs] to his people. . . . And may You be a help against his adversaries." These passages are speaking of the arrival of an ultimate King from Judah who would crush the head of the serpent and of his followers. After defeating the forces of wickedness, he will take his throne and rule with righteousness.

EXODUS 15:17

In the Song of Moses and of Israel in Exodus 15, Moses declares, "You will bring them and plant them in the mountain of Your inheritance, the place, O LORD, which You have made for Your dwelling, the sanctuary, O LORD, which Your hands have established" (v. 17). Jon Levenson points out that this "mountain of Your inheritance" is Mount Moriah—the temple Mount, "God's throne and his palace, from which he exercises cosmic sovereignty."[8] As Craig Blaising says, "Israel, then, becomes the

---

8. Levenson, *Sinai and Zion*, 136.

focal point for God's relations with humanity and His providence over the rest of creation."⁹

ISAIAH

By the time of the prophets, there was great anticipation of the Messianic Kingdom. This is especially true of Isaiah, although his only direct reference to this kingdom is found in Isaiah 9:7: "There will be no end to the increase of *His* government or of peace, on the throne of David and over his kingdom, to establish it and to uphold it with justice and righteousness from then on and forevermore. The zeal of the LORD of hosts will accomplish this." Even though this is Isaiah's only direct reference to the Kingdom, Isaiah and most of the other prophets have much to say about the coming of the King and the establishment of his Kingdom. In his book about Isaiah and God's Kingdom, Andrew Abernethy wrote, "Though the term 'kingdom' occurs infrequently in Isaiah, the concept is integral throughout."[10]

In the future, Messiah will come again, and when he comes, he will come with judgment against all unrighteousness and the nations that oppose Israel. Isaiah says, "He will strike the earth with the rod of His mouth, and with the breath of His lips He will slay the wicked" (Isa 11:4c). This is a frequent theme in Isaiah. In fact, Abernethy says, "The book of Isaiah regularly associates the throne of the Davidic king with the role of executing justice."[11]

Isaiah 35:5–10 presents a powerful and dramatic picture of the Kingdom:

> Then the eyes of the blind will be opened, and the ears of the deaf will be unstopped. Then the lame will leap like a deer, and the tongue of the mute will shout for joy. For waters will break forth in the wilderness, and streams in the Arabah. The scorched land will become a pool and the thirsty ground springs of water; in the haunt of jackals, its resting place, grass *becomes* reeds and rushes. A highway will be there, a roadway, and it will be called the Highway of Holiness. The unclean will not travel on it, but it *will* be for him who walks *that* way, and fools will not wander *on it*. No lion will be there, nor will any vicious beast go up on it;

---

9. Blaising, "The Kingdom of God in the Old Testament," 219.
10. Abernethy, *The Book of Isaiah and God's Kingdom*, 2.
11. Abernethy, *The Book of Isaiah and God's Kingdom*, 16.

these will not be found there. But the redeemed will walk *there*, and the ransomed of the LORD will return, and come with joyful shouting to Zion, with everlasting joy upon their heads. They will find gladness and joy, and sorrow and sighing will flee away.

This anticipation of the Messianic Kingdom runs like a river through the Hebrew Scriptures. Stephen Dempster notes, "Significantly, a key concept in the last narrative section of the Tanakh [i.e., the Old Testament] . . . is the term 'kingdom' (of God). The Tanakh ends on a note of hope, pointing to the future."[12] Of course, he is speaking of what we are calling the Messianic Kingdom. William Barrick comments: "The Lord's plan for His kingdom dominates history from the first creation to the new creation. The Old Testament predicts a coming earthly kingdom, a kingdom that will be fulfilled someday through Jesus Christ, the second Adam, and the One who fulfills the covenants of Scripture."[13]

INITIAL JUDGMENT

The Kingdom begins, however, with judgment against the Lord's enemies; it begins with justice and righteousness. This judgment is an expression both of God's holiness and his love for his people. As he crushes the forces of evil, he is zealously guarding and protecting his own.[14]

The prophet Zechariah describes the nations gathering to fight against Jerusalem in a great end-times battle. We call it the battle of Armageddon, but it appears to be fought on three fronts: Bozrah in Edom, Jerusalem, and Armageddon.[15] It is possible to understand the conflict in Bozrah as judgment on Esau and his descendants, as similar language is used both in Genesis 27:15 and in Isaiah 63:1. As Esau's garments were stained with blood so that they had an aroma "like the smell of the field" (Gen 27:27), so would Messiah's as he comes from battle.[16] If so, perhaps

---

12. Dempster, *Dominion and Dynasty*, 49.

13. Barrick, "The Kingdom of God in the Old Testament," 173.

14. Romans 2:9–10 indicates that judgment will come to some in Israel in the first place, and also to the nations.

15. For Bozrah, see Isa 63:1–6; Jer 49:22 (also Rev 19:6); for Jerusalem, see Zech 12; 14:1–5, 12–15; and for Har-Mageddon, see Rev 16:16 (also 14:19–20).

16. Zakovitch emends בגדי ... החמדת to בגדי ... החמצות (*bigdei hachamudot* to *bigdei hachamutsot*), from "best garments" to "clothes that were foul-smelling," due to being blood splattered. He thus claims an association with Esau. Zakovitch, *Jacob*, 39–45.

the conflict in Jerusalem should be seen as God's judgment on the false shepherds of Israel, and the great conflict at Armageddon as God's judgment on the nations.

The establishment of the Kingdom will be sudden and Messiah's victory decisive because it will mark the end of world empires, including the empire of Antichrist.[17] The psalmist also confirms this picture of judgment in Psalm 2:8–9, as the nations are given to the Son for judgment. The Son is told: "You shall break them with a rod of iron, You shall shatter them like earthenware" (v 9).

The Lord will take his stand on the Mount of Olives. It will be a most unusual day in the history of the world: Zechariah says, "In that day there will be no light; the luminaries will dwindle. For it will be a unique day which is known to the LORD, neither day nor night, but it will come about that at evening time there will be light" (Zech 14:6–7). Evidently, the river of life mentioned in Ezekiel 47:1–12 will flow out from Jerusalem, and at this time "the LORD will be king over all the earth" (Zech 14:9).

Earlier, we looked at Zechariah 6:12–13. Although this passage deals primarily with the Priest like Melchizedek, this priest would also be a king and is referred to as "the Branch." Verse 13 says, "Yes, it is He who will build the temple of the LORD, and He who will bear the honor and sit and rule on His throne." It should be noted that according to this passage, the Branch will sit and rule upon his throne *after* the temple is built.

ULTIMATE RESTORATION

There will initially be judgment, but his coming will also bring salvation and restoration to Israel. He will have previously restored the people to the Land of Israel, for Isaiah prophesied, "He will lift up a standard for the nations and assemble the banished ones of Israel, and will gather the dispersed of Judah from the four corners of the earth" (Isa 11:12). Likewise, the prophet Joel declared, "The LORD roars from Zion and utters His voice from Jerusalem, and the heavens and the earth tremble. But the LORD is a refuge for His people and a stronghold to the sons of Israel" (Joel 3:16).

Then he will restore the nation spiritually. The prophets of Israel said, "There will be no more gloom for her who was in anguish" (Isa 9:1), for "they will look on [Him] whom they have pierced; and they will mourn

---

17. Dan 9:26–27; also 2:34–35, 44–45; 7:13–14.

for Him, as one mourns for an only son, and they will weep bitterly over Him like the bitter weeping over a firstborn" (Zech 12:10). Again, Isaiah said, "Then the eyes of the blind will be opened, and the ears of the deaf will be unstopped" (Isa 35:5). That he is speaking of spiritual sight and hearing is made clear by his reference to them as "the redeemed" and as "the ransomed of the LORD" (vv. 9 and 19). Consequently, "a land [will] be born in one day" and "a nation [will] be brought forth all at once" (Isa 66:8), and all the tribes of Israel will be reunited.[18]

Eva Rydelnik comments about the additional prophecies of God pouring out his Spirit in conjunction with the establishment of the Kingdom:

> This outpouring of the Spirit is one aspect of the initiating of the millennial kingdom. Often prophets connect the establishment of the messianic kingdom with the coming of the Spirit upon His people (Ezek 36:27; Jl 2:28–32; Zch 12:10). At that time, it is God's Spirit that brings about transformation of the land and its inhabitants. The transformation from "desert" to "orchard" to "forest" ([Isa 32,] vv. 15–16) is similar to other prophetic descriptions of eschatological transformations (Isa 29:17–24; 44:3–5). This is a time of messianic plenty seen in the desert becoming an orchard, and the orchard like a forest, and more important, the bringing of peace to the land.[19]

Who can help but be moved by the beautiful descriptions in Scripture of the restoration of the people to the Land and the restoration of the Land to fruitfulness (see, for example, Amos 9:13–15)?[20] These are emotional passages of God's returned blessing upon his people.

Messiah will set up his Kingdom in Jerusalem, his throne in the rebuilt temple, and he will reign over Israel on the throne of David. But his empire will extend to the ends of the earth. As Zechariah says, "The LORD will be king over the whole earth." As the righteous Judge, he will "decide with fairness for the afflicted of the earth."[21]

The Scriptures say that he will restore all the created order so that "they will not hurt or destroy in all My holy mountain, for the earth will be full of the knowledge of the LORD as the waters cover the sea" (Isa 11:9). Not only will the nations finally beat their swords into plowshares

---

18. See also Isa 60:1–3; Jer 3:18; 50:4; Ezek 37:15–22.
19. E. Rydelnik, "Isaiah 32: 1–8; 33:17–24," 901.
20. See James, *New Creation Eschatology and the Land*.
21. Zech 14:9; Isa 11:4b.

and their spears into pruning hooks, but God will create a new heaven and a new earth, and the former things shall not be remembered or come to mind. All flesh shall come to worship before him.[22]

Now, we turn to the New Testament.

---

22. Cf. Isa 2:4; 65:17, 25; Mic 4:3.

17

The Messianic Kingdom in the New Testament Scriptures

SEVERAL YEARS AGO, I watched a short online video of a pastor who was leading the youth group from his church on a tour of Israel. In the clip, the pastor and the young people were near the Western Wall in Jerusalem, and they had engaged a rabbi in discussion. The pastor was trying to convince the rabbi that Jesus was the Messiah, and he used several messianic prophecies to make his case. The rabbi's response was that Jesus couldn't have been the Messiah, because he didn't establish his kingdom. The pastor met this objection by telling him that the kingdom was already here, but it was an invisible kingdom. With this, the rabbi could not contain himself—he was laughing out loud: "Oh, I see, it's an *invisible* kingdom!" The truth of the matter is that an invisible kingdom is foreign to the Hebrew Scriptures. It is always presented as physical and earthly.

For most of the past century it has been popular for Christians to believe that the Kingdom is already here, but it's not yet here in its fullness. For the present, it is spiritual, invisible, and ethereal. It is in the hearts of all believers. As we submit to the Lord's authority in our lives, we experience the Kingdom. Again, this is a departure from the teaching of the Old Testament. It may be due in part to the tendency to associate the Lord's authority with his role as King. But God's authority is characteristic of Jesus as Prophet, as Priest, and as King. As we have seen, the authority of Jesus is absolute, regardless of his role. It may also be a failure to distinguish between God's universal sovereignty and the Messianic Kingdom.

But notice, on the one hand, the universal sovereignty of God is non-apocalyptic and theocentric—that is to say, it is not particularly related to end times. God has exercised his sovereignty over the universe since Creation, and the focus is on the Father. The Messianic Kingdom, on the other hand, is apocalyptic and christological—that is to say, it is something to be anticipated. It is future, and it is focused on the Messiah, King Jesus. George R. Beasley-Murray says, "The teaching of Jesus on the Kingdom of God . . . was essentially Christological."[1] Regarding the apocalyptic nature of the Kingdom, Mark Saucy says, ". . . apocalyptic delineates a Jesus who acted and spoke out of an awareness of an eschatological calendar or sequence of events."[2] Again, we hear Paul say, "For our citizenship is in heaven, from which also we eagerly wait for a Savior, the Lord Jesus the Messiah" (Phil 3:20).

Often, those who believe the Kingdom has already been inaugurated do not see a vital role for Israel at present. But God is dealing with Israel at present, and the Kingdom is yet future.

In the Old Testament, the Messianic Kingdom is depicted as a physical kingdom on a renewed earth. When Jesus was in the synagogue in Nazareth, his use of messianic passages from Isaiah indicates that his view of the Kingdom was consistent with its portrayal in the Hebrew Scriptures.[3] This was also the case in his response to John the Baptist.[4] The times and circumstances in which we live do not reflect the picture of the Kingdom we find in Scripture. This is not a time of peace and righteousness. The lion is not lying down with the lamb. Needless to say, because the idea of an invisible kingdom doesn't find justification in the

---

1. Beasley-Murray, "Foreword," xiii.

2. M. Saucy, *The Kingdom of God in the Teaching of Jesus*, xxvi–xxvii.

3. Reference here is to Isaiah 61. Jesus quotes Isaiah 61:1–2a in Luke 4:18–19. Jesus quotes from the first portion of the chapter (vv. 1–3), which describes his ministry as the Servant. He does not quote from the second paragraph (vv. 4–9), which describes the restoration of the Land, the cities, and the people, under the rule of King Messiah. This is yet future.

4. In Matthew 11:4–15, Jesus quotes from Isaiah 35:5–6, a passage which speaks of a second exodus, a time of comfort and salvation. The same is true of Isaiah 40. Jesus also quotes Malachi 3:1 in reference to John. This verse speaks of preparing the way for the "messenger of the covenant," but the following verses that speak of judgment are not mentioned, for that aspect of Messiah's ministry is yet future.

Old Testament, it is unpersuasive for Jewish non-believers. Ultimately, the controversy resolves itself in answering the question, "Has Jesus established the kingdom on earth, and is he currently reigning as king?"

INTERPRETIVE PRINCIPLES

The promise of the Messianic Kingdom ties together all the threads of the biblical story. So why is the conversation confusing and sometimes controversial? Why do so many Christians believe the Kingdom is already here in an inaugurated form? First, there seems to be a misunderstanding of Jesus's messianic roles. Second, there is a failure to accept one or more of the following principles that should guide our interpretation:

1. We must distinguish between the *identity* of Jesus and his *function* at a given time.

2. We must distinguish between *God's universal kingdom* and *the Messianic Kingdom*. For example, it is possible to say that God's universal kingdom is "already," for it is eternal. But the Messianic Kingdom is "not yet." This is different from claiming that the Messianic Kingdom itself is "already" here, though "not yet" in its fullness.

3. We must interpret the more difficult verses on a particular topic in light of the verses that are clear.

4. We must understand the language of the Bible. The Bible often uses figures of speech. Sometimes, one thing is emphasized by substituting a related word or idea. Two of these figures of speech that use substitution are closely related: metonymy and synecdoche. Ken Rossoll expresses the difference this way: "*Metonymy* deals with the changing of one word for another to which it has a relation."[5] For example, in the Old Testament, "scepter" is often used as a figure of speech (metonymy) referring to Messiah's authority to rule.[6] A scepter is not essential for one to rule, but it is a word commonly associated with a ruling king.

A related figure of speech is synecdoche. Rossoll goes on to explain that synecdoche is a form of metonymy where the exchange of one word

---

5. Ken Rossoll, "Synecdoche, a Suburb of Metonymy," Figures of Speech in the Bible; accessed 12 April 2022 at https://figuresofspeechinthebible.net/?p=11481.

6. See Gen 49:10; Deut 33:21; Judg 5:15; 2 Sam 7:7; Ps 45:6; 76:1–2; 78:68–70.

for another expresses a change in quantity. He says, "Whether it be a part for the whole or the whole for a part, a quantity is being changed. A part is a lesser quantity or amount of the whole, and the whole is a greater part or quantity than the part."[7]

For an example where a part of a thing is used to represent the thing itself, consider Proverbs 1:16: "For their feet run to evil, and they hasten to shed blood." Their feet do not run without the people to whom they belong! In Psalm 73:9, the "tongue" of the wicked "parades through the earth." Look again at Isaiah 66:8: "Can a land be born in one day? Can a nation be brought forth all at once?" Here "land," a part of the nation, is used as a figure of speech for the entire "nation."

As we consider the Messianic Kingdom in the Old Testament, what are the essential parts of the whole? There must be (1) a king, the Messiah. He must possess (2) the authority and qualifications to be king. There must be (3) a standard for gaining citizenship, in order to have (4) citizens over whom he rules, and there must be (5) a territory or domain over which he reigns. These are all essential components or aspects of a kingdom.

A synecdoche can also involve a whole entity used for a part. This is called "synecdoche of the whole."[8] To take examples from the Hebrew Scriptures, in 1 Samuel 15, Samuel used "kingdom" to refer to Saul's right to rule: "So Samuel said to him, 'The LORD has torn the kingdom of Israel from you today and has given it to your neighbor who is better than you.'"[9] What was being taken from Saul was God's delegated authority to be king, but it is referred to as "the kingdom." This is using "kingdom" to refer to an essential aspect of the kingdom (a part), namely Saul's authority.

In 2 Samuel 7:16 God promised David: "Your house and your kingdom shall endure before Me forever; your throne shall be established forever." In this verse, God is promising David a dynasty of kings from his descendants. Here, a series of kings is referred to as David's "kingdom" and as his "throne."[10]

---

7. Rossoll, "Synecdoche, a Suburb of Metonymy," n. 401. Ethelbert Bullinger's definition is less clear. He says that metonymy is "a figure of speech by which one name or noun is used instead of another, to which it stands in a certain relation." Bullinger, *Figures of Speech Used in the Bible*, 538.

8. Bullinger, *Figures of Speech Used in the Bible*, 613.

9. 1 Sam 15:28; see also 10:16.

10. In 2 Chronicle 17:10, "kingdoms" is used of the kings of the surrounding nations.

In Exodus 19:6 God says of Israel, "and you shall be to Me a kingdom of priests and a holy nation." Here, "kingdom" is used of those who would be citizens of this future Kingdom.[11] "Kingdom" is also used of lands or cities over which a king would rule and of the king himself (1 Kgs 18:10). With these examples we see that "kingdom" is used of a king, of his right to rule, of a dynasty, of the citizens of a kingdom, and of the domain of a kingdom.

This is also the case in the New Testament, for example, when a city (a larger entity) is used to refer specifically to a part of a city, namely, its residents. Jesus said, "Woe to you, Chorazin! Woe to you, Bethsaida! For if the miracles had occurred in Tyre and Sidon which occurred in you, they would have repented long ago in sackcloth and ashes" (Matt 11:21). He was referring to the residents of these cities, not to the streets and buildings. In this case, the cities were the whole or larger entities, but reference was to the residents, who formed an essential part of the cities.

Likewise, in the Gospels, "kingdom" may refer to the king, the citizens of the coming Kingdom (Rev 5:9–10), or the standard for gaining citizenship in the coming Kingdom.[12] An example is found in Matthew 6:33: "But seek first His kingdom and His righteousness, and all these things will be added to you." How do we seek his Kingdom? What does "His righteousness" have to do with the Kingdom? "His righteousness" is a righteousness both imputed to us and worked out progressively in us when we place our faith in him and become his disciples. This is the way to acquire citizenship in his Kingdom and to be "fitted" or prepared for that Kingdom. To "seek . . . His kingdom" is to become his disciple. This is consistent with the Great Commission in Matthew 28:19–20: We are to "make disciples," then baptize and teach them to observe all that Jesus commanded. Understanding how "kingdom" is used will help us as we try to sort out the evidence from the Gospels regarding the Messianic Kingdom. If I have belabored this point, it is because it is a major problem when deciphering the teachings of the Gospels about the Kingdom.

---

11. See also 2 Kgs 19:19; 2 Chr 14:5.

12. Matt 4:23. In Matthew 21:43, "kingdom of God" seems to refer to the authority to proclaim the path to citizenship.

EVIDENCE PRIOR TO THE ASCENSION

Our examination of the messianic roles of prophet, priest, and king has shown that Jesus's role in his earthly ministry (as described in the Gospels) was that of the Prophet. Never again in the New Testament is he portrayed in that role. At present, he is our great High Priest, "according to the order of Melchizedek" (Heb 7:11). He is not referred to as a currently reigning king in the Epistles, not even once. This would seem to indicate that the Kingdom is in the future. But is there additional clear evidence before the ascension that would support this? There is.

The Kingdom is future. The model prayer (Matt 6:9–13) leads us to pray "Thy kingdom come" (v. 10a). Andrew Woods says, "The entire prayer ... revolves around a request for the coming kingdom and interim requests to be fulfilled during the kingdom's absence."[13] The prayer is for the coming of the Messianic Kingdom when God's will is done on earth as it is in heaven. In the meantime, the prayer is for daily provision ("daily bread"), forgiveness, and deliverance from temptation.[14] If the Kingdom was future and had not "come," then it obviously was not present at that time.

In Matthew 13, Jesus was at home in Capernaum. He went to the shore, and as a crowd gathered, he got into a boat and spoke to the crowd. On this occasion, he told eight parables in which he spoke of the Kingdom. Bruce Compton suggests,

> In effect, the first parable and its interpretation set the pattern by which the subsequent parables in this chapter are to be understood. With that in mind, the 'mysteries' of the kingdom of Heaven introduce the revelation that there will be an interval between ... Jesus' First and Second Advents, with his kingdom being established at his Second Advent.[15]

---

13. Woods, *The Coming Kingdom*, 193. See Toussaint, *Behold the King*, 108–12; D. Turner, *Matthew*, 187–88. See also the excellent discussion of the second petition in Quarles, *Sermon on the Mount*, 194–201.

14. Rheenen and Parker propose the following interpretation: "The phrase 'kingdom of God' is ... defined by the Lord's Prayer as 'God's will being done on earth'" [i.e., at present]. Van Rheenen and Parker, *Missions*, 188. For a compelling refutation, see A. Mitchell, "Your Kingdom Come, Your Will Be Done," 208–30. Mitchell says that to accept Rheenen and Parker's interpretation would be "to insert ourselves in the story where we were never intended to fit" ("Your Kingdom Come, Your Will Be Done," 229). This understanding is also consistent with the interpretation given above regarding Matthew 6:33.

15. Compton, "The 'Kingdom of Heaven/God' and the Church," 189.

After the first parable, his disciples asked him why he was teaching in parables. His answer revealed that he was teaching in parables to call out the remnant of the people who had "ears to hear."[16] He quoted from Isaiah 6:9–10, which is the classic passage on the judgment of spiritual blindness. He was speaking to those who had "ears to hear and eyes to see."

Through these parables, he was teaching about this interim time before the establishment of the Messianic Kingdom. He said that the gospel was to be preached widely, but the results would be inconsistent (vv. 1–23). It would be difficult, if not impossible, to evaluate the results (vv. 24–30, 34–43). Nevertheless, the numbers of disciples, the "sons of the kingdom," would multiply and spread to the nations (vv. 31–33). The remnant of Israel in the past, together with his own disciples, were precious to him, and he would go to extreme lengths to purchase them for himself (vv. 44–46). When he returns to establish his Kingdom, true disciples will be separated from the rest who are to be judged (vv. 47–50), and his disciples will constitute the citizens of this future Kingdom. More than this, the spiritual blindness of the majority of the nation will be removed, and Israel will say, "Blessed is He who comes in the name of the LORD" (Matt 23:39).

While the growth of the "kingdom of heaven" begins with a very small seed and grows to be a "tree" (Matt 13:31–32), the Kingdom established by the "God of heaven" will appear suddenly, bringing to an end all other earthly kingdoms (Dan 2:44–45). These passages can best be reconciled by understanding the parable of Jesus to be speaking of the growth in numbers of the citizens of the future Kingdom.[17]

Late in Jesus's ministry, there was a request for James and John to be given places of prominence in the Messianic Kingdom.[18] Jesus rebuked them for seeking places of prominence but indicated that the Kingdom was yet future. In spite of this, the expectation was strong that since Jesus, the King, was with them, and since they were making what would be their final ascent to Jerusalem, surely the establishment of the Kingdom was near!

On this same journey, most likely on the same day, as Jesus and his disciples neared Jerusalem, he told a parable because the disciples "supposed that the kingdom of God was going to appear immediately." In the parable, he spoke about "a certain nobleman [who] went to a

---

16. Matt 11:15; Mark 4:9, 23; Luke 8:8; 14:35. See also Rom 11:8.
17. Compton, "The 'Kingdom of Heaven/God' and the Church," 187–92.
18. Matt 20:20–28; Mark 10:35–45.

distant country to receive a kingdom for himself, and then return" (Luke 19:11–12). Here, Jesus was likening himself to this nobleman, and he was preparing his disciples for a long wait. However, while they waited for the Kingdom, they were to be busy, as good stewards of the resources he had given them. He wanted them to know that the Messianic Kingdom was not to appear immediately. It would come at some undisclosed time in the future. Here, late in Jesus's ministry, the Kingdom had not yet come.

Apparently, it was difficult for the disciples to wrap their minds around this truth. Jesus assured them that it would come, but not yet. In the meantime, he was gathering a people for his future Kingdom. It was this "delay" that came as a surprise to them, and he needed to teach them about the growth in the number and extent of his disciples in the interim.

At the triumphal entry in Mark 11:10, the crowds were shouting, "Blessed is the coming kingdom of our father David; Hosanna in the highest!" At the crucifixion, the penitent thief was saying, "Jesus, remember me when You come in Your kingdom!" (Luke 23:42). For the crowds and for the thief, the Kingdom was yet future, and Jesus did not offer any correction. Instead, he assured the thief that he would be with him in paradise, presumably until the Kingdom would be established.

Following his crucifixion, burial, and resurrection, Jesus taught his disciples about the Kingdom of God (Acts 1:3). Following this period of instruction about the Kingdom, his disciples asked him, "Lord, is it at this time You are restoring the kingdom to Israel?" (Acts 1:6–7). His response to the question was to dismiss it because it was not for them "to know the times or epochs" (v. 7), but the clear implication here is that the Messianic Kingdom had not yet been inaugurated; it was yet future.

The difficult passages. If the Kingdom was still in the future following the resurrection, then how are we to understand the passages in the Gospels that refer to the "gospel of the kingdom," or to the Kingdom being "near," "at hand," or "in the midst of you"? Is there a form of the Kingdom that is present now, after all? Was Jesus redefining the Kingdom as some kind of invisible or "spiritual" manifestation of the Kingdom? Or is there a better explanation?

Following the principle of interpreting the difficult verses in light of the clear passages, we will want to see if there are reasonable explanations for these passages that can be harmonized with the future view of the Kingdom that is taught in so many other places. As we have seen, one of the keys to understanding otherwise difficult passages is an awareness of the literary device of synecdoche—for example, using "kingdom" for an aspect or component of the Kingdom.

The citizens of the Kingdom. Kingdom language is used of the people God is preparing as citizens of the Kingdom. In Revelation 1:6, John says that Jesus has made us "a kingdom, priests." Here, he uses "kingdom" to refer to those who have been granted citizenship in that Kingdom through faith in Jesus. This is much like Jesus saying, "Truly, truly, I say to you, he who hears my word and believes Him who sent Me, has eternal life, and does not come into judgment, but has passed out of death into life" (John 5:2). As Craig Blaising points out, "In Revelation 1, John writes that the redemption accomplished by Christ has led to the present creation of a kingdom people." He continues: "In Revelation 5:9–10, John says that the Lamb has 'made them a kingdom.' But importantly, John adds, 'they shall reign on the earth,' pointing to the yet future manifestation of that kingdom."[19]

Here, it is the citizens of the Kingdom who are referred to as the Kingdom. As Jesus said in Luke 12:32: "Do not be afraid, little flock, for your Father has chosen gladly to give you the Kingdom." Though the Kingdom is yet future, our citizenship has changed! We now belong to this future Kingdom of God's beloved Son. Jesus told Nicodemus, "Unless one is born of water and the Spirit, he cannot enter into the kingdom of God" (John 3:5).

Spiritual authority to proclaim the gospel of the Kingdom. In Matthew 21:43 (HCSB) Jesus says to the religious leadership, "Therefore I tell you, the kingdom of God will be taken away from you and given to a nation producing its fruit." If the "kingdom of God" is to be equated with an invisible form of the Kingdom characterized by salvation and spiritual blessings, how could it have been transferred from the Sanhedrin? Here, Jesus uses "kingdom of God" to refer to the authority to announce the way to the Kingdom.[20] On other occasions this same authority is spoken of as the "keys of the kingdom"[21] or the "key of knowledge" (Luke 11:52).

---

19. Blaising, "A Theology of Israel and the Church," 94. It should be noted that Blaising believes the creation of a kingdom people indicates an inaugurated form of the Kingdom, while I understand these verses to be speaking of the present creation of the citizenry of the coming Kingdom.

20. D. Turner, "Matthew 21:43 and the Future of Israel," 46–61. It is interesting to note here that the vineyard (Israel) is neither abandoned, nor replaced (even temporarily).

21. Matt 16:19; 18:18.

What was God's design for the chief priests and the leadership of the nation? To recognize Jesus as the Messiah and to proclaim him to be the way to citizenship in the Kingdom. Instead, they opposed him. Since the scribes and Pharisees rejected Jesus, "the kingdom of heaven" was taken from them and given to the apostles. That is to say, the spiritual authority to proclaim the way to gain citizenship in the Kingdom (i.e., the authoritative preaching of the gospel) was being transferred to the apostles. Israel had not been replaced, but the nation was placed under new management. Better results were to be expected. Those results are found in the book of the Acts of the Apostles.[22]

The authority of Jesus also included authoritative teaching concerning how to prepare for life in the Kingdom.[23] In the same way, in Matthew 23:13, Jesus condemned the religious leaders, "because [they] shut off the kingdom of heaven from people; for [they] do not enter in [themselves], nor do [they] allow those who are entering to go in." They "shut off the kingdom of heaven from men" by their failure to tell them how to enter. New Testament commentator David Turner says, "The scribes and Pharisees, who claim to open the door to God, actually keep people out of the kingdom. Ironically, they 'are not leaders but misleaders.'"[24] My former colleague Noam Hendren says in reference to the Sermon on the Mount, "Throughout the sermon, Jesus pointed to himself as the 'gatekeeper' of the kingdom, so that one's relationship to him and obedience to his teaching would determine who would enter the kingdom and who would be judged."[25]

Jesus told Thomas, "I am the way, and the truth, and the life; no one comes to the Father, but through Me" (John 14:6). The way to gain citizenship in the Kingdom, to see the Kingdom of God, to enter into the

---

22. The judgment against the "vineyard" and its restoration are found also in Isaiah 5:1–7 and 27:2–6, respectively.

23. In a similar vein, Matthew 12:28 and Luke 11:20 speak of Jesus's authority over demons. On these occasions, Jesus says, "If it is by the Spirit/finger of God that I cast/drive out demons, then the kingdom of God has come upon you." The verb translated "has come" (ἔφθασεν) may well be understood as a timeless aorist with a future meaning, thus, "the kingdom of God will be upon you." Regardless, as we have seen in similar passages, here "the Kingdom of God" is most likely a reference to Jesus, the prince of that Kingdom, and explained as metonymy (i.e., the Prince and his power over Satan are essential aspects of the kingdom and are referred to as the Kingdom).

24. D. Turner, *Israel's Last Prophet*, 318–19. His quotation is from Davies and Allison, *Matthew 19–28*, 285.

25. Hendren, "The Kingdom of God in the Gospels," 222.

Kingdom of God, is through faith in Jesus, and the way to be prepared for the Kingdom is by accepting the role of a disciple of Jesus.

The Kingdom is "at hand" or "in the midst of you." Jesus used "kingdom" in connection with his own person, as the King of that coming Kingdom. When he said, "The kingdom of God is in your midst," he was referring to himself. John the Baptist had done the same thing. He had preached, "Repent, for the kingdom of heaven is at hand" (Matt 3:2). Jesus preached this same message.[26] This, again, is the use of synecdoche, referring to a part when indicating the whole.

The same phenomenon also explains the phrase "the kingdom of heaven is at hand" or "in the midst of you." In Luke 10:9, Jesus told his disciples (the seventy) that as they traveled, they were to tell those who extended hospitality that "the kingdom of God has come near to you." If the Kingdom is future, then how are we to understand these passages that seem to say it is already "in the midst of you" or "at hand"? If it is "near," is it "here"?

The first order of business is to understand the phrase "the kingdom of heaven is at hand." It was proclaimed by John the Baptist, Jesus, the apostles, and the seventy (Luke 10:9). We need to understand what each part of the phrase means. Often "Heaven," "the Name," or "Lord" were substituted for "Yahweh" or "God." Therefore, the phrase is speaking of the Kingdom of God. Since "kingdom" is never redefined in the New Testament, John the Baptist and the apostles were using it in its Old Testament sense—an earthly kingdom, centered in Jerusalem. It is the Messianic Kingdom.

That brings us to "at hand."[27] James 5:8 uses the same word to express nearness, not "here-ness." He says, "You too be patient; strengthen your hearts, for the coming of the Lord is near," or "*at hand.*" In the next verse, he says that "the Judge is standing right at the door." In other words, James is using this word to say that the Lord's return is near, not that it is here. Paul, like James, uses this word in Philippians 5:4 to say, "The Lord is near."[28] Luke is using the same word, even as James and Paul, to say that the Kingdom is among you (i.e., near you), not that it is within you, and therefore already here.

In Luke 17:20b–21 Jesus said, "The kingdom of God is not coming with signs to be observed; nor will they say, 'Look, here *it is*!' or 'There

---

26. Matt 4:17; Mark 1:15.

27. ἐγγίζω, *engízo*.

28. ὁ κύριος ἐγγύς, *ho Kyrios engys*.

it is!' For behold, the kingdom of God is in your midst."²⁹ Sometimes people read this and think it is saying that the Kingdom is in your heart; it is within you. Nothing could be farther from the truth. In context, Jesus was addressing the Pharisees. These were the men who were opposing Jesus. Certainly, Jesus was not claiming that the Kingdom was in their hearts! In rejecting the King, who was "in their midst," however, they were rejecting citizenship in the Kingdom.

Furthermore, as Woods puts it, "The Bible nowhere portrays the kingdom entering people. Rather, it is people who will one day enter the coming kingdom."³⁰ Finally, if this is to be taken as saying that the Kingdom is within believers, then "kingdom" has been redefined, and there is no place for a future, terrestrial kingdom. This would contradict the passages that speak of a future, earthly kingdom. You can't have it both ways.

The gospel of the Kingdom. When John the Baptist, Jesus, and the apostles "proclaimed the gospel of the kingdom," it might sound to some as though they were announcing the arrival of the Kingdom. Instead, they were not proclaiming that the Kingdom *had* come, but that it *would* come, and they were announcing how to become citizens of that Kingdom, namely by becoming disciples of Jesus.³¹ This gospel of the Kingdom was accepted by the remnant, but it was rejected by most of the nation (the "rest," in Rom 11:7).

Jesus has used "kingdom" in the same way earlier in the Sermon on the Mount, when he said, "Seek first His kingdom and His righteousness, and all these things will be added to you" (Matt 6:33). We have already seen in the preaching of the apostles in Luke 9 that "gospel" is used interchangeably with "the kingdom of God." This is an example of synecdoche, speaking of a part as if it were the whole. In this case, the way into the Kingdom is referred to as the kingdom.

---

29. ἐντὸς ὑμῶν ἐστιν, *entós humón estín*.

30. Woods, *The Coming Kingdom*, 112. Although unattributed, this thought almost certainly comes from Marshall, *The Gospel of Luke*, 655. However, cf. Toussaint, *Behold the King*, 164. See Matt 5:20; 23:13; John 3:5.

31. Woods notes that, following Pentecost, nowhere is there any reference to the "gospel of the kingdom" being preached (*The Coming Kingdom*, 61). This language may have been reserved for calling the remnant of Israel under the Mosaic Covenant to put their faith in Jesus as the Messiah. With the establishment of the New Covenant and the outpouring of the Holy Spirit, those who had received the gospel of the Kingdom became citizens of that kingdom.

SUMMARY

When we consider the evidence carefully, the clear testimony of Scripture is that the Kingdom was not inaugurated during the earthly ministry of Jesus. Prior to the ascension, there is nothing in the Gospel accounts that can overturn the entirely futuristic view of the Kingdom in Acts 1:6–8. The disciples asked: ". . . Lord, is it at this time You are restoring the kingdom to Israel?" He did not challenge their premise that it was yet future.

If the Kingdom were to have been established in any real sense before the time of Jesus's departure, this would have been the perfect time to clarify. If Jesus functioned exclusively as the Prophet like Moses and Suffering Servant of Isaiah in the days of his earthly ministry, his Kingdom was not inaugurated at that time. It then becomes important to examine the evidence following the ascension.

EVIDENCE FOLLOWING THE ASCENSION

Michael Vlach reports, "In Paul's writing there are fourteen direct references to God's 'kingdom.' This compares with 121 references to 'kingdom' in Matthew, Mark, and Luke."[32] Where it refers to the Messianic Kingdom, it is always pointing to a future Kingdom that will be inherited in the future.[33] No reference requires the Kingdom to be a present reality; it is always future, although believers are to adopt a lifestyle compatible with the Kingdom at the present time.[34] As Saucy writes, "The New Testament notably restricts usage of the *basileia*-language group [i.e., kingdom vocabulary] when addressing the function of the risen Christ. It is arguable that after Acts, Christ is not called 'king' or pictured as currently 'reigning' until in Revelation."[35]

Eckhard Schnabel, in his landmark work, *Paul the Missionary*, says:

> I do not explore the theme of the kingdom of God which some contemporary missiologists regard as a fundamental theological concept that encompasses everything that the church does. While Paul uses the phrase kingdom of God several times, clearly assuming that his readers know what he is talking

---

32. Vlach, "The Kingdom in Paul's Epistles," 3. Vlach's entire article is both relevant and excellent.

33. 1 Cor 6:9–10; 15:50; Gal 5:21; Eph 5:5

34. Rom 14:17; 1 Cor 4:20; 1 Thess 2:12; 2 Thess 1:5.

35. M. Saucy, *The Kingdom of God in the Teaching of Jesus*, 108.

about, it is not a central category for his theology as we encounter it in his letters.[36]

Some see the use of Psalm 110 in the New Testament as evidence of the present reign of Jesus as King. Saucy says: "Psalm 110, the most important passage through which early Christians came to view the status and function of the risen Christ, while capable of justifying a present reign for Christ, is never used that way in the New Testament."[37] He continues, "Christ's present posture towards his enemies does not appear to correspond to that of a ruling king."[38]

DOMINION, DOMAIN, AND KINGDOM

Salvation changes a person's status. He no longer belongs to the domain of Satan, but to the future Messianic Kingdom. Paul writes, "Grace to you and peace from God our Father and the Lord Jesus the Messiah, who gave Himself for our sins so that He might rescue us from this present evil age, according to the will of our God and Father" (Gal 1:3–4). This passage emphasizes our deliverance from an "evil age" which is "present," but nothing is said about a present manifestation of the Messianic Kingdom. Paul's message to the Philippians is clear: "For our citizenship is in heaven, from which also we eagerly wait for a Savior, the Lord Jesus the Messiah" (Phil 3:20).

The same could be said of Colossians 1:13: "He has rescued us from the domain of darkness and transferred us to the kingdom of His beloved Son." Some have taken this as evidence that there is a present reality of the Kingdom, for with salvation, one is transferred to a "kingdom." But this verse adds nothing to the discussion of the timing of the Kingdom. It could be a present kingdom, or it could refer to a kingdom that is entirely in the future.

However, transferring us to "the kingdom of His beloved Son" is most likely explained by Paul's commission, "to open ... [the Gentiles's] eyes so that they may turn from darkness to light and from the dominion of Satan to God, that they may receive forgiveness of sins and an *inheritance* among those who have been sanctified by faith in Me" (Acts 26:18).[39]

---

36. Schnabel, *Paul, the Missionary*, 14.
37. M. Saucy, *The Kingdom of God in the Teaching of Jesus*, 109.
38. M. Saucy, *The Kingdom of God in the Teaching of Jesus*, 110.
39. Emphasis added.

Here, this change of status entitles one to forgiveness of sins, the indwelling Spirit for the present, and a spiritual inheritance for the future. The Kingdom is to be "inherited" by the "heirs of the kingdom;"[40] that is, by those who through Messiah have gained entrance, or citizenship, in the Kingdom. Once again: "For our citizenship is in heaven, from which also we eagerly wait for a Savior, the Lord Jesus the Messiah" (Phil 3:20).[41]

RECEIVING A KINGDOM

In Romans 6:8–14, Paul uses dominion language to describe the life of sanctification to which believers are called. He speaks of "dominion" twice (vv. 9, 14),[42] and "reign" once (v. 12).[43] But he first uses "dominion" in connection with Jesus. In verse 9, he says that before the resurrection, death had dominion over Jesus.[44] If so, he could not have instituted his Kingdom until he had conquered death with the crucifixion and resurrection.

Romans 6:5 says that through baptism, we are identified with him in death and will be identified with him in resurrection. The inference, of course, is that we are presently under the dominion of death, even as he was, though we are no longer "enslaved" to sin. In the future, we will have complete victory over both sin and death through him.

If we are now under the dominion of death, how can we speak of the Kingdom being present? In this interim time, Paul says that we, as believers, should not allow sin to have dominion over us, but instead should live in light of the certain future of resurrection life before us;[45] that is to say, we are to live as citizens of a future kingdom.

Some may point to Hebrews 12:28, which says, "Therefore, since we receive a kingdom which cannot be shaken, let us show gratitude, by which we may offer to God an acceptable service with reverence and awe." In this verse, "receive" is a present participle, and the phrase could more accurately be translated, "since we are receiving a kingdom." Some say that since it is a *present* participle, it indicates that the Kingdom has

---

40. E.g., see Rom 8:17; Gal 4:7; 1 Pet 1:4; Jas 2:5.
41. See Vlach, "The Kingdom in Paul's Epistles," 19–20.
42. Gk, κυριεύει, *kurievei*.
43. Gk, βασιλευέτω, *basileveto*.
44. Gk, κυριεύει, *kurievei*.
45. Rom 6:12, 13b.

already been inaugurated. But the participle indicates a process begun now but continuing into the future—"we are receiving."

It would be like a father who wants to give a car to a teenage son. The car is in the shop being made ready with new tires, fresh oil, etc. Nevertheless, the dad hands his son a set of keys and says, "Since you are receiving a car, you will need to determine now how you are going to drive it. What disciplines should you put in place now?" We have citizenship in the Kingdom now, like the keys to the car, but it is being made ready for us. Jesus said, "I go to prepare a place for you" (John 14:3, NIV). It is not here yet, but we already have our citizenship, and even as our "place" is being prepared, we are being made ready for the Kingdom.

Peter depicts the status of believers at present as living in exile. Katie Marcar expresses it this way: "Believers in 1 Peter are to understand themselves as redeemed with the blood of Christ, but as still living in exile as resident aliens and sojourners."[46] This strongly suggests that the Kingdom is not here yet. How could Israel (and not just the remnant) be a holy nation or a priestly nation unless the new High Priest of an alternative order were also reigning as king? As Peter says, "The end of all things is near ["at hand"]; therefore, be of sound judgment and sober spirit for the purpose of prayer" (1 Pet 4:7). Car keys are not the car, and citizenship in the Kingdom is not the Kingdom. The gospel is the key to the Kingdom.

THE SEALED SCROLL

The book of Revelation also adds an important note we must not miss. In Revelation 5 we read of a book or scroll that is sealed with seven seals. What is this book, who can open it, and what is the significance of its opening?

Although there are many explanations, the one that most clearly considers the context of Revelation is that this scroll contains the knowledge of future events of judgment that will fall upon the earth during a relatively short period of time (Rev 6:1—8:1).

Robert Thomas says, "The second scene of chapter 5 (vv. 2–5) revolves about finding someone with the necessary credentials to break the seals on the scroll." At first no one is found, and John is left weeping. Then John is told that "the Lion that is from the tribe of Judah, the Root of David, has overcome so as to open the book and its seven seals" (v. 5).

---

46. Marcar, "Exodus in the General Letters," 174.

His credentials to open the scroll are derived from his office and his accomplishment. He is the Messiah, and as the Prophet and Servant of the Lord, he offered his life as an atonement for sin. So, he is referred to as the Lamb. This accomplishment was necessary in order for him to become our High Priest and to later take his throne as the Messianic King.

These issues have been dealt with in many commentaries,[47] but a secondary significance of the opening of this scroll has not been given enough attention. It is true that with the opening of these seals, a series of judgments is unleashed upon the earth. Yet this imagery is built upon a similar vision found in Isaiah 29.

Beginning in Isaiah 24, judgments are also here pronounced upon the nations of the earth, including judgments against Judah. However, Isaiah 29:11–12 says, "The entire vision will be to you like the words of a sealed book, which when they give it to the one who is literate, saying, 'Please read this,' he will say, 'I cannot, for it is sealed.' Then the book will be given to the one who is illiterate, saying, 'Please read this.' And he will say, 'I cannot read.'" No one is found who can open the scroll. Yet, in a short while, "the deaf will hear the words of a book, and out of their gloom and darkness, the eyes of the blind will see" (Isa 29:18).

In the context of Isaiah, this darkness and gloom is the result of Israel's spiritual blindness and deafness. It follows the enactment of the judgment of spiritual blindness on the majority of the people in Isaiah 6, as the Lord instructs the young prophet how to live in the land of the blind in chapter 8:11–22.[48]

But the gloom of Isaiah 8:22 is turned to glory in chapter 9, as "the people who walk in darkness will see a great light; those who live in a dark land, the light will shine on them" (9:2). And the time will come when "the government will rest on His shoulders; and His name will be called Wonderful Counselor, Mighty God, Eternal Father, Prince of Peace. There will be no end to the increase of His government or of peace, on the throne of David and over his kingdom" (9:6–7).

The removal of the gloom and darkness is the restoration of spiritual perception. It is the end of the judgment of spiritual blindness, and it is

---

47. Especially helpful is R. Thomas, *Revelation 1–7*.

48. For more on divine hardening, see Chisholm, Jr., "Divine Hardening in the Old Testament," 410–34; Eakin, "Spiritual Obduracy and Parable Purpose," 87–109.); Evans, *To See and Not Perceive*"; Evans, "The Function of Isaiah 6:9–10 in Mark and John," 124–38; Evans, "Obduracy and the Lord's Servant," 221–36; Räisänen, *The Idea of Divine Hardening*; and Sibley, "The Blindness of Israel and the Mission of the Church."

necessary for the establishment of Messiah's Kingdom. It remains a question whether this blindness will be lifted suddenly for the entire nation or progressively,[49] but the opening of the scroll in Revelation 5 also signifies the end of Israel's spiritual blindness, so that they will look on him whom they have pierced, "and they will mourn for Him, as one mourns for an only son" (Zech 12:10).

To have a kingdom, you must have an authorized and reigning king, certified citizens, and a domain (i.e., the territory of the kingdom). We have God's authorized King, who is not presently reigning but is preparing the citizens of His future Kingdom. Specifically, He is saving a remnant of the Jewish people and many people from the nations. At the end, the advent of the Kingdom will be marked by the removal of Israel's blindness, Israel's salvation, and the destruction of the Lord's enemies. The domain of the Messianic Kingdom is the Land of Israel,[50] at the center of a worldwide empire that includes all nations and peoples.

SUMMARY

Determining the timing of the arrival of the Kingdom is significant. In the first place, of course, is our desire to be faithful to the teaching of Scripture. To say that the Kingdom is already here is to undercut and diminish the anticipation of Messiah's return to establish his Kingdom. Some of the last words Paul penned are these:

> For I am already being poured out as a drink offering, and the time of my departure has come. I have fought the good fight, I have finished the course, I have kept the faith; in the future there is laid up for me the crown of righteousness, which the Lord, the righteous Judge, will award to me on that day; and not only to me, but also to all who have loved His appearing. (2 Tim 4:6–8)

A few verses later Paul wrote, "The Lord will deliver me from every evil deed, and will bring me safely to His heavenly kingdom" (v. 18). An expectancy for the coming Kingdom propels a believer to evangelism, missions, a life of sanctification, and perseverance in trials and persecution. C. S. Lewis once said, "If you read history, you will find that the Christians who did most for the present world were just those who

---

49. Larsen suggests a progression during the Great Tribulation from the two witnesses to the 144,000 to "all Israel." Cf., Larsen, *Jews, Gentiles, and the Church*, 293–95.

50. See James, *New Creation Eschatology and the Land*.

thought most of the next.... It is since Christians have largely ceased to think of the other world that they have become so ineffective in this."[51] Paul wrote, "Do this, knowing the time, that it is already the hour for you to awaken from sleep; for now salvation is nearer to us than when we believed. The night is almost gone, and the day is near. Therefore let us lay aside the deeds of darkness and put on the armor of light" (Rom 13:11–12).

We need to think deeply and often of our "other" citizenship and long for the coming of our righteous King. "For our citizenship is in heaven, from which also we eagerly wait for a Savior, the Lord Jesus the Messiah" (Phil 3:20). When we thank the Lord for our food (our daily bread), we should also pray for the coming of his Kingdom, for to him "be glory, majesty, dominion and authority, before all time and now and forever. Amen."[52]

> When He comes, our glorious king,
> All His ransomed home to bring,
> Then anew His song we'll sing:
> Hallelujah! What a Savior![53]

---

51. Lewis, *Mere Christianity*, 134.
52. Matt 6:9–13; Jude 25. See also Titus 2:11–15.
53. Bliss, "Hallelujah! What a Savior!" Public domain.

Epilogue
What Shall We Do?

BEFORE PETER HAD EVEN finished his sermon on the Day of Pentecost, his audience demanded, "Brethren, what shall we do?" (Acts 2:37). We should not end this study without asking what our response should be to this presentation of the roles of Jesus the Messiah as Prophet, Priest, and King, and of his future Kingdom.

OUR RESPONSE TO THE MESSIANIC PROPHET

God said, "Whoever will not listen to My words which he shall speak in My name, I Myself will require it of him" (Deut 18:19). As Isaiah presents this "new Moses" who will lead Israel and the nations in a new exodus, out of the oppression of sin and death, the Holy Spirit, in a sense, takes the pen from the old prophet's hand and records the cry of Messiah himself: "Seek the LORD while He may be found; call upon Him while He is near. Let the wicked forsake his way, and the unrighteous man his thoughts; and let him return to the LORD, and He will have compassion on him; and to our God, for He will abundantly pardon."[1] The urgency of this response was echoed by John the Baptist centuries later: "He who believes in the Son has eternal life; but he who does not obey the Son will not see life, but the wrath of God abides on him" (John 3:36).

One of the first commands Jesus ever uttered consisted of only two words: "Follow Me" (John 1:43).[2] The proper response to the Prophet like Moses, who suffered and died for us, is to repent of our sin, trust him for our salvation, and follow him as his disciple.

---

1. Isa 55:6–7.
2. See also Matt 4:19; 8:22; 9:9; 10:38; 16:24; 19:21; John 10:27; 21:19.

OUR RESPONSE TO THE MESSIANIC PRIEST

The author of Hebrews explains how Jesus is superior to Moses and how he is the ultimate object of our faith. Then he warns of the danger of unbelief. Next, the author of Hebrews devotes the largest portion of his letter to the most thorough discussion of Jesus as our great High Priest to be found in the New Testament (Heb 5:1—13:25). Surely, Hebrews can help us as we consider our proper response to Jesus as High Priest. Among the many exhortations in the letter, three stand out.

First, in Hebrews 3:1, we are told to "consider Jesus, the Apostle and High Priest of our confession." To "consider" Jesus means to shove aside all distractions. We must learn more of him, think of him often, and try to conform our lives to his purposes. "Consider him!"

Second, in Hebrews 6:1, we are exhorted to press on to maturity. This means that we are to go beyond the basics and go deeper in our understanding of him and of his Word. "Press on!"

Third, in chapter 10, we are exhorted to draw near (v. 22) to the Lord in a way that will produce boldness for him and encouragement for other believers. "Draw near!" Consider him, press on with him, and draw near to him, for he is preparing us for the Kingdom as we serve him here.

OUR RESPONSE TO THE MESSIANIC KING

Like Melchizedek's name implies, the Messiah will be the King of Righteousness and Peace—righteousness in himself (which he has imputed to his disciples) and peace which he has established with God and with the nations. His reign will be like a breath of fresh air. This King and his government will be a thing of beauty and joy, even in his violent destruction of the forces of evil that would threaten his people. Here is a realm in which there is no terror, no plague, no threat, no corruption, and no deceit.

In both the Old and New Testaments, the most common and appropriate responses to the King are submission and celebration. With his coming, every knee will bow, and every tongue confess that he is Lord. Hallelujah!

In the book of Psalms, worship is the appropriate response to the King. Songs of worship and praise are sung to give thanks for his acts of salvation. This worship is accompanied by joy and rejoicing, but it is also associated with trembling.[3]

In the book of Revelation, Messiah is the King of kings and Lord of lords (19:16) and the ruler of the kings of the earth (1:5). The saints and the heavenly beings demonstrate what a proper response should be to the King. They fall down at his feet[4] and worship him. This worship consists of giving him glory, honor, and gratitude for who he is and for what he has done.[5]

Revelation 15:3 mentions that the saints in John's vision sang "the song of Moses, the bond-servant of God, and the song of the Lamb." Worship is an expression of his worthiness. The basis of his worthiness is what he accomplished as the Prophet like Moses and Servant of the Lord. He is "the Lamb slain from the foundation of the world."[6] One hymn writer wrote of the hallelujahs of the angels but suggested that when we sing the song of our redemption, "they will fold their wings, for angels never felt the joy that our salvation brings."[7]

CONCLUSION

This "undercover Messiah" is Prophet, Priest, and King, but his humble work as the Prophet has revealed him to be worthy of all honor, praise, and glory.

> Being found in appearance as a man, He humbled Himself by becoming obedient to the point of death, even death on a cross. For this reason also, God highly exalted Him, and bestowed on Him the name which is above every name, so that at the name of Jesus every knee will bow, of those who are in heaven and on earth and under the earth, and that every tongue will confess that Jesus the Messiah is Lord, to the glory of God the Father. (Phil 2:8–11)

Maranatha!

---

3. Pss 2:11; 20:5; 21:13; 101; 132:7; 144:9.
4. Rev 1:17; 7:12; 11:16; 19:4.
5. Rev 4:8–10; 5:9–14; 7:9–12; 11:16; 14:3; 19:1–4, 5, 7.
6. Rev 13:8 (KJV). See also 1 Pet 1:19–20.
7. Oatman, "Holy Holy, Is What the Angels Sing."

Appendix 1

The Three Offices of Messiah

THE THREE OFFICES OF Messiah (Prophet, Priest, and King) are recognized in the literature of the church as early as the beginning of the fourth century. However, Donald Macleod notes that the early references to these three messianic offices "were passing allusions rather than systematic formulae."[1] This seems to have been the case until the Reformation.

JOHN CALVIN

John Calvin (AD 1509–64) was impressed by the fact that Messiah means "the Anointed One" and that these offices were those associated with an anointing. The office of prophet was problematic, for it did not seem to require an anointing with oil. But this was offset in his mind by Isaiah 61:1: "The Spirit of the Lord God is on me, because the Lord has anointed me to bring good news to the poor."[2] Therefore, Calvin concluded, "Prophets, as well as priests and kings were anointed with holy oil."[3] As Macleod says, "It was with these very words that Jesus himself began his prophetic ministry in the synagogue at Nazareth" (Luke 4:18).[4] Calvin's

---

1. Macleod, "The Work of Christ," 353.

2. In the Appendices, the *Holman Christian Standard Bible* [HCSB] is used, unless otherwise noted.

3. Calvin, *Institutes of the Christian Religion*, 2.15.1.

4. Macleod, "The Work of Christ," 355.

conclusion regarding the anointing of prophets with oil is debatable, but this was his position.

INFLUENCE OF RASHI VIA LYRA

Calvin's understanding of Jesus as a prophet was doubtless influenced by the commentaries of Rabbi Shlomo Yitzhaki (AD 1040–1105), commonly known as Rashi. He is still regarded as one of the most renowned of Jewish scholars, and he lived about four hundred years before Calvin.

Rashi's approach to the Scriptures was more literal, and this appealed to Nicholas de Lyra (c. AD 1270–349), a Franciscan monk, who wanted to free Christian interpretation of the Bible from the stifling effect of allegory and mysticism. Lyra had studied theology in Paris and mastered both Hebrew and Greek. Even though he lived before the Reformation, he saw in Rashi a way to return the church to a more literal hermeneutic.

Lyra's most famous work is his *Postilla*, originally a Latin term for a Bible commentary. The *Postilla* of Lyra is a commentary on the Old and New Testaments. It enjoyed great popularity and was often added to editions of the Vulgate. His commentary was based on Rashi's literal manner of interpreting Scripture. Rashi's influence was so great on Lyra's writings that critics called him "Rashi's Ape."

However, Rashi's method of interpreting Scripture was not only more literal, but it was also less messianic. For example, Rashi did not interpret Deuteronomy 18:15–19 as a messianic prophecy, but merely as a prophecy concerning a line of prophets that would succeed Moses. In keeping with the precedent of Peter and Stephen in the New Testament, the disciples of Jesus in Rashi's day used this passage to point to Jesus's identity as the Messiah. Rashi could not allow such a messianic interpretation. Rashi's perspective was also, if unwittingly, adopted by Lyra. It was reflected in his commentary, and it was adopted by the Reformers.

One mediatorial office. This perspective influenced Calvin, and his thoughts on the messianic offices were more fully developed in his 1539 edition of the *Institutes*. Just as Lyra and Rashi before him, Calvin did not recognize the prophecy in Deuteronomy 18:15–19 as referring to a specific and ultimate Prophet, but instead, as speaking of merely the function of the prophets of the Old Testament. He says, "God, by supplying an uninterrupted succession of prophets, never left his people destitute of useful doctrine."⁵ While this is certainly true, it ignores the clear promise of the passage.

Nevertheless, the provision of "useful doctrine" was, and is, a function of Messiah. He says, "In the doctrine which he delivered is substantially included a wisdom which is perfect in all its parts."⁶ The ministry of Jesus as prophet is seen by Calvin in relation to the doctrine He delivered to the church, not as an office he occupied or a position he exercised at any particular time.

The same perspective is found in his treatment of the functions of king and priest. Calvin writes regarding Messiah as king: "There can be no doubt that God here promises that he will be, by the hand of his Son, the eternal governor and defender of the Church."⁷ With respect to his office as priest, Calvin sees Messiah's sacrificial death as a priestly work. He says, "Because a deserved curse obstructs the entrance [i.e., into 'the favour of God'], and God in his character of Judge is hostile to us, expiation must necessarily intervene, that as a priest employed to appease the wrath of God, he may reinstate us in his favour."⁸

Calvin not only associates Messiah's death but also his intercession with a priestly function. He says, "From this again arises not only confidence in prayer, but also the tranquility of pious minds, while they recline in safety on the paternal indulgence of God, and feel assured, that whatever has been consecrated by the Mediator is pleasing to him."⁹ In all this, that which characterizes the essence of each of these offices also characterizes the three aspects of Messiah's one mediatorial office.

So effective was Calvin's description of a single, threefold office of Messiah—including the functions of prophet, priest, and king—that "after Calvin, the threefold office became a key formula in Reformed catechesis and theology."¹⁰ It was later incorporated into the Westminster Confession of Faith (8.3), the Westminster Larger Catechism (42–45), and the Westminster Shorter Catechism (23–26).¹¹ It was used by later Reformed scholars and even by some outside of Reformed circles.

---

5. Calvin, *Institutes of the Christian Religion*, 2.15.2. Here, he also cites Hebrews 1:1–2.

6. Calvin, *Institutes of the Christian Religion*, 2.15.2.

7. Calvin, *Institutes of the Christian Religion*, 2.15.3.

8. Calvin, *Institutes of the Christian Religion*, 2.15.6.

9. Calvin, *Institutes of the Christian Religion*, 2.15.6.

10. Macleod, "The Work of Christ," 354.

11. Macleod, "The Work of Christ," 354.

This threefold office has been dubbed the *munis triplex*, the triple cure. It is like the three facets of a prism—an interrelated unity. As Daniel Treier puts it, "As Messiah, God's Anointed One, the incarnate Son of God fulfilled three primary offices in a united, ultimate way."[12] Millard Erickson writes, "It will be important to maintain all three aspects of his work, not stressing one so that the others are diminished, nor splitting them too sharply from one another as if they were separate actions of Christ."[13] Following a discussion of Jesus's revelatory role, Erickson summarizes, "When the whole biblical picture of Jesus is taken into account, his work as revealer cannot be split from his work as ruler and reconciler."[14]

Calvin and those who follow him do not seem to give due significance to the chronological sequence presented in Hebrews. Jesus as the Prophet and the Servant of the Lord had to live a perfect life and die an atoning death in order to qualify as the Priest like Melchizedek. He could not have served as a priest until the establishment of the New Covenant at the time of his death on the cross (Heb 7:4–28).

In speaking of the rule of Messiah, Calvin conflates God's universal sovereignty over the cosmos with Jesus's reign over the Messianic Kingdom.[15] In addition, he does not seem to recognize that dominion over the kingdoms of the world has been given to Satan for the present time (Luke 4:5–6). Instead of seeing Messiah in three separate roles which are initiated sequentially and exercised cumulatively, Calvin sees these functions as descriptive of the relationship between Messiah and the redeemed in a unified and simultaneous manner.

The Calvinist understanding of the *munis triplex* is usually considered in discussions of the work of Messiah, but it is also related to the needs and identity of Christians and corresponds to the threefold nature of man. Macleod denies that Calvin adopted the *munis triplex* because "it corresponded neatly to man's threefold spiritual need (knowledge, forgiveness, and deliverance)."[16] Yet, Macleod implies that he and others do see this as significant. Indeed, Treier says, "It . . . helps those who are new in Christ to understand their redeemed identity."[17] It also defines our proper response to Messiah.

12. Treier, *Lord Jesus Christ*, 232.
13. Erickson, *Christian Theology*, 782.
14. Erickson, *Christian Theology*, 786.
15. Erickson, *Christian Theology*, 786.
16. Macleod, "The Work of Christ," 354.
17. Treier, *Lord Jesus Christ*, 233.

Treier explains:

> As Prophet, Christ is the revelatory Mediator, representing God to humanity, addressing our ignorance.... As Priest, Jesus is the redemptive Mediator, representing humanity before God, offering himself vicariously, addressing our enmity.... As King, Jesus Christ mediates divine rule as both God and man, addressing our bondage. The Mediator initiates our participation in God's reign over the cosmos.... Each office highlights facets of a unified Christological reality. Christ the Prophet proclaims truth, eliciting faith. Christ the Priest gives life, eliciting love. Christ the King leads the way, eliciting hope.[18]

Even so, he does seem to allow for a discrete role of Jesus as the ultimate Prophet in the past when he says, "The prophetic office was the only one that Jesus exercised during his earthly ministry,"[19] though he does not elaborate. Nevertheless, for the present, Treier says, "The threefold office celebrates the ultimate unification of these mediating offices in the incarnate Son."[20]

MARTIN LUTHER

Martin Luther (1483–1546) was also greatly influenced by Nicholas de Lyra—so much so that some of his contemporaries quipped, "If Lyra had not played, Luther could not have danced."[21] For this reason, Luther failed to recognize much of the messianic significance of the Hebrew Scriptures.

Luther may also have been influenced by Immanuel Tremellius, an eminent Hebraist, Jewish Christian, and close associate of Calvin, especially in Heidelberg. Tremellius's biographer establishes that "he was well versed in rabbinic literature."[22] As a professor at the University of Heidelberg, he was strategically placed to exert a major influence throughout Europe, and his writings and translations were widely acclaimed in Reformed circles. Nevertheless, in the Lutheran Church, Johann Gerhard (1582–1637) was the theologian who most fully developed the

---

18. Treier, *Lord Jesus Christ*, 233–34.
19. Treier, *Lord Jesus Christ*, 234.
20. Treier, *Lord Jesus Christ*, 235.
21. Pearl, *Rashi*, 100.
22. See Austin, *From Judaism to Calvinism*, 110–11. See also, Pool, "The Influence of Some Jewish Apostates on the Reformation," 340.

understanding of Jesus's mediatorial office as prophetic, priestly, and kingly.[23]

Calvinism and the Reformed tradition have transformed the three prophesied offices of Messiah into one office with three aspects. They have also relocated the study of the offices of prophet, priest, and king from their original position in biblical studies to a subcategory, *munis triplex*, under the heading "The Work of Christ" in theological studies (dogmatics). However, modern biblical studies are reclaiming these as the distinct roles of Messiah as they are presented in the Scriptures. Certainly, the expectation in the Gospels was for the Prophet (see Deut 34:10), one who would be similar to, but greater than, Moses, not merely someone whose role had a "prophetic aspect."

Many today still hold this view. Like a schoolboy who licked a frozen lamppost, they are stuck to the Reformer's misunderstanding of these three offices of Messiah. They still see them primarily as benefits for believers. The Reformed understanding has a point, but it has missed the main point. It is a half-truth, and one with which no one should be content. In Deuteronomy 18:15–19, God promised to "raise up" a Prophet like Moses. In 1 Samuel 2:35, God promised to "raise up" a faithful Priest. In Jeremiah 23:5, God promised to "raise up" the Messianic King. These are three distinct and important roles, not just things that characterize Messiah's ministry.

DISPENSATIONALISM

Biblical scholarship has moved on. Careful attention to the text of Scripture has helped us see that we are told of three distinct roles of Messiah and that they are initiated sequentially and exercised cumulatively. Some Dispensational authors hold to the more dominant Reformed views,[24] but many understand the prophecies as referring to three discrete roles or offices, each occupied in turn by the Messiah. These authors may differ on the details, but they usually see three offices rather than one, and these roles are fulfilled sequentially. This insight also supports the view that the Messianic Kingdom is yet future.

David L. Cooper writes:

---

23. See Dorner, "Jesus: Prophet, Priest, King," 226–29.
24. E.g., cf. Kreider, "Jesus the Messiah as Prophet, Priest, and King," 174–87.

In view of all these facts [i.e., the uniqueness of Moses, the prophecy of One like him, and the fact that this One had not arisen by the conclusion of the Old Testament period], one must conclude that God was speaking of a definite, specific person through whom He would speak in a special manner in fulfillment of Israel's request at Sinai. God gave a special revelation through Moses—the law. From time to time, He has spoken through His various prophets, but He spoke in a unique and special manner through Moses. His promise to raise up a prophet like Moses implies, therefore, that He would give a special revelation through this promised prophet.[25]

Arnold Fruchtenbaum says, "He does not function in all three offices contemporaneously or simultaneously, but rather chronologically."[26] Harold Willmington concludes his paper by laying out his view of the chronology:

Thus to summarize His three offices: His role as a prophet began at the River Jordan and ended at Calvary. His role as a priest began at Calvary (where He offered up Himself), and continues today in heaven (where He prays for His people), and will end at the Second Coming. His role as a king will begin at the Battle of Armageddon and continue through the Millennium.[27]

Not all would agree with Willmington's chronology, but these authors illustrate the view presented here.

---

25. Cooper, *Messiah*, 46.
26. Fruchtenbaum, *The Footsteps of the Messiah*, 18.
27. Willmington, "Jesus Christ as Prophet, Priest, and King," unpaginated.

Appendix 2

The "Generation" of Matthew 24:34

"WHEN WILL THESE THINGS HAPPEN?"

STUDENTS OF SCRIPTURE HAVE long wrestled with the meaning of Matthew 24:34: "I assure you: This generation will certainly not pass away until all these things take place." Typically, Matthew 24 is interpreted as though it were an answer to the disciples's question in verse 3: "Tell us, when will these things happen? And what is the sign of Your coming and of the end of the age?" This is similar to the question asked by the Pharisees as to when the Kingdom of God was coming in Luke 17:20. It is also similar to the question the disciples would later ask him in Acts 1:6: "Lord, are You restoring the kingdom to Israel at this time?" Since the questions are similar, perhaps it would be helpful to compare the answers Jesus gave.

In Luke 17:20, he answered the Pharisees by saying, "The kingdom of God is not coming with something observable." In Acts 1:7, he told his disciples, "It is not for you to know times or periods that the Father has set by His own authority." In neither case did he respond by giving a timetable. Likewise, here in Matthew 24:36 Jesus says, "Now concerning that day and hour no one knows—neither the angels in heaven, nor the Son—except the Father only." It is therefore unlikely that he is departing from this agnostic view of the timing of the Kingdom here in Matthew 24:34.

"THIS GENERATION"

Previous attempts to interpret "generation" in verse 34 have been hampered by the misperception that the main purpose of this verse is to contribute information about the timing of the Second Coming. Certainly, the order of future events is given, and the accompanying signs are described, but the time cannot be known. There are three commonly held interpretations. "Generation" may be understood as referring to one of the following: Jesus's generation, the "terminal" generation, or the people of Israel.

Those who see it as the generation living at the time of Jesus[1] must say that this generation would witness the *beginning* of these things. But verse 34 demands that they witness *all* these things. In any case, this interpretation adds nothing to an understanding of the timing of the events preceding the Second Coming.

Those who take it as referring to the "terminal" generation[2] can only say that this generation will know these end times events are happening when they see them. Again, this interpretation makes no contribution to a discussion of the timing of the Lord's return. Some see a dual fulfillment that begins with Jesus's generation but is ultimately fulfilled in end times.[3]

Finally, there are others who understand the Greek word *genea* as referring not to a specific "generation," but to an ethnic group or a physical lineage—namely, the people of Israel. That is to say, the people of Israel will endure to the end. But this is stated often in Scripture, and like the previous explanations, it adds nothing to an understanding of the timing of these events. This diversity of thought has led some to resist taking a position.[4]

---

1. See Blomberg, *Matthew*, 364; Carson, "Matthew," 507; Hagner, *Matthew 14–28*, 715; Luz, *Matthew 21–28*, 208; Turner, *Matthew*, 585–86; Cranfield, "The Parable of the Unjust Judge and the Eschatology of Luke-Acts," 300–301.

2. See Toussaint, *Behold the King*, 276–80; Vlach, *He Will Reign Forever*, 385. Vlach says, "No one knows when this period of tribulation that culminates in the coming of Jesus will take place, but when it does the generation who sees these events can grasp they are the ones who will see the coming of Jesus" (280).

3. Blaising, "A Case for the Pretribulation Rapture," 40; Pettegrew, "The Messiah's Lecture on the Future of Israel," 280–83; Stagg, "Matthew," 221.

4. See Gaebelein, *The Olivet Discourse*, 74–75; *The Ryrie Study Bible*, note on Matthew 24:34; Walvoord, *Matthew*, 192–94. None of these three (Gaebelein, Ryrie, or Walvoord) render a decision regarding the interpretation of the word.

THE CONTEXT: MATTHEW 24

In Matthew 24:4–14, Jesus characterizes the opposition and suffering to be endured by his disciples. In verses 15–28, he describes conditions during the Tribulation (v. 21). In verses 29–31, he speaks of the supernatural signs that will mark the end of the Tribulation and the arrival of "the Son of Man." This is followed by the illustration of the fig tree in verses 32–33: "As soon as its branch becomes tender and sprouts leaves, you know that summer is near. In the same way, when you see all these things, recognize that He is near—at the door!" The signs of verses 29–31 ("these things") indicate that the return of the Lord is very near, though the specific time cannot be known.

THE MEANING OF "GENERATION"

If Matthew 24:34 was not intended to address the timing of the return of Jesus, how should it be interpreted? The word behind this translation is the Greek word γενεά, or *genea*. It is most often understood as a generation. This is how most English translations translate it. But the word is actually "a term relating to the product of the act of generating and with special reference to kinship, frequently used of familial connections and ancestry. Generally, those descended from a common ancestor, a 'clan,' then those exhibiting common characteristics or interests."[5]

This secondary meaning, "those exhibiting common characteristics or interests," has not been given sufficient attention. This Greek word and its Hebrew equivalent (דור, *dor*) may, and often do, refer to a spiritual lineage, rather than a physical one. A spiritual lineage is characterized by "common characteristics."[6] This meaning of the Hebrew word *dor* and the Greek word *genea* seems to be well-established in biblical thought from the time of Moses and of the Exodus. In fact, even earlier, Cain and Abel, though brothers, were characterized by two different attitudes toward God. They seem to stand as the heads of two spiritual lineages— those who are trusting in the Lord and those who are rejecting the Lord.

---

5. BDAG, 191

6. See Konradt, *Israel, Church, and the Gentiles in the Gospel of Matthew*, 208–14. See also Evald Lövenstam, *Jesus and "This Generation."* For דור, *dor* (generation), *HALOT* includes the meaning, "class of persons, formally, generation, i.e., a group exhibiting similarities (Dt 32:5; Pr 30:11)."

When Moses described those who rebelled against him and against the Lord, he referred to them as "this evil generation"[7] or a "devious and crooked generation."[8] He was not condemning all Israelites within a specific age range (e.g., his contemporaries), for that would have included himself, Aaron, and Caleb. For the same reason, he was not condemning all the lineage of Abraham, Isaac, and Jacob (the Israelites) of that time. Instead, he was referring to a group (the vast majority, to be sure) within Israel—those who rejected his leadership and the Lord whom he represented.

Isaiah used different words but the same thought when he cried out, "Oh sinful nation, people weighed down with iniquity, brood of evildoers, depraved children! They have abandoned the Lord; they have despised the Holy One of Israel; they have turned their backs on Him." (Isa 1:4). Here, Isaiah uses "nation," "people," "offspring" (seed), and "sons" in the same way Moses used "generation." However, Isaiah had much to say about the preservation of a remnant (Isa 1:9, 26; 6:13; 10:20, etc.).

Jeremiah pleaded with the "generation" of evildoers in his day to "pay attention to" the word of the Lord, using language suggestive of the Exodus (Jer 2:31). The prophets used the Hebrew word for a generation, *dor*, in the same way Moses had. It was sometimes used of a group defined by their common characteristic of rebellion against the Lord.[9] For example, Exodus 20:5 threatens that God will visit the iniquity of the fathers on the children, "to the third and the fourth generations of those who hate Me."

The psalmist referred both to an evil generation and a righteous generation in Israel. On the one hand, we find references to the rebellious generation. Psalm 78:8 speaks of "a stubborn and rebellious generation, a generation whose heart was not loyal and whose spirit was not faithful to God." Psalm 95:10 speaks of a generation "whose hearts go astray; they do not know My ways."[10]

On the other hand, "generation" is also used in describing those who fear the Lord. Psalm 14:5 (KJV) says that "God is in the generation of the

---

7. Deut 1:35, הדור הרע הזה, *ha-dor ha-ra hazeh*.

8. Deut 32:5 (see also v. 20), דור עקש ופתלתל, *dor iqesh uphtaltol*; LXX, γενεὰ σκολιὰ καὶ διεστραμμένη, *genea skolia kai diestramene*. Numbers 32:13 refers to "the entire generation of those who had done evil in the sight of the Lord."

9. J. Hamilton claims that "the Bible commonly describes people figuratively as children of those whose characteristics they emulate." J. Hamilton, "The Skull Crushing Seed of the Woman," 33. See also 47–48, n. 32.

10. Psalm 95:10 is also quoted in Hebrews 3:10. See also Ps 12:7; 78:8; 95:10.

righteous." Psalm 24:6 speaks of the remnant of Israel as "the generation of those who seek Him, who seek the face of the God of Jacob." Psalm 112:2 declares that "the generation of the upright will be blessed." So, from a biblical perspective, Israel was composed of two spiritual lineages: the faithful remnant who sought the Lord and those who were rebellious, sinful, and stubborn.

Is it possible to find the same usage of "generation" in Matthew's Gospel? Addressing the scribes and Pharisees, Jesus tells the parable of the children in the market. In Matthew 11:16 he asks, "To what should I compare this generation?" He uses "generation" in this way, even as Moses had (Matt 12:39, 41–42, 45).[11] In Matthew 23:36, Jesus seems to use "generation" to refer to all those who had killed and persecuted God's messengers—the prophets and others whom God had sent, from the time of Abel to Zechariah.

After a thorough examination of Matthew's use of "generation" as a denunciation, Anthony Saldarini concludes:

> In sum, Matthew uses the sayings about "this [evil, adulterous] generation" to attack those who reject Jesus, especially the leaders of the Jewish community both in Jesus' day and his own. He does not condemn all of Israel, nor does he simply identify "this generation" with the crowds, who are sheep without a shepherd and who approach Jesus for healing and teaching. "This generation" is an expression which gains its precise meaning from its polemical contexts.[12]

When Peter preached on the Day of Pentecost, he "strongly urged them, saying, 'Be saved from this corrupt generation!'" (Acts 2:40). Paul speaks of these two groups within Israel in Romans 11: the "remnant" (v. 5) and the "rest" (v. 7). In Philippians 2:15, he refers to the "children of God who are faultless," who are "blameless and pure." Yet here he also speaks of "a crooked and perverted generation." Jude sketches the lineage of rebellion from Cain to Balaam to Korah to the false teachers of his day, and even to fallen angels (see Jude 4–6 and 12–16).

In light of this usage, I suggest that in Matthew 24:34, Jesus, as the Prophet like Moses, may be referring to a spiritual lineage rather than to either a physical lineage (the people of Israel) or a physical generation (i.e., a period of either forty or seventy years).

---

11. See also Matt 16:4; 17:17.
12. Saldarini, *Matthew's Christian-Jewish Community*, 41–42.

A MESSAGE TO HIS DISCIPLES

Identifying Jesus's audience can help us correctly interpret this verse. He is speaking to his disciples initially (Matt 24:1, 3), then to those in the Tribulation who will endure to the end (v. 13). Finally, he seems to be speaking to "the elect" who survive the Great Tribulation (vv. 22, 24, 31). Jesus, the Prophet like Moses, has divided Israel—many have rejected him, but others have turned to him in repentance and faith. It is to these faithful ones, his disciples both present and future, that he directs this message.

In Matthew 24, the Lord tells of the stages in God's future program. But it is for the purpose of giving assurance to his disciples that their proclamation of the gospel, in spite of the suffering they may endure, will not have been in vain. God will always preserve the generation of those who seek him, the faithful remnant of Israel (v. 34). Though many may die as martyrs, the people and purposes of God cannot be thwarted, and their suffering and possible martyrdom will not have been in vain.

This is similar to the Lord's prophecy in Matthew 10:16–23 of the suffering his disciples will endure for his sake, yet they will endure and remain faithful "before the Son of Man comes" (v. 23). In both passages, the emphasis seems to be on perseverance, with the knowledge that God will preserve the witness and the "generation" of those who are faithful to him.

In Matthew 23, he says to the scribes and Pharisees, "This is why I am sending you prophets, sages, and scribes. Some of them you will kill and crucify, and some of them you will flog in your synagogues and hound from town to town. . . . I assure you: All these things will come on this generation" (vv. 34, 36). This passage is to forestall despair and to offer hope. In the midst of this suffering and tribulation, God is in control.

Therefore, I believe it best to understand this passage to be an encouragement to the disciples of Jesus, in every period of time to endure, to persevere even unto death, with the certain knowledge that their testimony and witness will not be in vain. Revelation 12:11 reinforces this interpretation. Speaking of this remnant, the Lord says, "They conquered him by the blood of the Lamb and by the word of their testimony, for they did not love their lives in the face of death."

Appendix 3

Views of the Kingdom

MOST CHRISTIANS DON'T GIVE much thought to the Kingdom, but how we view this subject can have a surprising impact on many areas of the Christian life. An incorrect view of the Kingdom can lead to the "prosperity gospel," an emphasis on "signs and wonders," and a view of missions defined by social justice and political activism. We will begin with a brief survey of the major positions, but I want to especially evaluate the "Kingdom Offer" view.

REALIZED ESCHATOLOGY

Eschatology is the doctrine of last things. Realized Eschatology is a theological theory that the prophetic passages in the New Testament do not refer to the future at all, but instead refer to the ministry of Jesus while on earth and are spiritualized to extend to the present in and through his disciples. This position has no place for futuristic interpretations because it views them all as irrelevant. The only imperative is to follow Jesus in a life of obedience and discipleship. In contrast to the Jewish and traditional Christian view, this position insists that the Kingdom is not future at all—it is present.

This view is especially attractive to liberal Christians in mainline denominations who prefer to emphasize the love and goodness of God while rejecting the notion of righteous judgment. It has given rise to an emphasis on the "social gospel" and on addressing the issues of poverty and social oppression—an emphasis which led to Liberation Theology.

Realized Eschatology was popularized by Ethelbert Stauffer (1902-1979), C. H. Dodd (1884-1973), and others. Stauffer was a part of the "German Christian" movement in Germany, and its goal was to bring theology into alignment with Nazi ideology. In 1957, he acknowledged his anti-Semitic views and said, "The primary role of Jesus research is clear: De-Judaizing the Jesus tradition."[1] Eliminating the Jewish and biblical view of the Kingdom fit with his values, for it "de-Judaized" eschatology by eliminating any Jewish (or biblical) emphasis on the future Kingdom toward which history is moving.

INAUGURATED ESCHATOLOGY

When Realized Eschatology (which says the Kingdom is present) is combined with a more traditional view (which says the Kingdom is future), the result is Inaugurated Eschatology. This view, like Realized Eschatology, says that the end times were inaugurated in the life, death, and resurrection of Jesus. But proponents of this view also believe the Kingdom is future. There are features of the Kingdom that suggest it is "already" here to some extent, though "not yet" in its fullness.

This position was popularized by George Eldon Ladd, especially among American evangelicals. It is the dominant view at present. While the belief in a future aspect of the Kingdom is still preserved, the emphasis is on the present reality of the Kingdom. In most evangelical churches, seminaries, and mission boards, there is talk of doing "kingdom business," of raising up "kingdom leaders," and of involvement in "kingdom ministry." Few who hold this position recognize that the overwhelming, if not the only, emphasis in Scripture, is on the future Kingdom.

KINGDOM THEOLOGY

Kingdom Theology is similar to Inaugurated Eschatology but advocates the taking of initiatives now to establish the Kingdom on earth at present. Those who hold this view believe the Kingdom of God should be manifested today. They say that the purpose of both individual Christians and the church as a whole is to manifest the Kingdom of God on earth

---

1. Klee, *Das Personenlexikon zum DrittenReich*, 598.

by emphasizing political activism and social action along with personal evangelism and foreign missions.

This has given rise among evangelicals to an "incarnational" view of missions. This is not the same as what we mean when we speak of being incarnational, in the sense of effectively sharing the gospel by learning the language and adapting to the culture of the people we want to reach. Of course, missionaries should learn the language and culture of a people and communicate the gospel in terms they can understand and accept. But some believe we are to incarnate the mission of Jesus. This is interpreted as fighting for social justice, economic justice, ecological concern, activism against pharmaceutical companies, etc.[2]

In contrast, the traditional view is that we are not to duplicate the mission of Jesus, for his mission was unique, but we are to be representatives of Jesus. In the traditional view, we are to make disciples as he commissioned. This is an important topic, but one we cannot deal with here.[3] Kingdom Theology claims that though there is a future aspect to the Kingdom, the emphasis is on advancing the Kingdom in the present through social activism.

KINGDOM NOW THEOLOGY

Kingdom Now Theology, or a variant that is called Dominion Theology, is advocated by C. Peter Wagner. John Wimber, the founder of the Vineyard movement, also holds to this theology, emphasizing signs and wonders as the manifestation of the Kingdom. This theology says God is looking for people who will help him regain lost territory and take back dominion.

This theology has been adopted by the more Charismatic elements of evangelicalism because it provides a theological basis for the more spectacular manifestations of the Holy Spirit, such as healing ministries, attempts to raise the dead, etc.[4] The "Word of Faith" teaching and the "New Apostolic Reformation" have arisen out of this theology. Of course, as might be expected, the emphasis is on the present existence of the Kingdom.

2. See, for example, Wright, *The Mission of God*.

3. For an incisive (and brief) assessment of this incarnational view, see Donald Hesselgrave's book, *Paradigms in Conflict*, 141–65. For a full response, see DeYoung and Gilbert, *What Is the Mission of the Church?* DeYoung and Gilbert hold to inaugurated eschatology and Replacement Theology, but they address Incarnationalism very well.

4. See, M. Saucy, *The Kingdom of God in the Teaching of Jesus*, 305.

Most of these views either deny or de-emphasize the future Messianic Kingdom. Charles Horne says that a futuristic view of the Kingdom is important, "because it sounds a refreshing note of hope against the backdrop of the despair which has largely characterized our age in the West."[5] While this is true, more importantly, a futuristic view of the Kingdom is essential for it reflects the view of the Kingdom promised in the Old Testament and anticipated in the New Testament.

THE "KINGDOM OFFER" VIEW

Dispensationalism is divided on the subject of the Kingdom. On the one hand, much current Dispensational thought has embraced an inaugurated view of the Kingdom. This is especially the case with Progressive Dispensationalism (also known as "Redemptive Kingdom Theology"[6]). But, on the other hand, there are still others who claim that the Kingdom has been postponed since the First Century. Dispensationalism struggles to understand why the gospel seems to have gone predominantly to the Gentiles, while the majority of the people of Israel seems to have been left behind. I have previously addressed the inaugurated view but must now give attention to the "kingdom offer" view.

Why did Jesus prophesy the destruction of the temple and pronounce judgment on Jerusalem? The most common answer is that this judgment was due to Israel's rejection of the Kingdom. According to this view, Jesus offered the Kingdom to Israel during his earthly ministry, but Israel rejected the offer (Matt 12). As a consequence, the offer of the Kingdom was taken "off the table," and it will not be offered again unless and until Israel repents. According to this position, the Kingdom is not only in the future, but it is also contingent on Israel's response.[7] In the meantime, Israel has been "put on the shelf" to await its future. Evidence for such an offer is difficult to find. If the "Kingdom of God" is to be taken from Israel's leadership in Matthew 12, how is it then that Jesus says it will be taken from them and transferred to the apostles in Matthew 21:43?

---

5. Horne, "Eschatology—The Controlling Thematic in Theology," 55.

6. See Blaising, "A Theology of Israel and the Church," 88. On the same page, see n. 9. For more on Progressive Dispensationalism, see Blaising and Bock, eds., *Dispensationalism, Israel and the Church*; Blaising and Bock, *Progressive Dispensationalism*; R. Saucy, *The Case for Progressive*.

7. Woods, *The Coming Kingdom*. See especially pp. 53–177.

Jesus prophesies judgment on Jerusalem with a particular focus on the temple. He weeps over the city and says:

> If you knew this day *what would bring peace*—but now *it is hidden from your eyes.* For the days will come on you when your enemies will build an embankment against you, surround you, and hem you in on every side. They will crush you and your children within you to the ground, and they will not leave one stone on another in you, because *you did not recognize the time of your visitation.*[8]

Here, Jesus says the reason for the coming destruction is because they "did not recognize the time of [their] visitation" or "what would bring peace." This is explained with reference to the blindness of Israel—that is, the inability of most of the people to repent or to perceive essential spiritual truth.[9] Jesus says these conditions for peace "have been hidden from your eyes." There is no mention of a kingdom offer. In fact, this destruction of the city and temple had also been prophesied by Daniel, seven hundred years previously, in Daniel 9:26.

This judgment is completely in line with the warning God had given should the people refuse to heed the Prophet like Moses, for the words he would speak would be the very words of God. God said, "I will hold accountable whoever does not listen to My words that he speaks in My name" (Deut 18:19). Jesus preached the gospel of the Kingdom, or as Peter put it, the "words of eternal life" (John 6:68). Temporal consequences, such as the destruction of the temple, would follow the rejection of his call to repentance and faith, though they were much less significant than the eternal consequences of a failure to heed the Prophet like Moses.

This supposed "kingdom offer" is a teaching that needs to be addressed more fully than some of these other views. There are at least ten objections that must be raised.

1. What Jesus offered Israel was not the Kingdom but the gospel of the Kingdom. So, Israel did not reject the Kingdom itself, but the *gospel* of the Kingdom. As Paul put it, what they "rejected" was "salvation."[10] This was their "stumble," their "transgression," their "failure" (Rom 11:11–12, NASB95). In other words, the gospel of the Kingdom is the gospel of grace that is now offered to all.

---

8. Luke 19:42–44, emphasis added.
9. See Isa 6:10; 44:18.
10. Rom 11:11–15. See Sibley, "Has the Church Put Israel on the Shelf?", 571–81.

Some point to Matthew 3:1–2, where John the Baptist came preaching, "Repent, because the kingdom of heaven has come near!" They claim this was an appeal to receive Jesus as a king, and therefore to accept the Kingdom he would offer. Is this true? "Kingdom of heaven" is another way of referring to the "kingdom of God."[11] What is meant by "the kingdom of heaven" in this context?

When we turn back to the announcement of John's conception and birth in Luke 1:16–17, we read that he was to "turn many of the sons of Israel to the Lord their God." This is explained with the phrase, "to turn the hearts of fathers to their children, and the disobedient to the understanding of the righteous, to make ready for the Lord a prepared people" (Luke 1:17). Here, "the fathers" are the patriarchs of Israel: Abraham, Isaac, and Jacob.[12] John was to call the people to repentance as preparation for them to become disciples of Jesus, "to make ready for the Lord a prepared people." and this is referred to as preaching "the kingdom of heaven" (Matt 3:2).

In Mark 1:4, we are told that John the Baptist was preaching "a baptism of repentance for the forgiveness of sins," and this is also the report in Luke 3:3. We must conclude that when John was preaching that the "the kingdom of heaven has come near," he was calling people to repent and become citizens of the coming Kingdom through faith in Jesus.

In Luke 9, we read that Jesus sent his twelve disciples out to the towns and villages. They were to stay in homes where hospitality was extended to them. But what was their message? What were they to preach? They were to preach "the kingdom of God" (v. 2). What does this mean? Does it mean they were to extend the offer of the Kingdom? Verse 6 tells us very clearly: "So they went out and traveled from village to village, *proclaiming the good news* and healing everywhere."[13]

In this passage, it is clear that the phrase "kingdom of God" is sometimes used of the gospel—the good news that through faith in Jesus

---

11. See Matt 19:23–24.

12. When used as a plural, "fathers" always refers to "ancestors" in the Gospels. It is used of the Samaritan ancestors in John 4:20; of those ancestors who persecuted the prophets in Matthew 23:30, 32; Luke 6:23, 26; 11:47–48; of those ancestors of the Exodus generation in John 6:31, 49, 58; and of the ancestors of Israel in John 7:22 and here in Luke 1:17. The idea is that the people would be turned back to the faith of Abraham, Isaac, and Jacob. Here the people are called "disobedient" and "the fathers" are called "the righteous."

13. Emphasis added.

citizenship may be gained in the future Kingdom of God.[14] This was the gospel of the Kingdom that was preached by Jesus and his disciples and was rejected by the majority of the nation. This rejection brought judgment on that generation (see Appendix 2). Yet though they rejected him, he never rejected the nation, not even temporarily.[15]

Likewise, Matthew 4:23 says, "Jesus was going all over Galilee, teaching in their synagogues, preaching the good news of the kingdom, and healing every disease and sickness among the people."[16] In Matthew 11:5, this preaching is simply called "the good news." Since it is the gospel that is to be preached in the whole world (Matt 26:13), it certainly is not Israel's offer of the Kingdom that is to be preached. Neither is there any reference here to Jesus as King. It was not the Kingdom, but the *gospel* of the Kingdom that was offered.

2. The judgment of spiritual blindness had rendered the majority of Israel spiritually incapable of considering such an offer. John says that "they *did not believe* in Him" because "they *were unable* to believe."[17] That's the reason Jesus was always calling for those "who have ears to hear."[18] He was calling forth a believing remnant.

To imagine that it was the Kingdom that was being offered to the nation, if it would accept the King, ignores the biblical doctrine of spiritual blindness. This "kingdom offer" would be like offering a blind man a steak dinner if he could only pass a vision test! Such a proposal might be a cruel joke, but it could not be considered a genuine offer.

This judgment of spiritual blindness, enacted through Isaiah, provides the context in which Messiah could be sacrificed as an atonement for sin (Isa 53:1, 3–8). The blindness of the majority of the Jewish people allowed for, and actually led to, Jesus's crucifixion, and it also led to mercy first being shown to the Gentiles and then to Israel (Rom 11:30–32). Such

---

14. This "gospel" was different from the gospel as Paul defined it in 1 Corinthians 15:3–4: "that Christ died for our sins according to the Scriptures, that He was buried, that He was raised on the third day." At this point in Messiah's ministry, the good news was that by becoming his disciple and trusting in him as the Son of God and the Messiah of Israel, citizenship could be gained in the future Kingdom of God.

15. For a refutation of the interpretation of Romans 11:15 that claims God did reject Israel, albeit temporarily, see Sibley, "Has the Church Put Israel on the Shelf?"

16. See also Matt 9:35; 24:14; 26:13; Mark 1:1, 14–15; 13:10; 14:9; 16:15; etc.

17. John 12:37, 39, emphasis added.

18. Matt 11:15; 13:9, 43; Mark 4:9, 23; Luke 8:8; 14:35. For "ears to hear" in these verses, see NASB, KJV, NIV, and others. The reference is to Isaiah 6:9–10.

an offer of the Kingdom could not be considered a bona fide offer if the recipients were incapable of receiving it.

3. The rejection of Messiah, his abuse, and his death do not signal an unanticipated turn of events—it was not a surprising disappointment that necessitated a change of plans, but it was a part of God's plan from the beginning. Messiah was prophesied to be rejected by his own people (Ps 69:8; Isa 53). He was to be a "stone to stumble over and a rock to trip over" (Isa 8:14), and he was to be "the stone that the builders rejected" (Ps 118:22). He was to be the one who is "despised," "abhorred" by the nation" (Isa 49:7), and hated "without cause" (Ps 69:4). Daniel says that Messiah would be "cut off" before the destruction of the temple and that Jerusalem would be destroyed (Dan 9:26).

This was not a defeat, but the way of Moses and the prophets who succeeded him. They too were opposed and rejected. This was the way that led to the atoning sacrifice of Messiah. The psalmist's conclusion was that his rejection led to his exaltation. Therefore, "This came from the Lord; it is wonderful in our eyes. This is the day the Lord has made; let us rejoice and be glad in it" (Ps 118:23–24).

4. Scripture does not teach that Jesus would rule in a kingdom without first having provided atonement for sin. If Israel had accepted Jesus's "kingdom offer," would it have been possible to have had the Messianic Kingdom prior to his death, burial, and resurrection? Nowhere in Scripture is the Messianic Kingdom ever envisioned apart from atonement. In Philippians 2:8–10, we are told:

> [Jesus] humbled Himself by becoming obedient to the point of death—even to death on a cross. For this reason God highly exalted Him and gave Him the name that is above every name, so that at the name of Jesus every knee will bow—of those who are in heaven and on earth and under the earth.

Here we see the cross before the crown. That the cross came before the crown was God's plan all along. How could there be a kingdom with no cross? There could not be.

5. This theology requires a "parenthesis" in God's program for Israel, which amounts to a temporary replacement of Israel with the church. According to this view, because the Kingdom was rejected by Israel, Israel has lost its favored position and has been removed from its place of blessing. That place is now occupied by the church, for the "church age" has been inserted into this "gap" in God's program for Israel.

Scripture does not allow for such a view, "since," as Paul says, "God's gracious gifts and calling are irrevocable" (Rom 11:29). Some Dispensationalists deny they believe in Replacement Theology, because they define it solely in terms of the future. For example, Darrell Bock says, "[Replacement Theology] focuses on how the fate of Israel, either as a nation or as a people, is ultimately seen. In other words, Israel can be 'replaced for now' at the centre of God's programme without being permanently replaced."[19]

The arguments in favor of this interpretation are very similar to those used to support more comprehensive Replacement Theology. Likewise, the arguments against Replacement Theology also apply to this "temporary replacement" view. Practically speaking, this form of Replacement Theology may tend to make the Jewish people all but irrelevant as far as missions and evangelism are concerned, even as comprehensive Replacement Theology tends to do. For God has set them to the side for now, according to this view. It also undermines the significance of the remnant of Israel.

6. The blessings that would flow from God's dealings with Israel were not limited to Israel—Israel was to be a blessing to the nations. Genesis 12:3 singles out Israel from the nations and says that blessings for the nations will come through Israel, from the chosen lineage of Abraham, Isaac, and Jacob. Bock translates the last phrase, "so that all the families of the earth may receive blessing through you."[20] But if the Church Age interrupts God's plan for Israel, so that Israel is currently set aside, how is Israel blessing the nations at present?

7. God does not have a "Plan B." Some think that God's "Plan A" was that the Kingdom would be established with Israel, but when Israel rejected the Kingdom, the Kingdom was offered to the Gentiles or to the church. God's plan that salvation would go to the Gentiles prior to the national restoration of Israel is not a response to the nation's rejection of his offer. It was his plan from eternity past. In Romans 11, we see that Israel's "transgression" was their rejection of salvation (v. 11), which has now come to the Gentiles. Injecting the subject of the Kingdom into Romans 11 is completely unwarranted. In Romans 11:30–32, Paul says:

> As you [i.e., Gentiles, cf. v. 13] once disobeyed God, but now have received mercy through their [i.e., the majority of the

---

19. Bock, "Replacement Theology with Implications for Messianic Jewish Relations," 238. See also, Pettegrew, "An Assessment of Covenant Theology," 169–70; and Bookman, "A Whale and an Elephant," 246–47.

20. Bock, "Israel, the Land, and the Promise," 33.

Jewish people's] disobedience, so they too have now disobeyed, resulting in mercy to you, so that they also now may receive mercy. For God has imprisoned all in disobedience, so that He may have mercy on all.

In the verses that follow, Paul does not say that this plan reveals the rejection of an offer of the Kingdom, but instead, the wisdom of God (see Rom 11:33–36).

8. This position requires a reading of Matthew 23:39 that is questionable. Here Jesus says, "You will not see Me from now (ἀπ' ἄρτι, *ap' arti*) until (ἕως ἄν, *eos an*) you say, 'Blessed is He who comes in the name of the Lord.'"[21] These expressions give the beginning and the end of a chronological period of time. The most common translation of *eos* (ἕως) is "until."[22] The nation will not see Jesus "until" a time in the future. At that time, Israel will say, "Blessed is He who comes in the name of the Lord."

At this time, Jesus was teaching in the courts of the temple (Matt 21:23). When we come to our verse in Matthew 23:39, Jesus has reached the end of his time at the temple. He will leave the temple (Matt 24:1), probably pass through the Eastern Gate, cross the Kidron Valley, and deliver what is called the Olivet Discourse from the Mount of Olives (Matt 24:3).

The three major characteristics of the period of time Jesus has announced are: (1) the removal of Jesus from their sight, (2) the continuation of the blindness of the majority of the people, and (3) the desolation and destruction of the temple.

In the first place, as we have seen, Jesus has already told his disciples repeatedly of his coming departure. He would not be physically present with them.

Secondly, apart from the believing remnant, the nation could not see who he was at that time. John 12:39 indicates that because of their spiritual blindness, "they were unable to believe." The judgment of spiritual blindness did not come upon the majority of the people as a result of anything that happened during the span of Jesus's earthly life and ministry, but it began in the days of Isaiah (Isa 6:9–10). This blindness will not be lifted until the Second Coming. Jesus is pointing here to his return, when their blindness will be removed. As Zechariah prophesied, "They will look at [Him] whom they pierced. They will mourn for Him as one mourns for an only child and weep bitterly for Him as one weeps

---

21. Author's translation.

22. See Alford, *Alford's Greek Testament*, 234; Quarles, *Matthew*, 279; and Bock, "God's Plan for History," 164–66.

for a firstborn" (Zech 12:10). Paul adds, "And in this way all Israel will be saved" (Rom 11:26). In Matthew 23:39, Jesus points to that time when they will say, "Blessed is He who comes in the name of the Lord."

Thirdly, this period would be characterized by the desolation and destruction of the temple. With Jesus's departure from the temple, it was deserted. God's presence would have departed. The temple had been desecrated (Matt 21:12–17), it would now be desolate, and eventually, it would be destroyed (Matt 24:2). This period would begin with Jesus's departure from the temple and would end with his return to the temple from the Mount of Olives.[23]

God is adamant that this period is not characterized by his rejection of Israel (Rom 11:1). On the basis of Romans 11:15, some say God has temporarily rejected Israel. A careful study of the passage, however, reveals that, rather than God rejecting Israel, the majority of Israel has rejected salvation (see n. 15, above). But the Lord still weeps for Israel and longs for the time when he will gather them under his wings (Matt 23:37).

9. This position fails to understand that Israel did not reject Jesus or the gospel of the Kingdom, but Israel was divided by these issues. In fact, according to Scripture, Israel has always been composed of two spiritual lineages that are sometimes referred to as "generations" or "nations." If one "generation" rejected the gospel of the Kingdom, the other accepted it. See Appendix 2.

10. Finally, just like every other people, Israel has provided more than enough evidence that it is incapable of meeting God's requirements. God is not to give Israel another chance; Israel doesn't need another chance. It needs God's rescue—his deliverance. Actually, Paul tells us what the "trigger" is for Israel's repentance and for the inauguration of the Kingdom. It is "the full number of the Gentiles," not Israel's acceptance of the Kingdom. Paul says, "A partial hardening has come to Israel *until the full number of the Gentiles has come in*. And in this way *all Israel will be saved.*"[24] With Israel's restoration, it will be able to fulfill its purpose.[25]

---

23. Cf. Ezek 10; 43:1–5.

24. Rom 11:25–26. Emphasis added.

25. Israel's "calling" was to be "a kingdom of priests and a holy nation" (Exod 19:6). This "calling" is "irrevocable" (Rom 11:29) and is currently being fulfilled partially, but it can only be fully realized when "the full number of the Gentiles has come in" (Rom 11:25). See Allison, "Romans 11:11–15," 30.

This unbiblical theory of a kingdom offer must be rejected for all these reasons. This view should not be embraced or taught if it cannot answer these objections.

EVALUATION

Has the Kingdom been inaugurated? Has it been postponed? Neither of these positions seems to best fit the biblical texts. We must hold to the view of the Kingdom promised in the Old Testament and anticipated in the New Testament. It is our inheritance and our blessed hope.

Bibliography

Abernethy, Andrew T. *The Book of Isaiah and God's Kingdom: A Thematic-Theological Approach*. Downers Grove, IL: InterVarsity, 2016.

Alexander, T. Desmond. "Further Observations on the Term 'Seed' in Genesis." *Tyndale Bulletin* 48 (1997) 363–67.

Alford, Henry. *Alford's Greek Testament: An Exegetical and Critical Commentary*. Vol. 1. Reprint of 7th ed. Grand Rapids: Baker Book House, 1980.

Allen, David L. *Hebrews*. The New American Commentary 35. Nashville, TN: B&H, 2010.

———. *Lukan Authorship of Hebrews*. NAC Studies in Bible and Theology. Nashville, TN: B&H Academic, 2010.

Allison Jr., Dale C. *The New Moses: A Matthean Typology*. Minneapolis, MN: Fortress, 1993.

———. "Romans 11:11–15: A Suggestion." *Perspectives in Religious Studies* 12 (1985) 23–30.

Anderson, Robert T., and Terry Giles. *Tradition Kept: The Literature of the Samaritans*. Peabody, MA: Hendrickson, 2005.

Attridge, Harold W. "How Priestly Is the 'High Priestly Prayer' of John 17?" *Catholic Biblical Quarterly* 75 (2013) 1–14.

August, Jared M. "The Messianic Hope of Genesis: The *Protoevangelium* and Patriarchal Promises." *Themelios* 42 (2017) 46–62.

Auler, Samuel. "More Than a Gift: Revisiting Paul's Collection for Jerusalem and the Pilgrimage of Gentiles." *Journal for the Study of Paul and His Letters* 6 (2016) 143–60.

Austin, Kenneth. *From Judaism to Calvinism: The Life and Writings of Immanuel Tremellius (1510–1580)*. Aldershot, England: Ashgate, 2007.

Baigent, John W. "Jesus as Priest: An Examination of the Claim That the Concept of Jesus as Priest May Be Found in the New Testament Outside the Epistle to the Hebrews." *Vox Evangelica* 12 (1981) 34–44.

Bailey, Kenneth E. "A Banquet of Death and a Banquet of Life: A Contextualized Study of Mark 6:1–52." *Theological Review* (Beirut) 29 (2008) 67–82.

Baldwin, Joyce G. *Haggai, Zechariah, and Malachi*. Tyndale Old Testament Commentary. Downers Grove, IL: InterVarsity, 1981.

Baron, David. *Rays of Messiah's Glory*. 2nd ed. London: Hodder and Stoughton, 1888.

———. *The Visions and Prophecies of Zechariah: "The Prophet of Hope and of Glory,"* an *Exposition*. London: Marshall, Morgan & Scott, 1918.
Barrick, William D. "The Kingdom of God in the Old Testament." *Masters Seminary Journal* 23 (2012) 173–192.
Bateman IV, Herbert W. "Psalm 110:1 and the New Testament." *Bibliotheca Sacra* 149 (1992) 452–53.
Bateman IV, Herbert W., Darrell L. Bock, and Gordon H. Johnston. *Jesus the Messiah: Tracing the Promises, Expectations, and Coming of Israel's King*. Grand Rapids: Kregel Academic, 2012.
Bauckham, Richard. *Jesus and the God of Israel: God Crucified and Other Studies on the New Testament's Christology of Divine Identity*. Grand Rapids: Eerdmans, 2008.
Bauer, Walter, Frederick W. Danker, W. F. Arndt, and F. W. Gingrich. *Greek-English Lexicon of the New Testament and Other Early Christian Literature*. 3rd ed. Chicago: University of Chicago Press, 2000.
Bavinck, Herman. *Sin and Salvation in Christ*. Vol. 3 of *Reformed Dogmatics*. Edited by John Bolt and translated by John Vriend. Grand Rapids: Baker Book House, 2006.
Beale, G. K. *A New Testament Biblical Theology*. Grand Rapids: Baker Academic, 2011.
Beasley-Murray, George R. "Foreword." In *The Kingdom of God in the Teaching of Jesus, in Twentieth Century Theology*, by Mark Saucy, xiii–xiv. Dallas, TX: Word, 1997.
———. *John*. Word Biblical Commentary 36. 2nd ed. Grand Rapids: Thomas Nelson, 1999.
Belcher, Richard P. *Prophet, Priest, and King: The Roles of Christ in the Bible and Our Roles Today*. Harmony Township, NJ: P&R, 2016.
Blackburn, Barry. *Theios Anēr and the Markan Miracle Traditions: A Critique of the Theios Anēr Concept as an Interpretive Background of the Miracle Traditions Used by Mark*. Wissenschaftliche Untersuchungen zum Neuen Testament 2/40. Tübingen: Mohr Siebeck, 1990.
Blaising, Craig. "A Case for the Pretribulation Rapture." In *The Rapture, Pretribulation, Prewrath, or Postribulation*, edited by Stanley N. Gundry and Alan Hultberg, 25–73. Grand Rapids: Zondervan, 2010.
———. "The Kingdom of God in the Old Testament." In *Progressive Dispensationalism*, edited by Craig A. Blaising and Darrell L. Bock, 212–31. Grand Rapids: Baker, 1993.
———. "A Theology of Israel and the Church." In *Israel, the Church, and the Middle East: A Biblical Response to the Current Conflict*, edited by Darrell L. Bock and Mitch Glaser, 85–100. Grand Rapids: Kregel, 2018.
Blaising, Craig A., and Darrell L. Bock, eds. *Dispensationalism, Israel and the Church*. Grand Rapids: Zondervan, 1992.
Blaising, Craig A., and Darrell L. Bock. *Progressive Dispensationalism*. Grand Rapids: Baker, 1993.
Bliss, Philip P. "'Man of Sorrows,' What a Name." In *Baptist Hymnal*, 56. Nashville, TN: Convention Press, 1975. Public domain.
Block, Daniel I. "Bringing Back David: Ezekiel's Messianic Hope." In *The Lord's Anointed: Interpretation of Old Testament Messianic Texts*, edited by Philip E. Satterthwaite, Richard S. Hess, and Gordon J. Wenham, 167–88. Eugene, OR: Wipf & Stock, 1995.
———. "My Servant David: Ancient Israel's Vision of the Messiah." In *Israel's Messiah in the Bible and the Dead Sea Scrolls*, edited by Richard S. Hess and M. Daniel Carroll, 17–56. Grand Rapids: Baker Academic, 2003.

Blomberg, Craig L. *Matthew: An Exegetical and Theological Exposition of Holy Scripture*. The New American Commentary 22. Nashville, TN: Holman Reference, 1992.

Bock, Darrell L. "God's Plan for History: The First Coming of Christ." In *Dispensationalism and the History of Redemption: A Developing and Diverse Tradition*, edited by D. Jeffrey Bingham and Glenn R. Kreider, 153–68. Chicago, IL: Moody, 2015.

———. "Israel, the Land, and the Promise." In *Upholding God's Word: Reaching God's Chosen: A Festschrift in Honor of Mitchell L. Glaser*, edited by Jim Melnick, Zhava Glaser, Gregory Hagg, et al, 31–37. New York: KIFM, 2022.

———. "The Reign of the Lord Christ." In *Dispensationalism, Israel and the Church: The Search for Definition*, edited by Craig A. Blaising and Darrell L. Bock, 37–67. Grand Rapids: Zondervan, 1992.

———. "Replacement Theology with Implications for Messianic Jewish Relations." In *Jesus, Salvation and the Jewish People*, edited by David Parker, 235–47. Milton Keynes, England: Paternoster, 2011.

Boda, Mark J. "Figuring the Future: The Prophets and Messiah." In *The Messiah in the Old and New Testaments*, edited by Stanley E. Porter, 35–74. Grand Rapids: Eerdmans, 2007.

Bolen, Todd. "A Case for a Messianic Reading of Psalm 18." In *To Seek, To Do, and To Teach: Essays in Honor of Larry D. Pettegrew*, edited by Douglas D. Bookman, Tim M. Sigler, and Michael J. Vlach, 48–64. Cary, NC: Shepherds, 2022.

Bookman, Douglas D. "The Nature of the Old Testament Theocracy." In *Forsaking Israel: How It Happened and Why It Matters*, 2nd ed., edited by Larry D. Pettegrew, 351–55. The Woodlands, TX: Kress Biblical Resources, 2021.

———. "A Whale and an Elephant." In *Forsaking Israel: How It Happened and Why It Matters*, 2nd ed., edited by Larry Pettegrew, 241–72. The Woodlands, TX: Kress Biblical Resources, 2021.

Brooks, Phillips. "O Little Town of Bethlehem," 1868. In *Baptist Hymnal*, 85. Nashville, TN: Convention Press, 1975, public domain. 7

Brown, Francis, S. R. Driver, and Charles A. Briggs. *Hebrew and English Lexicon of the Old Testament*. Oxford: Clarendon, 1907.

Brown, Jeannine K. "Exodus in Matthew's Gospel." In *Exodus in the New Testament*, Library of New Testament Studies 663, edited by Seth M. Ehorn, 31–47. London: T & T Clark, 2022.

Brown, J. K., and K. A. Roberts. *The Gospel of Matthew*. Two Horizons New Testament Commentary. Grand Rapids: Eerdmans, 2019.

Brown, Michael L. "Yeshua the Prophet: A Threat to the Establishment." *The Chosen People* 28:9 (2022) 5.

———. "Zechariah 6:9–15: The Royal Priesthood of Messiah." In *The Moody Handbook of Messianic Prophecy: Studies and Expositions of the Messiah in the Old Testament*, edited by Michael Rydelnik and Edwin Blum, 1247–59. Chicago: Moody, 2019.

Brown, Raymond E. *The Gospel According to John I–XII*. The Anchor Bible. Garden City, NY: Doubleday, 1966.

———. *The Gospel According to John XIII–XXI*. The Anchor Bible. Garden City, NY: Doubleday & Herman Bavinck, 1987.

Bullinger, Ethelbert William. *Figures of Speech Used in the Bible*. New York: E. & J. B. Young & Co., 1898.

Calvin, John. *Institutes of the Christian Religion*. Translated by Henry Beveridge. Christian Classics Ethereal Library. https://ccel.org/ccel/calvin/institutes.toc.html.

Carson, D. A. *Matthew*. In vol. 8 of *The Expositor's Bible Commentary*, edited by Frank E. Gaebelein and J. D. Douglas, 1–599. Grand Rapids: Regency Reference Library, 1984.

Chen, Kevin S. *The Messianic Vision of the Pentateuch*. Downers Grove, IL: IVP Academic, 2019.

Childs, Brevard S. *Introduction to the Old Testament as Scripture*. Minneapolis, MN: Fortress Press, 1979.

Chisholm Jr., Robert B. "Divine Hardening in the Old Testament." *Bibliotheca Sacra* 153 (1996) 410–34.

Cho, Sukmin. *Jesus as Prophet in the Fourth Gospel*. New Testament Monographs 15. Sheffield, England: Sheffield Phoenix, 2006.

Chou, Abner. "Ezekiel 21:25–27: The Hope of Israel." In *The Moody Handbook of Messianic Prophecy: Studies and Expositions of the Messiah in the Old Testament*, edited by Michael Rydelnik and Edwin Blum, 1073–81. Chicago: Moody, 2019.

Cockerill, Gareth Lee, Craig G. Bartholomew, and Benjamin T. Quinn, eds. *Divine Action in Hebrews, and the Ongoing Priesthood of Jesus*. Grand Rapids: Zondervan Academic, 2023.

Cohen, Abraham. *The Teachings of Maimonides*. New York: KTAV, 1968.

Cole, Robert. "Psalm 3: Of Whom Does David Speak, of Himself or Another?" In *Text and Canon: Essays in Honor of John H. Sailhamer*, edited by Robert L. Cole and Paul J. Kissling, 137–48. Eugene, OR: Pickwick, 2017.

———. "Psalm 3: The Victory of the Messiah." In *The Moody Handbook of Messianic Prophecy: Studies and Expositions of the Messiah in the Old Testament*, edited by Michael Rydelnik and Edwin Blum, 491–502. Chicago: Moody, 2019.

———. "Psalm 23: The Lord Is Messiah's Shepherd." In *The Moody Handbook of Messianic Prophecy: Studies and Expositions of the Messiah in the Old Testament*, edited by Michael Rydelnik and Edwin Blum, 543–58. Chicago: Moody, 2019.

———. "Psalm 90: The Fulfillment of the Davidic Covenant." In *The Moody Handbook of Messianic Prophecy: Studies and Expositions of the Messiah in the Old Testament*, edited by Michael Rydelnik and Edwin Blum, 645–61. Chicago: Moody, 2019.

———. "Psalms 86–88: The Suffering, Death, and Resurrection of the Messianic King." In *The Moody Handbook of Messianic Prophecy: Studies and Expositions of the Messiah in the Old Testament*, edited by Michael Rydelnik and Edwin Blum, 617–30. Chicago: Moody, 2019.

Collins, Jack. "A Syntactical Note (Genesis 3:15): Is the Woman's Seed Singular or Plural?" *Tyndale Bulletin* 48 (1997) 139–48.

Coloe, Mary L. "Welcome into the Household of God: The Foot Washing in John 13." *Catholic Biblical Quarterly* 66 (2004) 400–15.

Comfort, Philip W., and David P. Barrett, eds. *The Complete Text of the Earliest New Testament Manuscripts*. Grand Rapids: Baker Books, 1999.

Compton, R. Bruce. "The 'Kingdom of Heaven/God' and the Church: A Case Study in Hermeneutics and Theology." In *To Seek, To Do, and To Teach: Essays in Honor of Larry D. Pettegrew*, edited by Douglas D. Bookman, Tim M. Sigler, and Michael J. Vlach, 176–202. Cary, NC: Shepherds, 2022.

Congdon, Jim. "The Mosaic Law and Christian Ethics: Obligation or Fulfillment?" In *Jews and the Gospel at the End of History: A Tribute to Moishe Rosen*, edited by Jim Congdon, 145–54. Grand Rapids: Kregel Academic and Professional, 2009.

Cook, Ryan J. "Psalm 109: The Betrayal of the Messiah." In *The Moody Handbook of Messianic Prophecy: Studies and Expositions of the Messiah in the Old Testament*, edited by Michael Rydelnik and Edwin Blum, 663–71. Chicago: Moody, 2019.
Cooper, David L. *Messiah: His Historical Appearance*. Los Angeles, CA: Biblical Research Society, 1958.
Craigie, Peter C. *Psalms 1–50*. Word Biblical Commentary. Dallas, TX: Word, 1983.
Cranfield, C. E. B. "The Parable of the Unjust Judge and the Eschatology of Luke-Acts." *Scottish Journal of Theology* 16 (1963) 297–301.
Dahood, Mitchell. *Psalms I, 1–50*. The Anchor Bible. Garden City, NY: Doubleday, 1965.
Davies, W. D., and Dale C. Allison. *Matthew 19–28*. International Critical Commentary. Edinburgh: T&T Clark International, 1997.
Deenick, Karl. "Priest and King or Priest-King in 1 Samuel 2:35." *Westminster Theological Journal* 73 (2011) 325–39.
Dekker, Jaap. "The High and Lofty One Dwelling in the Height and with His Servants: Intertextual Connections of Theological Significance between Isaiah 6, 53 and 57." *Journal for the Study of the Old Testament* 41 (2017) 475–91.
Delitzsch, Franz. "The Prophecies of Isaiah." In *Biblical Commentary on the Old Testament*, 6 vols., edited by Carl Friedrich Keil and Franz Delitzsch, 1867–89. Reprint, Grand Rapids: Associated Publishers and Authors, n.d.
Dempster, Stephen G. *Dominion and Dynasty: A Theology of the Hebrew Bible*. New Studies in Biblical Theology, edited by D. A. Carson. Downers Grove, IL: InterVarsity, 2003.
DeYoung, Kevin, and Greg Gilbert. *What Is the Mission of the Church? Making Sense of Social Justice, Shalom, and the Great Commission*. Wheaton, IL: Crossway, 2011.
Dorner, I. A. "Jesus: Prophet, Priest, King." In *Nineteenth Century Evangelical Theology*, Christian Classics, edited by Fisher Humphreys, 226–29. Nashville, TN: Broadman, 1981.
Eakin Jr., Frank E. "Spiritual Obduracy and Parable Purpose." In *The Use of the Old Testament in the New and Other Essays: Studies in Honor of William Franklin Stinespring*, edited by James M. Efird, 87–109. Durham, NC: Duke University Press, 1972.
Edersheim, Alfred. *The Temple, Its Ministry and Services as They Were at the Time of Jesus Christ*. 1880. Reprint, London: Religious Tract Society, London: James Clarke & Co., 1959.
Ellis, E. Earl. *The Gospel of Luke*. The New Century Bible Commentary. Rev. ed. Grand Rapids: Eerdmans, 1974.
———. *The Old Testament in Early Christianity: Canon and Interpretation in the Light of Modern Research*. Grand Rapids: Baker Book House, 1992.
Ellison, H. L. *The Centrality of the Messianic Idea for the Old Testament*. Leicester, UK: Theological Students Fellowship, 1953.
Erickson, Millard J. *Christian Theology*. 2nd ed. Grand Rapids: Baker, 1998.
Eusebius. *The History of the Church from Christ to Constantine [Ecclesiastical History]*. Translated by G. A. Williamson. New York: Dorset, 1965.
Evans, Craig A. "Exodus in the New Testament." In *The Book of Exodus: Composition Reception, and Interpretation*, Supplements to *Vetus Testamentum*, edited by Thomas R. Dozeman, Craig A. Evans, and Joel N. Lohr, 440–64. Leiden: Brill, 2014.

———. "The Function of Isaiah 6:9–10 in Mark and John." *Novum Testamentum* 24 (1982) 124–38.

———. "Obduracy and the Lord's Servant: Some Observations on the Use of the Old Testament in the Fourth Gospel." In *Early Jewish and Christian Exegesis: Studies in Memory of William Hugh Brownlee*, edited by Craig A. Evans and William E. Stinespring, 221–36. Atlanta, GA: Scholars, 1987.

———. "Prophet, Sage, Healer, Messiah, and Martyr: Types and Identities of Jesus." In *Handbook for the Study of the Historical Jesus*, bilingual ed., edited by Tom Holmén and Stanley E Porter, 1217–43. Leiden: E. J. Brill, 2010.

———. *To See and Not Perceive: Isaiah 6:9–10 in Early Jewish and Christian Interpretation*. Journal for the Study of the Old Testament Supplement Series 64. Sheffield, UK: JSOT Press, 1989.

Fee, Gordon D. "Baptism in the Holy Spirit: The Issue of Separability and Subsequence." *Pneuma: The Journal of the Society for Pentecostal Studies* 7 (1985) 87–99.

Feiler, Paul Frede. "Jesus the Prophet: The Lukan Portrayal of Jesus as the Prophet Like Moses." PhD diss., Princeton Theological Seminary, 1986.

Finkbeiner, David. "Hosea 3:4–5: Israel's Present Estrangement and Future Restoration." In *The Moody Handbook of Messianic Prophecy: Studies and Expositions of the Messiah in the Old Testament*, edited by Michael Rydelnik and Edwin Blum, 1153–66. Chicago: Moody, 2019.

Fletcher, Michelle. "Reading Exodus in Revelation." In *Exodus in the New Testament*, Library of New Testament Studies 663, edited by Seth M. Ehorn, 182–201. London: T & T Clark, 2022.

Fretheim, Terence E. *Exodus*. Interpretation: A Bible Commentary for Teaching and Preaching. Louisville, KY: John Knox, 1991.

Fruchtenbaum, Arnold G. *The Footsteps of the Messiah: A Study of the Sequence of Prophetic Events*. Rev. ed. San Antonio, TX: Ariel Ministries, 2020.

Gaebelein, A. C. *The Olivet Discourse: An Exposition of Matthew XXIV and XXV*. Grand Rapids: Baker Book House, 1969.

Gaines, Timothy R., and Kara Lyons-Pardue. *Following Jesus: Prophet, Priest, King*. Antioch, Garsiel, Moshe. *From Earth to Heaven: A Literary Study of the Elijah Stories in the Book of Kings*. Bethesda, MD: CDL, 2014.

Glasson, Francis. *Moses in the Fourth Gospel*. Studies in Biblical Theology. 1963. Reprint, Eugene, OR: Wipf and Stock Publishers, 2009.

Godet, Frederic. *Introduction to the New Testament: The Collection of the Four Gospels and the Gospel of St. Matthew*. Edinburgh: T. & T. Clark, 1899.

Goheen, Michael W. *A Light to the Nations: The Missional Church and the Biblical Story*. Grand Rapids: Baker Academic, 2011.

Goldstein, Rich. "Superman Is Jewish: The Hebrew Roots of America's Greatest Superhero." *Daily Beast*, July 26, 2017.

Grogan, Geoffrey W. *Psalms*. The Two Horizons Old Testament Commentary. Grand Rapids: Eerdmans, 2008.

Grossman, Jonathan. *Esther: The Outer Narrative and the Hidden Reading*. Winona Lake, IN: Eisenbrauns, 2011.

Gurtner, Daniel M. "'Old Exodus' and 'New Exodus' in the Gospel of Mark." In *Exodus in the New Testament*, Library of New Testament Studies 663, edited by Seth M. Ehorn, 48–60. London: T & T Clark, 2022.

Hagner, Donald A. *Matthew 14–28*. Word Biblical Commentary 33b. Nashville, TN: Thomas Nelson, 1995.

Hamilton, James. "The Skull Crushing Seed of the Woman: Inner-Biblical Interpretation of Genesis 3:15." *Southern Baptist Journal of Theology* 10 (2006) 30–54.

Hamilton, Victor P. *Exodus: An Exegetical Commentary*. Grand Rapids: Baker Academic, 2011.

Harmon, Matthew S. *The Servant of the Lord and His Servant People: Tracing a Biblical Theme through the Canon*. New Studies in Biblical Theology 54. Downers Grove, IL: Apollos/IVP Academic, 2020.

Harrison, Everett F. *John: The Gospel of Faith*. Chicago, IL: Moody, 1962.

Heim, Knut M. "The Perfect King of Psalm 72: An 'Intertextual' Inquiry." In *The Lord's Anointed: Interpretation of Old Testament Messianic Texts*, edited by Philip E. Satterthwaite, Richard S. Hess, and Gordon J. Wenham, 223–48. Eugene, OR: Wipf and Stock, 1995.

Hendren, Noam. "The Kingdom of God in the Gospels." In *A Handbook on the Jewish Roots of the Gospels*. Peabody, MA: Hendrickson, 2021.

Hesselgrave, Donald. *Paradigms in Conflict*. Grand Rapids: Kregel, 2005.

Hindson, Edward E. "Isaiah 61:1–6: The Spirit-Anointed Messiah and His Promise of Restoration." In *The Moody Handbook of Messianic Prophecy: Studies and Expositions of the Messiah in the Old Testament*, edited by Michael Rydelnik and Edwin Blum, 983–96. Chicago: Moody, 2019.

Ho, Peter C. W. "The Shape of Davidic Psalms as Messianic." *Journal of the Evangelical Theological Society* 62 (2019) 515–31.

Hoehner, Harold W. *Ephesians: An Exegetical Commentary*. Grand Rapids: Baker Academic, 2002.

Holladay, William L. *A Concise Hebrew and Aramaic Lexicon of the Old Testament*. Grand Rapids: Wm. B. Eerdmans, 1971.

Horne, Charles M. "Eschatology—The Controlling Thematic in Theology." *Journal of the Evangelical Theological Society* 13 (1970) 53–63.

Hugenberger, G. P. "The Servant of the Lord in the 'Servant Songs' of Isaiah: A Second Moses Figure." In *The Lord's Anointed: Interpretations of Old Testament Messianic Texts*, edited by Philip E. Satterthwaite, Richard S. Hess, and Gordon J. Wenham, 105–40. Grand Rapids: Baker Books, 1995.

James, Steven L. *New Creation Eschatology and the Land: A Survey of Contemporary Perspectives*. Eugene, OR: Wipf & Stock, 2017.

Jervell, Jacob. "The Divided People of God." In *Luke and the People of God: A New Look at Luke-Acts*, 41–74. Minneapolis, MN: Augsburg, 1972.

———. "The Lost Sheep of the House of Israel: The Understanding of the Samaritans in Luke-Acts." In *Luke and the People of God: A New Look at Luke-Acts*, 113–32. Minneapolis, MN: Augsburg, 1972.

———. "The Mighty Minority." In *The Unknown Paul: Essays on Luke-Acts and Early Christian History*, 26–51. Minneapolis, MN: Augsburg, 1984.

Johnson, Alan. *Revelation*. In vol. 12 of *The Expositor's Bible Commentary*, edited by Frank E. Gaebelein and J. D. Douglas, 399–603. Grand Rapids: Zondervan, Regency Reference Library, 1981.

Kaiser Jr., Walter C. *Exodus*. In vol. 2 of *The Expositor's Bible Commentary*, edited by Frank E. Gaebelein and Richard P. Polcyn, 287–497. Grand Rapids: Zondervan, Regency Reference Library, 1990.

———. *The Messiah in the Old Testament*. Studies in Old Testament Biblical Theology. Grand Rapids: Zondervan, 1995.

———. "Until Messiah Comes to Whom the Crown Rightfully Belongs: Ezekiel 21:18–27." In *Upholding God's Word, Reaching God's Chosen: A Festschrift in Honor of Dr. Mitchell L. Glaser*, edited by Jim Melnick, Zhava Glaser, Gregory Hagg, et al, 155–61. New York: KIFM, 2022.

———. "2 Samuel 7: The Davidic Covenant (I)." In *The Moody Handbook of Messianic Prophecy: Studies and Expositions of the Messiah in the Old Testament*, edited by Michael Rydelnik and Edwin Blum, 385–97. Chicago: Moody, 2019.

Kaplan, Arie. "Supermensch!" *Utne Magazine*, 1 January 2004, 93–94.

Kidner, Derek. *Psalms 1–72*. The Tyndale Old Testament Commentaries. Leicester, England: Tyndale, 1973.

Kinzer, Mark S. *Postmissionary Messianic Judaism: Redefining Christian Engagement with the Jewish People*. Grand Rapids: Baker Academic/Brazos, 2005.

Kissling, Paul J. "The Testament of Jacob and the Blessing of Moses: A Narrative Approach." In *Text and Canon: Essays in Honor of John H. Sailhamer*, edited by Robert L. Cole and Paul J. Kissling, 1–15. Eugene, OR: Pickwick, 2017.

Kistemaker, Simon J. *Exposition of the Epistles of Peter and of the Epistle of Jude*. New Testament Commentary. Grand Rapids: Baker Book House, 1987.

Klee, Ernst. *Das Personenlexikon zum DrittenReich* [The Encyclopedia of Supporters of the Third Reich]. 2nd ed. Frankfurt am Main: Fischer Taschenbuch Verlag, 2005.

Klink III, Edward W. *John*. Zondervan Exegetical Commentary on the New Testament 4. Grand Rapids: Zondervan, 2016.

Konradt, Matthias. *Israel, Church, and the Gentiles in the Gospel of Matthew*. Translated by Kathleen Ess. Waco, TX: Baylor University Press, 2014.

Köhler, Ludwig, and Walter Baumgartner. *The Hebrew and Aramaic Lexicon of the Old Testament*. Edited by Johann Jakob Stamm. Leiden; New York: E.J. Brill, 1994–2000.

Köstenberger, Andreas J. "Exodus in John." In *Exodus in the New Testament*, Library of New Testament Studies 663, edited by Seth M. Ehorn, 88–108. London: T & T Clark, 2022.

Kreider, Glenn R. "Jesus the Messiah as Prophet, Priest, and King." *Bibliotheca Sacra* 176 (2019) 174–87.

Larsen, David L. *Jews, Gentiles, and the Church: A New Perspective on History and Prophecy*. Grand Rapids: Discovery House, 1995.

Levenson, Jon D. *Sinai and Zion: An Entry into the Jewish Bible*. San Francisco, CA: Harper and Row, 1985.

Lewis, C. S. *God in the Dock: Essays on Theology and Ethics*. Edited by Walter Hooper. Grand Rapids: Eerdmans, 1970.

———. *The Lion, the Witch and the Wardrobe*. The Chronicles of Narnia. New York: Harper Collins Publishers, 1950.

———. *Mere Christianity*. Rev. and amp. edition. New York: Harper Collins e-books, 2021.

Limbaugh, David. *The Emmaus Code: Finding Jesus in the Old Testament*. Washington, DC: Regnery, 2015.

Lindsey, F. Duane. "The Call of the Servant in Isaiah 42:1–9." *Bibliotheca Sacra* 139 (1982) 12–31.

———. "The Commitment of the Servant in Isaiah 50:4–11." *Bibliotheca Sacra* 139 (1982) 216–29.

———. *The Servant Songs: A Study in Isaiah*. Chicago, IL: Moody, 1985.
Longenecker, Richard N. *Biblical Exegesis in the Apostolic Period*. Grand Rapids: Eerdmans, 1975.
Lövenstam, Evald. *Jesus and "This Generation": A New Testament Study*. Coniectanea Biblica New Testament Series 25. London: Coronet Books, 1996.
Luz, Ulrich. *Matthew 21-28: A Commentary*. Hermeneia: A Critical and Historical Commentary on the Bible, edited by Helmut Koester. Minneapolis, MN: Augsburg, 2005.
Lyte, Henry F. "Abide with Me." In *Baptist Hymnal*, 217. Nashville, TN: Convention Press, 1975. Public domain.
Macleod, Donald. "The Work of Christ." In *Reformation Theology: A Systematic Summary*, edited by Matthew Barrett, 347-92. Wheaton, IL: Crossway, 2017.
Mannhardt, Yiffat. "Superman Returns," movie review. *Yediot Ahronot*, 7 July 2006.
Marcar, Katie. "Exodus in the General Letters." In *Exodus in the New Testament*, Library of New Testament Studies 663, edited by Seth M. Ehorn, 164-81. London: T & T Clark, 2022.
Maronde, Christopher A. "Moses in the Gospel of John." *Concordia Theological Quarterly* 77 (2013) 23-44.
Marshall, I. Howard. *The Gospel of Luke*. The New International Greek Testament Commentary. Grand Rapids: Eerdmans, 1978.
Mathews, Joshua G. *Melchizedek's Alternative Priestly Order: A Compositional Analysis of Genesis 14:18-20 and Its Echoes throughout the Tanak*. Bulletin for Biblical Research Supplement 8. Winona Lake, IN: Eisenbrauns, 2013.
McClain, Alva J. *The Greatness of the Kingdom: An Inductive Study of the Kingdom of God as Set Forth in the Scriptures*. Grand Rapids: Zondervan, 1959.
McConville, J. Gordon. "Messianic Interpretation of the Old Testament in Modern Context." In *The Lord's Anointed: Interpretation of Old Testament Messianic Texts*, edited by Phillip E. Satterthwaite, Richard S. Hess, and Gordon J. Wenham, 1-17. Grand Rapids: Baker, 1995.
McKinion, Randall L. "Psalm 69: The Lament of the Messiah." In *The Moody Handbook of Messianic Prophecy: Studies and Expositions of the Messiah in the Old Testament*, edited by Michael Rydelnik and Edwin Blum, 591-603. Chicago: Moody, 2019.
Merrill, Eugene H. "Genesis 49:8-12: The Lion of Judah." In *The Moody Handbook of Messianic Prophecy: Studies and Expositions of the Messiah in the Old Testament*, edited by Michael Rydelnik and Edwin Blum, 271-84. Chicago: Moody, 2019.
———. "Royal Priesthood: An Old Testament Messianic Motif." *Bibliotheca Sacra* 150 (1993) 50-61.
Mitchell, Andrew. "Your Kingdom Come, Your Will Be Done: A Study of Matthew 6:10." *Bulletin for Biblical Research* 30 (2020) 208-30.
Mitchell, David C. *The Message of the Psalter: An Eschatological Programme in the Book of Psalms*. Glasgow, Scotland: Campbell, 2003.
Moessner, David P. *Lord of the Banquet: The Literary and Theological Significance of the Lukan Travel Narrative*. Minneapolis, MN: Fortress, 1989.
Moffitt, David M. "Atonement at the Right Hand: The Sacrificial Significance of Jesus' Exaltation in Acts." *New Testament Studies* 62 (2016) 549-68.
———. "Exodus in Hebrews." In *Exodus in the New Testament Library of New Testament Studies* 663, edited by Seth M. Ehorn, 146-63. London: T & T Clark, 2022.
Moore, Anthony M. *Signs of Salvation: The Theme of Creation in John's Gospel*. Cambridge: James Clarke, 2013.

Moore, Nicholas J. "Sacrifice, Session and Intercession: The End of Christ's Offering in Hebrews." *Journal for the Study of the New Testament* 42 (2020) 521–41.
Moreau, A. Scott, Gary R. Corwin, and Gary B. McGee. *Introducing World Missions: A Biblical, Historical, and Practical Survey*. Grand Rapids: Baker Academic, 2004.
Motyer, J. Alec. *The Prophecy of Isaiah: An Introduction and Commentary*. Downers Grove, IL: InterVarsity Press, 1993.
Muilenburg, James. "Form Criticism and Beyond." *Journal of Biblical Literature* 88 (1969) 1–18.
Munck, Johannes. *Paul and the Salvation of Mankind*. Richmond, VA: John Knox, 1959.
Newman, Randy. *Mere Evangelism: 10 Insights from C. S. Lewis to Help You Share Your Faith*. Charlotte, NC: The Good Book, 2021.
Oatman, Johnson. "Holy Holy, Is What the Angels Sing." In *Seventh-day Adventist Hymnal*, 425. Hagerstown, MD: Review and Herald Publishing Association, 1985. Public domain.
Ortlund, Dane C. "'And Their Eyes Were Opened, and They Knew': An Inter-canonical Note on Luke 24:31." *Journal of the Evangelical Theological Society* 53 (2010) 717–28.
———. "The Old Testament Background and Eschatological Significance of Jesus Walking on the Sea (Mark 6:45–52)." *Neotestamentica* 46 (2012) 319–37.
Ortlund, Gavin. "Resurrected as Messiah: The Risen Christ as Prophet, Priest, and King." *Journal of the Evangelical Theological Society* 54 (2011) 749–66.
Oswalt, John N. *The Book of Isaiah, Chapters 40–66*. The New International Commentary on the Old Testament. Grand Rapids: Eerdmans, 1998.
Pao, David W. *Acts and the Isaianic New Exodus*. Grand Rapids: Baker Academic, 2000.
Pearl, Chaim. *Rashi*. New York: Grove, 1988.
Perrin, Nicholas. *Jesus the Priest*. Grand Rapids: Baker Academic, 2018.
———. "Jesus as Priest in the Gospels." *Southern Baptist Journal of Theology* 22 (2018) 81–99.
Peters, George N. H. *The Theocratic Kingdom of Our Lord Jesus, the Christ*. 3 vols. New York: Funk and Wagnalls, 1884.
Peterson, David G. *The Acts of the Apostles*. The Pillar New Testament Commentary. Grand Rapids: Eerdmans, 2009.
———. "Luke's Theological Enterprise: Integration and Intent." In *Witness to the Gospel: The Theology of Acts*, edited by I. H. Marshall and David Peterson, 521–44. Grand Rapids: Eerdmans, 1998.
Pettegrew, Larry D. "An Assessment of Covenant Theology." In *Forsaking Israel: How It Happened and Why It Matters*, 2nd ed., edited by Larry D. Pettegrew, 169–206. The Woodlands, TX: Kress Biblical Resources, 2021.
———. "The Messiah's Lecture on the Future of Israel." In *To Seek, To Do, and To Teach: Essays in Honor of Larry D. Pettegrew*, edited by Douglas D. Bookman, Tim M. Sigler, and Michael J. Vlach, 280–83. Cary, NC: Shepherds, 2022.
Pool, David de Sola. "The Influence of Some Jewish Apostates on the Reformation." *Jewish Review* 2:7–12 (May 1911–March 1912).
Porter, Stanley E., and Bryan R. Dyer. *Origins of New Testament Christology: An Introduction to the Traditions and Titles Applied to Jesus*. Grand Rapids: Baker Academic, 2023.
Postell, Seth D. "Abram as Israel, Israel as Abram." In *Text and Canon: Essays in Honor of John H. Sailhamer*, edited by Robert L. Cole and Paul J. Kissling, 16–35. Eugene, OR: Pickwick, 2017.

———. "Genesis 3:15: The Promised Seed." In *The Moody Handbook of Messianic Prophecy: Studies and Expositions of the Messiah in the Old Testament*, edited by Michael Rydelnik and Edwin Blum, 239–50. Chicago: Moody Publishers, 2019.

———. "Messianism in the Psalms." In *The Moody Handbook of Messianic Prophecy: Studies and Expositions of the Messiah in the Old Testament*, edited by Michael Rydelnik and Edwin Blum, 457–75. Chicago: Moody, 2019.

———. "Numbers 24:5-9, 15-19: The Distant Star." In *The Moody Handbook of Messianic Prophecy: Studies and Expositions of the Messiah in the Old Testament*, edited by Michael Rydelnik and Edwin Blum, 285–308. Chicago: Moody, 2019.

———. "Typology in the Old Testament." In *The Moody Handbook of Messianic Prophecy: Studies and Expositions of the Messiah in the Old Testament*, edited by Michael Rydelnik and Edwin Blum, 161–75. Chicago: Moody Publishers, 2019.

Postell, Seth D., Eitan Bar, and Erez Soref, *Reading Moses, Seeing Jesus: How the Torah Fulfills Its Goal in Yeshua*. Wooster, OH: One For Israel Ministry and Weaver Book Co., 2017.

Prettel, Juan David. "Messianic Judaism and Tradition: A Critical Engagement with Mark S. Kinzer." Ph.D. dissertation, Southwestern Baptist Theological Seminary, 2022.

Provan, Ian W. "The Messiah in the Books of Kings." In *The Lord's Anointed: Interpretation of Old Testament Messianic Texts*, edited by Phillip F. Satterthwaite, Richard S. Hess, and Gordon J. Wenham, 67–85. Grand Rapids: Baker, 1995.

Quarles, Charles L. *Matthew*. Exegetical Guide to the Greek New Testament. Nashville, TN: B&H, 2017.

———. *Sermon on the Mount: Restoring Christ's Message to the Modern Church*. Nashville, TN: B & H Academic, 2011.

Räisänen, Heikki. *The Idea of Divine Hardening: A Comparative Study of the Notion of Divine Hardening, Leading Astray and Inciting to Evil in the Bible and the Qurʾā[set macro over a]n*. Publications of the Finnish Exegetical Society 25. 2nd ed. Helsinki: The Finnish Exegetical Society, 1976.

Ramsey, Arthur Michael. *The Glory of God and the Transfiguration of Christ*. London: Longmans, Green and Co., 1949.

Ravens, David. *Luke and the Restoration of Israel*. Journal for the Study of the New Testament Supplement Series 119. Sheffield: Sheffield Academic, 1995.

Raymer, Roger. *1 Peter*. In vol. 2 of *The Bible Knowledge Commentary: An Exposition of the Scriptures by Dallas Seminary Faculty*, edited by John F. Walvoord and Roy B. Zuck, 837–58. Wheaton, IL: Victor Books, 1983.

Robinson, J. Armitage. *St. Paul's Epistle to the Ephesians: A Revised Text and Translation with Exposition and Notes*. London: Macmillan, 1903.

Rossoll, Ken. "Synecdoche, a Suburb of Metonymy." https://figuresofspeechinthebible.net/?p=11481.

Rydelnik, Eva. "Isaiah 32:1-8; 33:17-24: The Righteous and Majestic King." In *The Moody Handbook of Messianic Prophecy: Studies and Expositions of the Messiah in the Old Testament*, edited by Michael Rydelnik and Edwin Blum, 897–905. Chicago: Moody, 2019.

Rydelnik, Michael. "The Davidic Covenant as Messianic Prophecy: 2 Samuel 7:1-17." In *Upholding God's Word, Reaching God's Chosen: A Festschrift in Honor of Dr. Mitchell L. Glaser*, edited by Jim Melnick, Zhava Glaser, Gregory Hagg, et al, 175–86. New York: KIFM, 2022.

———. "Joel 2:23: The Teacher of Righteousness." In *The Moody Handbook of Messianic Prophecy: Studies and Expositions of the Messiah in the Old Testament*, edited by Michael Rydelnik and Edwin Blum, 1167–85. Chicago: Moody, 2019.

———. *The Messianic Hope: Is the Hebrew Bible Really Messianic?* NAC Studies in Bible and Theology. Nashville, TN: B&H Academic, 2010.

———. "Psalm 110: The Messiah as Eternal King Priest." In *The Moody Handbook of Messianic Prophecy: Studies and Expositions of the Messiah in the Old Testament*, edited by Michael Rydelnik and Edwin Blum, 673–91. Chicago: Moody, 2019.

———. "2 Samuel 23:1–7: David's Last Words." In *The Moody Handbook of Messianic Prophecy: Studies and Expositions of the Messiah in the Old Testament*, edited by Michael Rydelnik and Edwin Blum, 399–409. Chicago: Moody, 2019.

Rydelnik, Michael, and Edwin Blum, eds. *The Moody Handbook of Messianic Prophecy: Studies and Expositions of the Messiah in the Old Testament*. Chicago: Moody Publishers, 2019.

Rydelnik, Michael, and Michael Vanlaningham, eds. *The Moody Bible Commentary*. Chicago: Moody Publishers, 2014.

Ryken, Philip. *The Messiah Comes to Middle-Earth: Images of Christ's Threefold Office in The Lord of the Rings*. Downers Grove, IL: IVP Academic, 2017.

The Ryrie Study Bible. New American Standard Translation, with introduction, notes, etc. by Charles Caldwell Ryrie. Chicago, IL: Moody, 1978.

Sailhamer, John H. "The Canonical Approach to the OT: Its Effect on Understanding Prophecy." *Journal of the Evangelical Theological Society* 30 (1987) 307–15.

———. *Genesis*. In vol. 2 of *The Expositor's Bible Commentary*, edited by Frank E. Gaebelein and Richard P. Polcyn, 3–284. Grand Rapids: Zondervan, Regency Reference Library, 1990.

———. "Hosea 11:1 and Matthew 2:15." *Westminster Theological Journal* 63 (2001) 87–96.

———. *Introduction to Old Testament Theology: A Canonical Approach*. Grand Rapids: Zondervan, 1995.

———. *The Meaning of the Pentateuch: Revelation, Composition and Interpretation*. Downers Grove, IL: IVP Academic, 2009.

———. "Messiah and the Hebrew Bible." In *The Moody Handbook of Messianic Prophecy: Studies and Expositions of the Messiah in the Old Testament*, edited by Michael Rydelnik and Edwin Blum, 41–60. Chicago: Moody, 2019.

———. *The Pentateuch as Narrative: A Biblical-Theological Commentary*. Grand Rapids: Zondervan, 1992.

Saldarini, Anthony J. *Matthew's Christian-Jewish Community*. Chicago: University of Chicago Press, 1994.

Saucy, Mark. *The Kingdom of God in the Teaching of Jesus, in 20th Century Theology*. Dallas, TX: Word, 1997.

Saucy, Robert L. *The Case for Progressive Dispensationalism*. Grand Rapids: Zondervan, 1993.

Schnabel, Eckhard J. *Early Christian Mission: Jesus and the Twelve*. Downers Grove, IL: InterVarsity, 2004.

———. *Paul, the Missionary: Realities, Strategies and Methods*. Downers Grove, IL: IVP Academic, 2008.

Schnittjer, Gary Edward. *Old Testament Use of Old Testament: A Book-by-Book Guide*. Grand Rapids: Zondervan Academic, 2021.

Schreiner, Patrick. *The Ascension of Christ: Recovering a Neglected Doctrine*. Bellingham, WA: Lexham, 2020.

Schrock, David. *The Royal Priesthood and the Glory of God*. Short Studies in Biblical Theology. Wheaton, IL: Crossway, 2022.

Schultz, Richard. "The King in the Book of Isaiah." In *The Lord's Anointed: Interpretation of Old Testament Messianic Texts*, edited by Phillip F. Satterthwaite, Richard S. Hess, and Gordon J. Wenham, 141–65. Grand Rapids: Baker, 1995.

Seder Moed. Vol. 2 of *Mishnayot*. Translated and annotated by Philip Blackman. Gateshead, UK: Judaica Press, 2000.

Shepherd, Michael B. *A Commentary on the Book of the Twelve: The Minor Prophets*. Grand Rapids: Kregel Academic, 2018.

Sherman, Robert J. *King, Priest, and Prophet: A Trinitarian Theology of Atonement*, Theology for the 21st Century. London: T&T Clark, 2004.

Shomron. "The Taheb, the Restorer, A Prophet like Moses." http://members.tripod.com/~osher_2/html_articles/taheb1.htm.

Sibley, James Ray. "The Blindness of Israel and the Mission of the Church." Ph.D. diss., Southwestern Baptist Theological Seminary, 2012.

Sibley, Jim R. "The 'Cinderella' of Messianic Prophecy." Paper presented at the annual meeting of the Pre-Trib Research Center, Irving, TX, 12 December 2019.

———. "Deuteronomy 18:15–19: The Prophet Like Moses." In *The Moody Handbook of Messianic Prophecy: Studies and Expositions of the Messiah in the Old Testament*, edited by Michael Rydelnik and Edwin Blum, 325–41. Chicago: Moody, 2019.

———. "Has the Church Put Israel on the Shelf? The Evidence from Romans 11:15." *Journal of the Evangelical Theological Society* 58 (2015) 571–81.

———. "The Jewish Disciples in the Book of Acts." In *A Handbook on the Jewish Roots of the Christian Faith*, edited by Craig A. Evans and David Mishkin, 206–13. Peabody, MA: Hendrickson Publishers, 2019.

———. "The Messianic Jewish Apologetic Purpose of John 9." Paper presented at the annual meeting of the Evangelical Theological Society, San Antonio, TX, 16 November 2016.

———. "'You Talkin' to Me?' 1 Peter 2:4–10 and a Theology of Israel." *Southwestern Journal of Theology* 59:1 (Fall 2016) 59–75.

Snearly, Michael K. "Psalm 118: The Rejected Stone." In *The Moody Handbook of Messianic Prophecy: Studies and Expositions of the Messiah in the Old Testament*, edited by Michael Rydelnik and Edwin Blum, 693–700. Chicago: Moody, 2019.

Spencer, James. "Psalm 72: The Messiah as Ideal King." In *The Moody Handbook of Messianic Prophecy: Studies and Expositions of the Messiah in the Old Testament*, edited by Michael Rydelnik and Edwin Blum, 605–15. Chicago: Moody, 2019.

Squires, John T. "The Plan of God." In *Witness to the Gospel*, edited by I. Howard Marshall and David Peterson, 19–39. Grand Rapids: Eerdmans, 1998.

———. *The Plan of God in Luke-Acts*. Society for New Testament Studies Monograph Series 76. Cambridge: Cambridge University Press, 1993.

Stagg, Frank. "Matthew." In *General Articles, Matthew–Mark*, vol. 8 of *Broadman Bible Commentary*, edited by Clifton J. Allen, 261–253. Nashville, TN: Broadman, 1969.

Stutz, Andreas. "Jesus as Messiah in the Synoptic Gospels." In *A Handbook on the Jewish Roots of the Gospels*, edited by Craig A. Evans and David Mishkin, 148–55. Peabody, MA: Hendrickson, 2021.

Tabb, Brian J., and Steve Walton. "Exodus in Luke-Acts." In *Exodus in the New Testament, Library of New Testament Studies* 663, edited by Seth M. Ehorn, 61–87. London: T & T Clark, 2022.

Tannehill, Robert C. "The Story of Israel within the Lukan Narrative." In *Jesus and the Heritage of Israel: Luke's Narrative Claim on Israel's Legacy*, edited by David Moessner, 325–39. Harrisburg, PA: Trinity Press International, 1999.

Thomas, John Christopher. *Footwashing in John 13 and the Johannine Community*. Sheffield, UK: Journal for the Study of the New Testament Publishers, 1991.

Thomas, Robert L. *Revelation 1–7: An Exegetical Commentary*. Chicago, IL: Moody, 1992.

———. *Revelation 8–22: An Exegetical Commentary*. Chicago, IL: Moody, 1995.

Toussaint, Stanley D. *Behold the King: A Study of Matthew*. Portland, OR: Multnomah, 1980.

Treier, Daniel. *Lord Jesus Christ*. New Studies in Dogmatics. Grand Rapids: Zondervan Academic, 2023.

Tsedaka, Benyamin. *Understanding the Israelite-Samaritans, From Ancient to Modern*. Jerusalem: Carta Jerusalem, 2017.

Turner, David L. *Israel's Last Prophet: Jesus and the Jewish Leaders in Matthew 23*. Minneapolis, MN: Fortress, 2015.

———. *Matthew*. Baker Exegetical Commentary on the New Testament. Grand Rapids: Baker Academic, 2008.

———. "Matthew 21:43 and the Future of Israel." *Bibliotheca Sacra* 159 (2002) 46–61.

Turner, George Allen, and Julius R. Mantey. *The Gospel According to John*. The Evangelical Commentary 4. Grand Rapids: Eerdmans, n.d.

Unger, Merrill F. *Zechariah: Prophet of Messiah's Glory*. Grand Rapids: Zondervan, 1963.

Van Groningen, Gerard. *Messianic Revelation in the Old Testament*. Grand Rapids: Baker, 1990.

VanGemeren, William A. *Psalms*. In vol. 5 of *The Expositor's Bible Commentary*, edited by Frank E. Gaebelein and Richard P. Polcyn, 3–880. Grand Rapids: Zondervan, Regency Reference Library, 1991.

Van Rheenen, G., and A. Parker, *Missions: Biblical Foundations and Contemporary Strategies*. 2nd ed. Grand Rapids: Zondervan Academic 2014.

Varner, William. *Messiah's Ministry: Crises of the Christ*. Dallas, TX: Fontes, 2021.

Vlach, Michael J. *He Will Reign Forever: A Biblical Theology of the Kingdom of God*. Silverton, OR: Lampion, 2017.

———. "The Kingdom in Paul's Epistles." In *To Seek, To Do, and To Teach: Essays in Honor of Larry D. Pettegrew*, edited by Douglas D. Bookman, Tim M. Sigler, and Michael J. Vlach, 2–25. Cary, NC: Shepherds, 2022.

Vos, Geerhardus. "The Priesthood of Christ in the Epistle of Hebrews." *Princeton Theological Review* 5:3 (1907) 423–47.

Waltke, Bruce K., and M. O'Connor. *An Introduction to Biblical Hebrew Syntax*. Winona Lake, IN: Eisenbrauns, 1990.

Walvoord, John F. *Matthew: They Kingdom Come*. Chicago, IL: Moody, 1974.

Wesley, Charles. "Come, Thou Long Expected Jesus," 1744. In *Baptist Hymnal*, 79. Nashville, TN: Convention Press, 1975, public domain.

Westcott, B. F. *The Gospel According to St. John*. 1881. Reprinted with corrections, Grand Rapids: Eerdmans, 1981.

Wilkinson, Paul R. *Israel: The Inheritance of God*. 2nd ed. San Antonio, TX: Ariel Ministries, 2022.

Willmington, Harold. "Jesus Christ as Prophet, Priest, and King." *The Second Person File*, 2017. https://digitalcommons.liberty.edu/ cgi/viewcontent.cgi?article=1062&context=second_person.

Wilson, Gerald Henry. *The Editing of the Hebrew Psalter*. Society of Biblical Literature Dissertation Series 76. Chico, CA: Scholars, 1985.

Wodrow, Robert. *Sermons by the Rev. Robert Bruce, Minister of Edinburgh, Reprinted from the Original Edition of 1590 and 1591, with Collections for His Life*. Edited by William Cunningham. Edinburgh: Printed for the Wodrow Society, 1843.

Woods, Andrew M. *The Coming Kingdom: What Is the Kingdom and How Is Kingdom Now Theology Changing the Focus of the Church?* Duluth, MN: Grace Gospel, 2016.

Wright, Christopher J. H. *The Mission of God: Unlocking the Bible's Grand Narrative*. Downers Grove, IL: IVP Academic, 2006.

Yarbrough, Mark. "Israel and the Story of the Bible." In *Israel, the Church, and the Middle East: A Biblical Response to the Current Conflict*, edited by Darrell L. Bock and Mitch Glaser, 47–61. Grand Rapids: Kregel, 2018.

Yee-cheung, Wong. *A Text-Centered Approach to Old Testament Exegesis and Theology and Its Application to the Book of Isaiah*. Hong Kong: Alliance Bible Seminary, 2001.

Young, Edward J. *The Book of Isaiah*. 3 vols. The New International Commentary on the Old Testament. Grand Rapids: Eerdmans, 1972.

Youngblood, Ronald F. *1, 2 Samuel*. In vol. 3 of *The Expositor's Bible Commentary*, edited by Frank E. Gaebelein and Richard P. Polcyn, 553–1104. Grand Rapids: Zondervan, Regency Reference Library, 1992.

Zakovitch, Yair. *Jacob: Unexpected Patriarch*. Translated by Valerie Zakovitch. New Haven, CT: Yale University Press, 2012.

Scripture Index

Genesis

1–2:22	30
1	45
1:28	35
2:8	34
2:9	34
2:17	16
2:23	30
2:24	30
3:1–2	61
3:4	61
3:13–14	61
3:15	5, 32, 35, 84, 173, 200
12:1–3	22, 35
12:3	34, 123, 168, 192, 250
14	56, 151
14:18–20	25, 36, 59
14:18	149, 150, 190
14:19–20	67, 141, 150
14:20	26
14:22	25
15	22
15:1	26
15:2	150
15:6	26, 169
17:4	22
18:4	135
19:2	135
20:7	14
22:17–18	2
22:18	22, 72
24:43	135
26:4	22
26:5	169
27:15	202
27:27	202
28:14	22
34	27
37:31	104
41:45	149
43:9	152
43:24	135
44:32	152
45:2	170
49	34
49:1	32
49:5–7	27
49:8–12	5, 32, 33, 35, 36
49:8	31, 33
49:9	34
49:10–12	31
49:10	13, 15, 33, 36, 63, 98, 114, 173, 176, 200, 208
49:11–12	33, 104

Exodus

1:15–22	13
2	28
2:1–2	13
2:10	13
2:14	13, 121

Exodus (*cont.*)

3	16	18	56
3:1	149	18:4	150
3:11	26	18:5	28
3:13	26	18:7	28
3:14	116	18:8–12	28, 36
4	28	18:8–11	150
4:1–10	26	18:10–11	150
4:1–3	51	18:10	67
4:6–7	135	18:12	151
4:13	26	18:13	124
4:14–16	26	18:19–22	124
4:14	28	18:21	124
4:16	51	19	58
4:20	51, 128	19:3	24
4:22	98, 103	19:4	22
4:27	28	19:5–6	22
6:6–7	22	19:5	22, 23, 187
7:9–10	51	19:6	2, 23, 49, 210, 252
7:11–12	125	19:8	24
7:19–20	51	19:9	117
7:22	125	19:10–24	24
8	94	19:10	138
8:5	51	19:13	24
8:8	91	19:14	138
8:16	51	19:16–19	14
8:19	94	19:22–23	138
8:28	91	19:24	24
9:23	51	20:5	239
10:13	51	20:19–21	14
10:16–17	91	23:24–25	102
12:3–5	61	24	116, 126
12:5	143	24:1–8	197
12:23	144	24:1	117
13:1–2	138	24:4	118
14:6	51	24:8	126
15:1–18	31	24:16	116, 117
15:11	188	28–29	24
15:13	51	29:1	143
15:17	200	30:17–21	135
16:8	53	30:30	27
17:1–7	23	31:1–6	26
17:1–6	107	31:18	84
17:2	102	31:36–39	26
17:4	18, 121	32	102
17:5–7	51	32:11–13	17, 91
17:8–16	150	32:28	27
17:8–13	51	32:30–32	50
		32:30	91

32:32	17, 91, 123	14:11	54, 121
33–34	115, 137	14:12	91
33:19	115	14:13–19	92
33:22	115	14:19	92
34:6–7	115	16	123
34:6	44	16:22	92
34:28	101	16:46–48	18
34:29	109	20:1–11	107
40	135	21:7	18
40:15	149	21:16–18	107
40:34–38	197	21:18	107
43:28	140	23	32
		23:22	98

Leviticus

		24	32
1:3	143	24:5–9	32, 36
1:10	143	24:7	98
3:1	143	24:8	98
4—7:10	126	24:9	34
4:3	60	24:14	32
4:14	60	24:16–19	173
4:21	151	24:17–19	31, 35
4:23	60	24:17	35
4:28	60	27:15–17	48
8	24	27:17	51
8:12	27		

Deuteronomy

11:32	103	1:35	239
15:25–30	134	4:12	117
16:6	138	4:22	17
16:17	151	4:25–31	17
16:21	136	6:13	102
16:22	138	6:16	102
17:11	60, 126	6:24–26	59
23:26–32	151	7:6	22
23:29	129	8:2	102
23:33–43	119	8:3	102
23:33	120	9:9	108
23:36	120	9:10	94
23:39	120	9:26–29	92
24:5–9	177	10:8	25
		10:17	189

Numbers

		11:1	169
6:24–26	136, 140, 141	16:13	120
11:17	17	16:15	120
11:25	17	17:12	29
12:6–8	16	18	16, 81, 85, 88, 106, 110, 118, 128, 129
12:7	16		
14:10	18, 121		

Deuteronomy (*cont.*)

18:9–14	15, 110, 125
18:9	15
18:12	15
18:15–19	10, 14, 15, 36, 46, 52, 85, 88, 96, 105, 108, 114, 230, 234
18:15	15, 17, 20, 53, 89, 110, 117, 123, 128, 193
18:18	15, 50, 57, 89, 193
18:19	16, 17, 53, 89, 110, 129, 225, 246
18:20–22	110
18:22	50
19:4	23
23:25	177
26:8	48
29:4–5	23
29:4	54
30:1–10	17
31:3–5	17
31:28–29	32, 35
31:29	17
32	32, 137
32:5	238, 239
33	137
33:4–7	32, 35, 36
33:7	36
33:21	33, 208
34:10	18, 19, 36, 46, 85, 88

Joshua

1:1	134

Judges

4:21–22	35
5:15	33
9:53	35

1 Samuel

2:17	56
2:22	56
2:27–28	57
2:27	56
2:30–34	56
2:30–31	57
2:35	57, 58, 167, 193, 234
3:20	57
10:1	100
10:10	100
15	98
15:28	209
16:11–13	177
16:12–13	176
16:13	180
21:6	177
22:2	176

2 Samuel

1:23	43
2:4	176
5:1–4	176
5:3–4	176
6:13–17	59
6:14	59
6:18	59
7	52, 63, 174
7:7	33, 208
7:12–13	10
7:12	57, 69, 193
7:14	89
7:16	10, 58, 69, 84, 209
8:11	138
15	44
17:21—18:33	44
20	44
23:1–5	42
23:1	43, 193
23:2	43
24	59

1 Kings

12	106
18:4	43
18:10	210
18:13	43
19:10	43
19:16	100

SCRIPTURE INDEX

2 Kings

2:8	99
2:9–11	112
2:9	100
4:8–37	111
4:18–37	112
5:25–27	107
6:1–7	99
13:20 21	112
17:17–24	112
19:1–7	92
19:19	210
20:11	92
24:17	61
24:19–20	62

1 Chronicles

6:15	65
16:22	100
17:10	209

2 Chronicles

3:1	59
14:5	210
25:4	4

Ezra

2–5	72
7:11–26	67
7:27	67

Nehemiah

8:1	4
9:26	43

Esther

3:1	98

Job

31:36	65

Psalm

2	71
2:6–9	71
2:7	89, 101, 134
2:8–9	203
2:11	227
2:12	89
3–31	41
3	44, 45
5	45
6	45
7	45
12:7	239
13	45
14:5	239
16:10	44
17	45
18	71
20–21	71
20:5	227
21:13	227
22	6, 45
22:1–18	173
22:1–2	44
22:6–8	44
22:14–18	44
23	44, 45
23:2	45
23:6	45
24	45
24:6	240
25	45
26–28	45
28	71
28:9	44
34:20	44
39	45
42	45
43	45
45	71
45:3	71
45:6	33
51–72	41
54–57	45
59	45
61	45, 71
64	45
69:4	249
69:8	249
69:17	43
69:19–21	44

Psalm (cont.)

69:19	43
69:20	44
69:21	43
70	45
71	45
72	71, 173
72:11	43
73:9	209
76:1–2	33, 208
77:19–20	51
78:8	239
78:52–53	51
78:68–70	33, 208
78:71	42
80:1	44, 51
85:10	190
86	41, 45
86:2	44
86:4	44
86:9	43
86:15	44
86:16	44
89	71
89:24–37	6
90	110
95:10	239
99:6	27
101–3	41
101	71, 227
105:6	2, 49
105:15	100
107–9	59
108–10	41
110	59, 63, 71, 81, 189, 219
110:1–4	60
110:1	59, 83, 146, 147, 152, 175
110:4	2, 10, 49, 59, 146, 148, 151, 152
111–13	59
112:2	240
118	181, 182
118:2–24	182
118:22	183, 249
118:23–24	249
118:26	181
119	31
132	71
132:7	227
138–45	41
141	45
142	45
144:9	227

Proverbs

1:16	209
30:4	89
30:11	238

Ecclesiastes

2:5	34
2:11	34

Isaiah

1:2–4	70
1:3	31, 84
1:4	239
1:9	239
1:26	239
2:2–4	73
2:2–3	66
2:4	205
4:2	64
5:1–7	215
5:7	31
6	222
6:1	70
6:9–10	54, 70, 84, 212, 248, 251
6:10	246
6:13	239
7:14	84, 89, 174
8:11–22	222
8:14	249
8:18	73
8:21–22	84
8:22	222
9:1	97, 203
9:2	222
9:6–7	173, 222
9:6	53, 86, 89, 177

9:7	174, 201	43:12	50
9:9	204	43:16–21	48
9:19	204	44:1	2, 47
10:20	239	44:3–5	204
11	19	44:18	70, 246
11:1–2	101	45:4	47
11:1	64	48:20	47
11:4	201, 204	49:1–13	47
11:9	204	49:1–6	46
11:10	19	49:3	2, 47
11:12	203	49:5	2, 47
20:3	47	49:6	2, 47
24	222	49:7	249
24:5	50	50:4–11	47
24:23	71	50:4–9	46
27:2–6	199, 215	50:4	49
29	222	50:10	2
29:9–12	70	51:9–10	47
29:11–12	222	52:13—53:12	46, 47, 126, 173
29:17–24	204	52:13–15	54
29:17–18	70	52:13	47, 70, 74
29:18	222	52:14	53
30:10–11	70	53	6, 61, 64, 85, 142, 143, 184, 193, 249
32:1	71	53:1	53, 54, 248
32:3–4	70	53:2	13
32:15–16	204	53:3–8	248
33:17	71	53:3	54, 174, 182
33:23	70	53:6–7	61
35:4–6	71	53:7	60, 126
35:5–10	201, 204	53:8	74
35:5–6	70, 207	53:9	127
35:5	204	53:10	60, 74, 127
37:35	47	53:11–12	61
40–55	47, 53	53:11	47, 48, 74
40:1–11	48	53:12	50, 126, 127
40:11	48	55:6–7	225
41:8–9	2, 49	55:12–13	48
41:8	47	59:10	70
42:1–9	47, 180	59:17–20	6
42:1–4	6, 46	60:1–3	204
42:1	2, 47, 49, 100, 101, 117, 170	60:21	169
42:6	50	61	179
42:7	70	61:1–3	46, 180, 207
42:9	50	61:1–2	50, 179, 183, 207
42:18–20	70	61:1	229
43:3–5	48	61:4–9	207
43:8	70	61:6	61, 108, 112

Isaiah (cont.)

61:8	50
63:1–6	173, 202
63:1	202
63:11	47
64–65	92
65:17	205
65:25	205
66:8	204, 209

Jeremiah

2:31	239
3:18	204
4:2	72
10:23–25	92
11:21	43
14:7–9	92
18:7–10	168
23:5–6	190
23:5	64, 66, 72, 193, 234
27:18	92
30:8–9	57
30:9	193
31:6	73, 127
31:15–17	13
31:31–34	50
31:33	23, 169
33:15	66
38:4–6	43
49:22	202
50:4	204
50:20	61, 169
53:2–3	62

Ezekiel

3:24–25	57
9–11	198, 199
9:8	92
10	252
11:13	92
11:16–20	92
20:1–33	62
21:1–17	62
21:10	63
21:12	63
21:25–27	61, 62, 66
21:26	63
21:27	33, 63
34:23–24	52, 57, 177
34:24	86
36–37	168
36:26	120
36:27	204
37:15–22	204
37:24	23, 169
43:1–9	199
43:1–5	73, 252
43:7	72
45:25	120
47:1–12	203

Daniel

2:34–35	203
2:44–45	203, 212
2:47	189
3:25	89
6:10	92
7:13–14	203
8:23	73
8:25	73
9:4–19	92
9:18–19	93
9:25	13, 53, 73, 86, 177
9:26–27	203
9:26	73, 176, 246, 249

Hosea

3:5	57
11:1	98

Joel

2:17	92
2:28–32	204
2:28–29	120
2:28	100
3:16	203

Amos

7:2	92
7:5	92
9:11	193
9:13–15	204

Micah

4:1–5	73
4:1–2	66
4:3	205
5:2	84, 174
7:14–20	92

Habakkuk

3:2	92

Zechariah

1:18–21	174
2:10–13	6
3	64
3:1–5	64
3:1	64, 166
3:2	64, 166
3:3	64
3:4	64
3:6–7	64
3:7	65
3:8	64, 72
3:9	64
6:9–15	64, 65
6:9–11	65
6:11	65
6:12–13	66, 72, 203
6:13	203
9	182
9:9–10	6
9:9	85, 87, 173, 181, 182
9:10	182
12	202
12:10	61, 170, 204, 223, 252
13:1	61
13:7–9	55
14:1–5	202
14:2–9	173
14:6–7	203
14:8	120
14:9	203, 204
14:12–15	202
14:16–21	119

Malachi

3:1	112, 207

Matthew

1:1–17	175
1:20	15
1:21	81, 193
2	102
2:2	86, 177. 179, 183
2:15	98
2:17–18	13
3	102
3:1–2	247
3:2	216, 247
3:11	159
3:12	86
3:15	101
3:17	101, 102, 134, 180, 198
4	102
4:2	101
4:10	102
4:12–16	97
4:17	216
4:19	225
4:23	210, 248
5	108
5:1	109
5:17–19	110
5:20	217
6:5–15	136
6:9–13	211, 224
6:9–10	192
6:33	210, 217
7:7–11	136
7:15	110
7:24	110
7:26	110
7:28	88
8:1–4	134
8:1	109
8:2	134
8:22	225
9:9	225
9:17	104
9:20	175
9:27	175

Matthew (cont.)

9:35	248
10:2–3	118
10:16–23	241
10:23	241
10:32	136
10:38	225
10:40	89
11:1–15	94
11:1	88
11:4–15	207
11:5	248
11:15	212, 248
11:16	240
11:21	210
12	245
12:1–8	177
12:6	135
12:8	177
12:18	100
12:23	175
12:28	215
12:36–37	165
12:39–40	113
12:39	240
12:41–42	240
12:41	113, 135
12:42	235
12:45	240
13	211
13:1–23	212
13:9	248
13:24–30	212
13:31–33	212
13:31–32	212
13:34–43	212
13:43	248
13:44–46	212
13:47–50	212
13:53–58	113
13:53	88
13:54–58	108
13:57	113
14:13–21	114
14:24–33	115
14:27	116
15:22	175
15:24	89
16:4	240
16:19	214
16:21–23	139
16:24	225
17:1–9	118
17:1–8	116
17:1	116, 117
17:5	117, 180, 198
17:17	240
17:22–23	139
18:18	214
19:1	88
19:16—20:16	118
19:21	225
19:23–24	247
19:28	118, 124
20:17–19	139
20:20–28	212
20:30–31	175
21:5	182
21:9	175, 181
21:11	123
21:12–17	252
21:15	122, 175
21:23	121, 251
21:33–41	198
21:43	122, 198, 210, 214, 245
21:45	122
22:5	175
22:42	175
22:45	175
23	123
23:13	122, 215, 217
23:30	247
23:32	247
23:34	241
23:36	240, 241
23:37–39	136
23:37	89, 252
23:38	199
23:39	212, 251
24:1	241, 251
24:2	252
24:3	236, 241, 251
24:4–14	238
24:4–5	125

24:4	125	6:32–44	114
24:9	125	6:35	114
24:11	125	6:47–52	115
24:13	241	6:48	115
24:14	125, 248	8:11–12	121
24:15–28	238	8:31–32	139
24:16–18	125	9:2–8	116
24:21	238	9:7	117
24:22	241	9:12	7
24:23–26	125	9:30–32	139
24:24	125, 241	9:37	89
24:29–31	238	10:17–31	118
24:31	241	10:32–34	139
24:32–33	238	10:35–45	212
24:34	125, 236, 237, 238, 240, 241	10:47–48	175
		11:10	213
24:36	236	13:10	248
26:1	88	14:3	135
26:6	135	14:7	139
26:13	248	14:9	248
26:17–30	126	14:12–25	126
26:24	7	14:21	139
26:29	150	14:24	126
27:11	183	14:61–62	120
27:29	183	15:2	183
27:37	183	15:9	183
27:38	127	15:12	183
28:19–20	210	15:18	183
28:20	157	15:43	127
		16:15	248
		16:19	152

Mark

1:1	248		
1:4	247	**Luke**	
1:8	247	1:16	247
1:14–15	248	1:17	112, 247
1:15	216	1:21–22	140
1:40–45	134	1:32–33	179
2:27	177	1:32	175
2:28	121	1:43	86
4:9	212, 248	1:68	86
4:23	212, 248	1:69	86
4:41	116	1:71	86
5:24–34	124	1:77	86
5:25–34	124	2:25	86
6	116	2:26	86
6:1–6	108	2:30	86
6:31–32	114	2:32	86

Luke (*cont.*)

2:34	86
2:38	85, 86
2:46–47	121
3:3	247
3:16	159
4:1–13	140
4:2	101
4:5–6	232
4:6	83
4:14—9:50	118
4:14	179
4:16–30	108
4:18–19	207
4:18	89
4:21	179
4:24	108, 180
4:25–27	108
4:43	89
5:12–16	134
5:20–21	120
6:12	136
6:23	247
6:24–25	181
6:26	247
7:11–17	111
7:16	111, 112
7:18–23	112
7:22	112
7:24–29	112
7:26	112
7:27	112
7:28	112
7:40	96
8:8	212, 248
8:40–42	112
8:42–48	134
8:43–48	134
8:49–56	112
9:1—19:44	118
9	217
9:2	247
9:6	247
9:10–17	114
9:21–22	139
9:28–36	116
9:28–31	113
9:31	117
9:43–45	139
9:48	89
9:51—18:14	118
10:9	216
10:13–15	181
10:16	89
11:1	136
11:17–18	94
11:19	94
11:20	94, 215
11:47–48	247
11:52	214
12:8	136
12:32	214
13:2–5	181
13:34	89
14:35	212, 248
17:11–19	135
17:20–21	216
17:20	236
18:18–30	118
18:31–34	139
18:38–39	175
19:11–27	181
19:11–12	213
19:11	181
19:12	124
19:13	192
19:38	181
19:42–44	246
19:43–44	181
22:7–23	126
22:22	139
22:32	136
22:45	136
22:69	152
23:2	183
23:3	183
23:37	183
23:42	213
23:51	127
24:16	128
24:19	96, 127
24:25	7, 128
24:27	3, 7, 75
24:31	128
24:32	130

SCRIPTURE INDEX 283

24:44	128
24:50–51	141

John

1	103
1:14	199
1:17	101
1:20–23	87
1:29	86, 126
1:32–33	159
1:34	86
1:36	86
1:43	7, 103, 225
1:45	103
1:49	103, 179
2	103
2:11	103
3:2	94
3:5	158, 214, 217
3:16	89
3:36	99, 225
4	105, 120
4:4	90
4:7–15	106
4:10	107
4:14	107
4:16–18	106
4:19	106
4:20	247
4:22	168
4:34	90
5:2	214
5:17–18	120
5:22	124
5:39–40	7
5:45–47	7
5:45–46	114
5:45	114
5:46	19
6–9	114
6:1–15	114
6:14	114
6:15	179, 182
6:16–21	115
6:20	116
6:31	247
6:49	247
6:58	247
6:68	246
7:10	119
7:14–24	120
7:19–27	96
7:22	247
7:37–40	96
7:37–38	120
7:40	120
7:52	96
8:14	139
8:21	139
9	96, 121
9:17	122
9:24–33	7
10:11–16	53
10:11	55
10:27	225
11:1–44	112
12:13	181
12:14–15	182
12:31	95
12:32	95
12:37	54, 122, 248
12:38	54
12:39	248, 251
12:47–48	181
12:49–50	50
13	126
13:3	139
13:5	135
13:33	139
13:36	139
14–17	137
14:1–3	139
14:2–4	139
14:3	221
14:6	215
14:7–10	90
14:12	139
14:15–24	137
14:15	155
14:16	139
14:18	139
14:25–26	139
14:26	156
15:26–27	156
15:26	156

John (cont.)

16:5	139
16:7–15	156
16:8	157
16:13–15	156
16:16–19	139
16:28	139
17	137, 138
17:17–19	137, 138
18:13	183
19:3	183
19:31–33	144
19:39–43	127
20:20	139
20:22	139
20:25	144
20:30–31	94
20:31	103
21:19	225

Acts

1:3	140, 213
1:5	159
1:6–8	218
1:6	213, 236
1:7	213, 236
1:8	192
2	120, 159
2:2	199
2:17	130
2:29–32	175
2:30–32	147
2:30–31	44
2:33	156
2:36	185
2:37	225
2:40	240
2:47	185
3:15	86, 177
3:22–23	128, 185
4:27	100
4:29	186
4:31	186
5:30–31	144
5:31	86, 152, 177
6:2	186
6:4	186
6:7	186
7	129
7:37	129
8:4	185, 186
8:14	186
8:25	186
9:4	54, 164
10:38	100
10:44–46	130
11:1	186
11:14	186
11:15–16	159
11:19–21	185
12:24	186
13:5	186
13:7	186
13:30–35	147
13:44	186
13:46	186
13:47	171
13:48	186
13:49	186
17:7	184
18:24–26	130
19:1–6	130
19:20	186
20:28–32	185
26:18	219

Romans

1:1	156
1:3–4	148
1:3	175
2:9–10	202
6:3–7	99
6:5	220
6:8–14	220
6:9	83, 220
6:12–13	220
6:12	220
6:14	220
8:9	158
8:17	219
8:28	164
8:29	164
8:34	152, 158, 165
11:1–6	168
11:1	252

11:5	240	3:16	2, 49
11:7–10	168	3:19	49
11:7	217, 240	3:24	7
11:8	212	4:4–5	104
11:11–24	168	4:7	219
11:11–15	246	5:21	218
11:11–12	168, 246		
11:11	250	## Ephesians	
11:15	248, 252	1:7	146
11:25–26	168, 252	1:11	145
11:26	61, 170, 252	1:12	145
11:29	250, 252	1:13	158
11:30–32	168, 248, 250	1:18–20	145
11:33–36	251	1:20	146, 152
12	161	2:1	160
12:2	165	2:2–3	160
12:5	164	2:4–6	146
13:11–12	224	2:5	160
14:17	17	2:6	160
15:16	155, 170, 171	2:7	160
		2:10	166
## 1 Corinthians		2:11–22	160, 164
1:26–29	162	2:11–12	168
3:16	164	2:20	156
4:20	218	3:5	156
6:2–3	124	3:17	164
6:9–10	218	3:20	146
10:1–5	101	3:30	122
10:1–2	99	4:4–6	159
10:17	164	4:11–13	155
11:2	142	4:11	160
12:4–11	161	4:12–13	161
12:13	130, 159	4:12	164
12:27	164	4:23	163
15:3–4	248	5:5	218
15:20	127		
		## Philippians	
## 2 Corinthians		2:5–8	83
1:21–22	130	2:5	163
1:22	158	2:8–11	227
5:20	158	2:8–10	249
5:21	65	2:9–10	192
		2:10–11	81
## Galatians		2:13	166
1:3–4	219	2:15	240
1:10	156	3:20	195
		5:4	216

Colossians

1:13	184, 219
3:1–2	160, 163

1 Thessalonians

2:3–4	122
2:6	122
2:12	218
4:16–17	167

2 Thessalonians

1:5	218

1 Timothy

6:13–15	184
6:15	186, 189

2 Timothy

2:8	175
3:8	125
4:6–8	223
4:18	223

Titus

2:11–15	224

Hebrews

1:1–4	142
1:1–2	146, 231
1:2	134
1:3	142, 146, 147, 152, 198
1:5	134
1:8	134, 184, 186
1:13	83, 152
2:1	129, 130
2:4	130
2:6	134
2:8	83
2:17	139, 142, 155
3:1	139, 149, 155, 158, 226
3:2–6	90, 91
3:5–6	134
3:6	58
3:8–11	23
3:10	239
4:12	156
4:14–15	139, 155, 158
4:15	144, 192
5:1—13:25	226
5:1	155
5:5–6	158
5:5	155
5:6	148, 155
5:8–9	142
5:8	134
5:9–10	147
5:10	139, 155, 158
6:1	226
6:19–20	147, 165
6:20	148, 155, 158
7:1—8:14	158
7:1–2	190
7:1	155
7:3	148, 155
7:4–28	232
7:5	155
7:11	155, 211
7:12	142, 155
7:14–15	155
7:16	143
7:17	148, 155
7:20–22	151
7:21	148, 155
7:22	127, 152
7:23–24	155
7:24	148
7:25	138, 148, 158
7:26–28	155
7:28	148, 151
8:1	147, 151, 152, 155
8:3–4	155
8:6	127
8:13	143
9:6–7	155
9:11–14	60
9:11	155
9:15	142
9:24–28	82
9:24	147
9:25	155

9:28	193
10:11	155
10:12	142, 152
10:21	155
10:22	226
12:2	142, 146, 152
12:23	158
12:28	220
13:3	164
13:10–12	142
13:11	155
13:20–21	142
13:20	53

James

1:1	156
2:5	219
4:4–5	164
4:17	165
5:8	216

1 Peter

1:1	58
1:4–5	164
1:4	219
1:10–12	5
1:19–20	227
1:19	61
2	187
2:5	155, 170
2:9–10	24, 58, 187
2:9	155, 170
2:25	53
3:22	152
4:7	221
5:2	53
5:4	53

2 Peter

1:1	156
1:16–18	199

1 John

2:1	165
2:27	160
3:4	165

Jude

1	156
4–6	240
12–16	240
25	224

Revelation

1	214
1:1–3	188
1:1	156
1:4–8	188
1:4	170, 187
1:5–7	187
1:5	83, 187, 189, 227
1:6	155, 170, 187, 214
1:17	227
1:19	188
2–3	188
3:21	153
4–22	188
4:8–10	227
5	221, 223
5:2–5	221
5:5	133, 221
5:8–10	170
5:9–14	227
5:9–10	187, 210, 214
5:10	155, 170
5:12	191
6:1—8:1	221
7:9–12	227
7:12	227
7:17	53
11:15	188
11:16	227
12:11	241
13:8	227
13:11–18	130
14:3	227
14:19–20	202
15:3–4	188
15:3	188, 227
16	188
16:16	202
17:14	188, 189
19:1–4	227
19:4	227

19:5	227	19:16	188, 189, 227
19:6	202	20:6	155, 171
19:7–9	150	22:16	175
19:7	227		

For more information about the author
or to access free resources, please use the QR code.

www.ingramcontent.com/pod-product-compliance
Lightning Source LLC
Chambersburg PA
CBHW050839230426
43667CB00012B/2064